To the Summit and safe return

When I set out to summit Mount Everest in 1996, I disciplined my focus through programming my brain – my subconscious - with my self-invented Mantra. "To the Summit and Safe return".
Unknowingly I invented 3 simple universal mental steps to scale and survive the highest mountain in the world – Mount Everest.
Over the past 20 years - Neuroscience has developed and today we know so much more about the brains plasticity. The fact is that it is truly possible to cultivate character traits through focused thinking and acting.
The extreme experiences of climbing Everest – has been my lifelong inspiration – propelling me onwards in pursuing my passion to innovate Humans through simple mental disciplining.
Human Innovation through NeuroLeadership.
Mount Everest 1996 is where my lifepassion for mobilizing Human Potential in as many as possible all started.
Grand leaders are rare – so I focus on mobilizing excellent leadership – Decency Leadership – across the Globe. Because we can change the World – together.
One Brain at the Time – The Everest Way.

To the Summit and safe return is my personal account of Everest. The foundation for neuro based strategies for personal and professional fulfillment

I sincerely wish you a fulfilling life
Yours
Lene Gammelgaard
Top 10 Motivational Speaker and bestselling author of Climbing High

Content

1. "Get busy living or get busy dying"
2. One question changed my life - Do you have a vision?
3. You must dare to risk creating a better
4. People of mediocre ability can achieve outstanding
5. Keep it simple
6. Test you limits, to know what they are
7. Find out what you can pursue with passion
8. Make it happen and have fun
9. Your vision must mobilize you from within
10. If your vision excites you, you can achieve it
11. Determine what your goals are, plan, take action
12. If you are going through hell, keep going
13. Mountains have the power to call us into their realms
14. Your life is your responsibility
15. Mountains are democratic. They makes all equal
16. Utilize your resources strategically to achieve your goals
17. What is the purpose of your life?
18. Mobilize your untapped potential
19. Summit fever
20. There are no guarantees in life - fight for what you want
21. Coping with unfulfilled expectations
22. What do you truly want from life?
23. To the summit and safe return

24. How to persevere where others give up
25. Never give up - your willpower makes a difference
26. Keep moving - no matter what
27. Take action - inspire change
28. How to go on - when you can not
29. Perseverance - recommitment
30. Nobody experiences continuous success
31. What can we learn from the past?
32. Mount Everest is a mirror for humanity
33. The fulfillment of one grand vision is just a new beginning
34. Simple living – Serenity – Age
35. About Lene Gammelgaard - www.lenegammelgaard.com

Mobilize your future today

"Defeat is not the worst of failures. Not to have tried is the true failure"
                                                George Edward Woodberry

- What do you dream about?
- Do you want your life to be an exact copy of today in 5 years' time? If not, what will you do to influence the direction?
- When will you start?
- Who would you be and what would you do if your inner doubts, fears, feelings of defeat and exhaustion and the cynicisms that come with life's experiences did not hold you back?

Everest is extremely unsentimental and so should we, those of us who challenge our self-quest on the highest mountain in the world. Everest offers sobering yet viciously elemental circumstances, confronting you with who and what you are, as well as the contrary: who and what you are not.
We who climb high are brutally exposed to the elements, for ourselves and the world to judge. Those who immerse themselves in this extraordinary quest of testing themselves on Mount Everest, display crucial courage while risking the willingness of getting past the worry that accompanies pursuing unknown territory.
  There is not only death and survival here, but also grandiosity, breathtaking and tear inducing magnificence. The human spirit; apart from luck, turns out, has much to do with how we approach and cope with the equalizing merciless environment we venture

into. Is it in pursuit of a passion-driven life? The life of passion materializes when an emotional nature meets a consuming vocation.

To be passionate is to impart yourself with something you value highly, but have yet to fully control and master. To be passionate is to risk, to put oneself out there and to accept menace as an inevitable component of existence.

Disaster struck on May 10 1996 as four different expedition members attempted to reach the summit of the highest mountain in the world. At almost midnight May 9 we all embarked from Camp 4 at 8000 meters, within one hour of each other. At around noon May 10, a powerful unforeseen storm speedily rose up Mt. Everest from the lower regions of the Indian Plateau trapping those of us who were descending in a precarious position.

The upper reaches of Mount Everest are a death zone. This is a mountaineering term for altitudes above a certain height - around 8000 m (26,000 ft.), with less than 356 millibars of atmospheric pressure. We were so high above sea level that the oxygen density was not sufficient to sustain human life. Several deaths in high-altitude mountaineering have been caused by the effects of the death zone, either directly: loss of vital functions or indirectly: unwise decisions made under stress or physical weakening leading to accidents. In the death zone, the human body cannot acclimatize, as it uses oxygen faster than it can replenish. An extended stay at 8000 meters and above without supplementary oxygen will result in deterioration of bodily functions, loss of consciousness and ultimately death within 5 to 24 Hours.

I was stuck in the death zone, above 8000 meters, where subzero temperatures and oxygen deprivation paralyzes your will to act and preserve yourself. Our bodies try to keep us alive for as long as possible and therefore closes down blood circulation in the extremities first. Fingers, hands, toes and feet swiftly turn from useful tools into lumps of ice.

The monstrous storm significantly increased our risk of frostbites, as the high wind speed was combined with abnormally low temperatures. The hazardous wind chill temperatures might have been as low as -50°C, causing any exposed tissue to freeze.

If exposed to the wind and cold above 8000 meters for longer than two minutes, human beings begin to die. Genetic survival and self-preserving instincts help the organism to protect the brain and heart by centering the nourishing blood to sustain these two vital organs for as long as possible. Exposure to extreme cold for any prolonged period makes the task of attempting to keep the brain and heart functioning no longer possible.

The brain shuts down even though you are still alive because it takes longer to freeze to death. Moreover, I instantly begun to feel the excruciating pain but never slipped into unconsciousness. I therefore have no firsthand experience of the hallucinations that seem to precede death from hypothermia. Most mountaineers who succumb to subzero temperatures take off their clothes in the process of becoming extinct, as they feel as if they are burning from the inside. Everest veterans, strong and experienced mountaineers such as, Scott Fischer and Rob Hall did not make it. They pursued their vision of summiting the Everest, with as many clients reaching the top and no casualties. Their quest was to survive Mount Everest, as a means of making a living and expanding their business opportunities based on their freedom loving lifestyles.

I knew when I set out to climb Everest that it would have a price. I just didn't realize what complex, brutal recompense Mother Goddess of the Earth would crave. Mount Everest is a mighty, yet simple universe. A dramatic scene, mirror for all humankind of how we can or cannot conduct ourselves and how swiftly we might elevate life or perish. Everest - pure, unearthly, vast and pristine, yet gruesome, deadly and profoundly rewarding for a short while - just as life can be anywhere. Climbing Everest takes one and a half months - a fragment of time- compared to the decade's most humans drag themselves through obligatory so called daily lives. The imprints and life altering mountain is incomparable to anything else in anybody's life span. Those who climb construct themselves inwardly by expressing themselves outwardly. Everest can bring coherence to the scattered impulses we are all born with. By investing in this extreme outward activity, we define and attempt to understand ourselves and expand our capacities in the process. Living the risk of pursuing oneself out in the unknown requires courage as well as risk willingness. People with passion have the courage to confront and deal with their issues. We all have certain core concerns that preoccupy us through life.

Passionate people often discover themselves through their pursuits and use their imagination to open up possibilities, discerning or creating visions for their next life chapter.

They invest in understanding their emotional luggage in pursuit of becoming liberated from unconscious, socialized inner patterns that might not be conducive to who they are and who they must become in order to find meaning in life. They delight in new ways to expand their personalities and move toward their goals. People with passion have the courage to be who they are with abandon. Those who are driven from within, somehow get to the other side of fear, beyond the blur of the unknown that is scary to approach, the dread of the unknown that keeps people from altering their lifestyles. Once through their inner qualms - they have more freedom to navigate. They opt out of things, relations, situations that are repetitive and deadening. Sometimes there is recklessness and a willingness to throw their imperfect selves out in public view, while not really bothered by how people will react. Driven individuals are just unwilling to be ruled by the tyranny of public opinion. People who expose their contradictions confront the rest of humankind with the question I perpetually utilize in my pursuit of touching people through my mobilizing speeches.

    I am convinced that individuals, who desire to risk climbing Everest, live with a craving for passion, starting out with an especially intense desire to complete themselves. When we ponder about living with passion, what does it mean exactly? Human beings seem to be the only species that are propelled into developmental processes that bring them to integration and coherence. Some people are seized by this task with a fierce longing, which maybe be mobilized by emotional wounds that need fundamental healing, by a fear of oblivion or fragmentation or maybe a drive fueled some glorious fantasy to make a mark on the world. Nevertheless, they often have an unquenchable thirst to find some activity they can pursue wholeheartedly, without reservation.

    Modesty might be a virtue; however, I do not believe modesty is a virtue when it comes to self-assessment and goal setting. I do not care who you are or what difficulties you face in your life, you should make plentiful plans for your future. There is few limits to what you can accomplish in life if you dream big, commit yourself to work hard, for as long as it takes for you to accomplish what you must, to find fulfillment in your existence. As long as we have freedom to choose, we have the personal responsibility to reflect inwards, to perceive what is crucial to lend meaning to our lives. With freedom of choice follows self-responsibility as well as consequences. Everest is a constant reminder to humankind of what passion can transcend. It mercilessly shows you what you are made of in that brief period that seems like a lifetime. This dramatic life-pursuing quest for some becomes the end of their existence, for me, Everest stands out as the grandest adventure I have ever experienced.

    I had the great good fortune of scaling Everest in a historic context in 1990. After the demolition of the Berlin Wall, we experienced global optimism, we had seen the end of histories tendency to repeat itself in up and down turns. The trend seemed to be towards implementation of worldwide democracies. Liberalism and human rights appeared an inevitable consequence of the world order, where trade barriers gave way to peace and poverty reduction. The 1990s fulfilled our inborn desire for a never ending upward trend and an end to all ideological and religious conflicts. No more devastating random wars and our global world order illusion seemed to do fantastic for a decade. Our scaling naivety was confronted with what Time Magazine called "A Decade from Hell". The constructive belief in a democratic world order, resembling what we know in the west was disrupted by the impact of 11th September 2001. We are now faced with humongous human initiated catastrophes that have no simple solutions and are changing our existences as we know them. There are no guarantees that the world will become a better place for the majority of the growing number of inhabitants. Captivating that the unrest as well as potential solutions, all stem from thoughts produced in a human brain and beliefs transformed into action. Devastating or the contrary all wars begin in one brain and so do all solutions, I utilized my brains capacity for unconscious programming to achieve a seemingly unreachable goal and my company- Human Innovation-focusing explicitly on how we can employ our brain capacities to initiate change. I transform my findings into strategies which I share worldwide as a Global Motivational Speaker, installing renewed fighting spirit. I summited the Everest during the Global upward trend: allowing myself to dwell in untainted adventurous attentiveness.

I am profoundly grateful.

1

"Get busy living or get busy dying"
Lene Gammelgaard

"Confronted with the petty concerns of my ordinary life, I feel empty, as if I am wasting a priceless gift... the brief time that is allotted for each human for creativity. Days pass and my work does not generate the strength and eagerness to live, which memories of the mountains inspires in me. Perhaps this melancholy will pass when there is another magnificent peak. In truth, I do not know. I want to achieve something essential in life, something that cannot be measured by wealth or position in society. I want to respect myself. From the first day, I knew I belonged in those heights, that it was my destiny to climb high. I knew that, for me, mountaineering would be about the human struggle with altitude. In the mountains, I attempt to understand my life"
Anatoli Boukreev

I am acutely aware that life is short. Since I lost my younger brother in a motorbike accident when he was twenty and I was twenty two, I have been stressed by my inner confrontation, "Get busy living or get busy dying". This is a gift and a curse, reminding us to be alert to the frailty of life. Each day I consider if I am wasting too much time carrying out trifling chores so as to make life for my three kids function within the framework of established societal norms. I get up in the morning, go to school and cram all the desired free time activities pressed into the remaining waking hours. What approach is unsurpassed; to truly be present in the short time span we have available in our lives? How can we utilize life to its fullest? Living with the factual undercurrent, that life might suddenly end: that there are no guarantees. This experience-based matrix is the foundation on which I decided to attempt climbing Everest instead of abstaining. I made the conscious choice of risking being fully and passionately alive, living the greatest adventure presented to me and I chose life.

When you commit to climb Everest, you will face the dangers of falling off the mountain, tripping into huge crevices and asphyxiation from low oxygen levels, avalanches and falling rocks, as well as meteorological conditions that can unexpectedly change drastically in mere minutes.

At the summit, winds often reach hurricane strength literally blowing people off the mountain. Oxygen levels leave us gasping for breath while our oxygen-deprived brains, leave us unable to make rational decisions. Mount Everest requires the ability to shift course of action based on new information and to address multiple goals and changing circumstances. Surviving Everest requires leaders, individuals and teams to establish enough freedom from external restraints, obligations, commitments and sufficient liberty from past routines, habits and traditions to respond to complexities and contingencies. It demands the ability to draw conclusions from present experiences, the capacity to distinguish the irrelevant and insignificant from the important, especially in the myriad situations of high complexity and inherent risk that require a process of continuous adaptation, ability to solve problems and to deal with changing psychological and physiological needs and chaos that arise on an Everest expedition.

The truth is surviving Everest craves a great deal of random luck. Therefore, you must be somewhat accustomed to face and cope with life and death situations. Some mountaineers stop for a brief rest only to slowly drift into an unfathomable sleep, never to wake up. Most of the people who lose their lives attempting to scale Everest still linger on the mountain, their dead bodies in such a cold environment stay perfectly preserved. Given that a person can die between breaths, many who expire are not recognized as such, until quite some time after they succumb. In an environment where every step is a struggle, rescue of the dying is all but impossible and stiff frozen corpses are almost always irretrievable.

The solid to the core iced up bodies become part of the landscape and more spectacularly become 'landmarks' that future climbers use as way markers during their climb.

One of the most thought provoking deaths in modern Everest history - raising fundamental questions about the human ethics of those who pursue the summit, I find, is the fate of David Sharp who got stuck in a cave known as *'Green Boots Cave'*, just below the peak of Mount Everest. David Sharp attempted the climb in 2005 and near the top, stopped in this cave to rest, as many have done before him. His body eventually froze in place, rendering him unable to move, although still alive. More than 30 climbers passed by him as he sat there - high on the mountain - freezing to death. Some heard faint moans and realized he was still alive, they stopped and spoke with him. David Sharp was able to identify himself but was unable to move. Some more compassionate climbers brought him out into the sun in an attempt to thaw him but eventually, realizing

David would be unable to move, abandoned him to die. What is certain is that every single one of the 30-odd climbers pursuing the summit that day gave up on the man. Either by choice, by ignorance, or by misjudging him as a corpse they already expected to see in that infamous cave, they left him out in the sun with the hope that he would warm up and be able to get himself out of the death zone. Because the climbers are limited by their time above 8000 meters, there was only so much they could do. He was found dead the following day where he had been left and brought back into the cave with the other dead Indian climber; his face covered by his pack. His body is no longer in the cave because the following season it was moved from the cave by fellow climbers who interred him off the trail at the request of his family.

While chilling in itself, the incident supports the bigger context of the deadliness of Mount Everest.

The highest recorded death count prior to the earthquake disaster in 2015 was in 1996, which saw 15 people die throughout the year due to reasons such as falls, rope accidents, exposure and altitude sickness. Before 1996, it was recorded that one in four climbers died when trying to scale the mountain. In 1974, the number of climbers who reached the summit was zero as in 2015. The West Ridge Direct of the peak was attempted by a French expedition team, however all six members were killed by an avalanche. Today, the Mount Everest death toll stands at 275 people: four per cent of the 6958 people who have attempted the climb.

On 18th April 2014, 16 high-altitude workers, including 13 Sherpas, were killed in the Khumbu Icefall below Camp 1 following a Serac collapse on the mountain's west shoulder. It was the worst single loss of life in the mountain's history. Despite this tragedy, the fatality rate on the Everest has been dropping in recent years, both for foreign climbers and hired highaltitude workers. The grim reality of the horrific conditions of the final push in the Death Zone is that 150 bodies have never been, and will likely never be recovered. They are all still there, located, almost without exception, in the Death Zone. David Sharp's body, which sat in that cave prior to its retrieval, served as a guiding beacon for other mountaineers nearing the summit. Tangible gruesome evidence of the conditions on Everest, both the brutal forces of nature in this outlandish environment as well as the modus operandi of the people who pursue this kind of conquest, ought to serve as evidence- based examples of human egocentrism.

2

The Question that changed my life….

"Big mountains are a completely different world: snow, ice, rocks and thin air. You cannot conquer them, only rise to their heights for a short time and for that, they demand a great deal. The struggle is with yourself, with the feelings of weakness and inadequacy. That struggle appeals to me. It is why I became a mountaineer. You arrive at the top having renounced everything that you think you must have to support life and are alone with your soul. That empty vantage point lets you reappraise yourself and every relationship and object that is part of the civilized world with a different perspective."

Anatoli Boukreev

- Do you have a vision? If not, start chasing your innermost desires. Finding out what we truly dream about is often the most confronting and distressing process, as we do not seem to truly know.
- If you do not know what you want, how can you initiate the strategic steps necessary to accomplish what will give you lasting meaning?
- If you have a year to spend doing anything you want, what would you do?

It's early morning 1995 on the Baltoro Glacier in Pakistan, Scott and I are headed for Concordia, a giant crossroad created by some of the largest glaciers in the Himalayas. I have just spent a month with Scott in Pakistan, trekking to Broad Peak Base Camp in the Karakoram Range. Broad Peak (26,402 feet/8,047 meters), neighbor to the second highest mountain in the world, notorious K2, is the target of Scott's climbing expedition this July. I am on my way out of Base Camp to meet up with my team to climb the steep 7,300 m of Gondogoro La Pass. Scott insists on joining me on this two-hour hike and like kids playing in the rain, we laugh as we jump the small melted water floods crisscrossing abound the glaciated surface and competing about who finds our way the fastest and smartest among the labyrinth of ice pinnacles.

Scott is amazed and impressed by my burning desire to take a bath in the screamingly chilly just unfrozen glacier ponds and I just can't help it. I am irresistibly drawn down into the blue transparent chill. I once again experience that I am slightly better at finding my way through the glacier, repeatedly acknowledging that I do not have the same brutal body strength that Scott possesses. How can I? Confronting me over and over again is the fact that if I want to play with the big boys, I must utilize my limited resources intelligently to be able to perform to the standards that are necessary to survive at the altitude. Enormous massifs surround us: Gasherbrum II, III, and IV, Mitre Peak, Chogolisa, Broad Peak and behind us, the characteristic pyramid shape of K2. Here on the glacier, just before our paths part, Scott pops the question that will profoundly change my life.

"Do you want to climb Everest with me in the spring in 1996?"

It takes only a split second from the moment Scott's question hits the receptors of my brain for me to impulsively exclaim my response.

"Yes!"

No doubt, no anxiety, no second thoughts. Nothing: just inner certainty. I know he is not just teasing; he is serious about his invitation. Circumventing mudslides, crossing raging torrents, diplomatically coping with the tensions of the trekking group at altitude, Scott ought to have some valid insights as to why he poses this invitation to me right here and now. After sharing a full month in some of the roughest terrain in the Pakistan Himalayas, had Scott formed the impression that I have what it takes? My "yes" unleashes a quanta jump expansion groundswell and within me a point of no return. A tsunami of unprecedented desires, wants, untapped resources and exploding inner drives that propelled my every thought, step and action in the year to come. I have been initiating and living adventurous voyages since I was 18, crossed the Atlantic - pursuing my first daring dream; however, I have never experienced a developmental momentum equated to whatever is mobilized through Scott's invitation on that glacier in Pakistan and my accepting it. It is a 'Yes' that unbolts the floodgates of my core.

All blocked energy is now roaring beyond obstructions, wanting Mount Everest! Climbing the highest mountain in the world with a kindred spirit tempts me beyond reason and I am at a turning point in my life. I have been living alone in a two-room apartment in a nice intellectual corner of Copenhagen. Having been divorced from my husband, I fell hopelessly in love with a new man, who turned out to be a clean addict and HIV positive. So instead of devouring in a customary love life with him, we co-founded a drug treatment center where I worked one full week every month until I parted for good - for Everest.

Maintaining my inborn and habitual gravitation towards freedom above stability I am a contemporary nomad, unattached by proprietorship and an ambitious overachiever not able to comply with the rules of civilized society. I want more of life. I want something different. I know that this ginormous energy release is more than the desire to summit Everest, much more than the rather superficial act of climbing to the top of the world, even though it is the highest mountain on earth. For periods of my life I have hidden from the world's opportunities, not knowing how to gain renewed momentum, due to the meaninglessness following negative life shocks. I withdrew from age relevant living, stifled in anguish and hopelessness-when my younger brother was killed in an accident and when I divorced my harsh husband - because I needed to grieve, withdraw to reposition myself and align with yet another unwanted life experience. It is obvious that I am now ready to grow and I must propagate. I cannot escape to strive to reach my full potential in spite of my desire to escape the responsibility and tough investments that follow. I have experienced death, defeat, failures and having to restore myself to new life zest time after time. I have developed a modus operandi to reawaken the desire to cope with existence once again. For me serenity and daily satisfaction is learning to accept reality with all its myriads of contradictions and paradoxes, the formidable and discouraging aspects, as well as the pristine and invigorating and adapting into the freedom that lies in acknowledging limitation.

Therefore, it is possible for me - with no doubt whatsoever - to want Everest one hundred percent. My "yes" is a tribute to the subtlety of life, a return to innocence, re-igniting my zest for life and leaving the defeats and sorrows of the past behind. It is a "yes" to trusting my own strength to carry this mission through successfully. Life zest is one of the fortes possessed by humanity. It encompasses approaching life as an adventure.

Zest is essentially a concept incorporating courage and involves acquiring the motivation to complete undertakings, re-invigorated by thought provoking circumstances or tasks in spite of challenging conditions. Those who possess life zest exude excitement, anticipation, enthusiasm and energy when approaching life. Hence, the concept of zest involves accomplishing visions wholeheartedly, whilst being adventurous, vivacious and energetic. Zest discourages focus on the negative and in order to truly understand, you must observe people that 'live well'.

Zestful people simply enjoy things more than people who lack zest. It is a positive trait reflecting on a person's life approach. My 'yes' is a yes to life's grandeur, promise and hope. It's a 'yes' to a naiveté that does not correspond with my life experiences and cynicism, but rather the pureness that might follow the total resignation of a human being. And why shouldn't I climb the highest mountain in the world? But first Scott has to survive guiding Broad Peak.

"I am grateful to inform you that Scott Fischer and two clients' summited Broad Peak this morning at 9:05. More are headed for the summit. We wish them all good luck and a safe trip down and send our best regards to you.
All the best Abdul Quddus Nazir Sabir Expeditions".

Later that day on August 1995 I receive an update from Scott himself on my answering machine, back in Copenhagen.

"I reached the summit and am safe down in Base Camp. Do you still want to climb that 'Big Thing' with me?"

Finally, it's time to work towards Everest, to intensify my climbing training and to pursue sponsors to cover my share of the expenses. Three days later, I receive a letter from Scott composed in Broad Peak Base Camp on August 16, 1995

Dear Lene,

Thanks so much for your letters. The crisis right now is seven deaths on K2. On the 13th we all summited Broad Peak, and Mountain Madness did well. Late afternoon an extreme wind came up - we were already down to Camp 3. It killed those still on K2. They called from the summit at 6:00 P.M. - that's the last we ever heard from them. My friends Rob Slater, Geoff Lakes and Alison Hargreaves all died. Plus three Spaniards and a guy from New Zealand. The only contact we have with the outside world is our illegal satellite phone... It makes me realize how frail we actually are. That we are playing a deadly game. I don't want to be dead - I want to be alive....Did you get my message at your machine? I do hope so. This is all pretty painful. Alison leaves two kids. Same age as mine. A lot of tears... Major bummer. Don't let me die, Lene. Keep me humble. (I am probably not humble, but I need to be.) The mountains are supreme. Most powerful. You should have seem it, Lene; the wind came up and just killed them. Geoff Lakes turned around and found his way back down to Camp 4, but an avalanche that hit the tent during the night killed him. Bivvier came as far down as Camp 2, where his friends were, but died during the night. None of the remaining managed to climb down. We can see a corpse on the slopes. It's a major tragedy. Alison was the driving force toward the summit, with little respect for the power of K2. K2 won. What strikes me just now is that I trust my survival skills totally. But I had the same trust in their ability to survive - those who are now dead - and they had similar confidence in themselves. And they died. I must be careful….The expedition blues are here. I will start hiking…..

3

"Personal risk is the prerogative for human innovation"
Lene Gammelgaard

- Give yourself a stake in the vision.
- Positive stress from fear.
- You can innovate by engaging in risk taking and acting boldly.

Success in almost any undertaking that requires you engage in risk taking and with risking the unknown the element of fear rises. How you respond to your fear will determine the difference between success and failure. Stress and fear is your psyche's way of responding to challenges. If you let angst lead you to abstain from initiating and exploring new opportunities and seeking cover at the first hint of resistance, you will fail.

If you confront your inner anxieties, decide to fight them and let your positive stress mobilize you to take action, you will succeed. When everything is at stake, existential fear concentrates your mind superbly. Healthy fear of how you will be capable of coping with your future, how to overcome financially; often provoke the most creative and surprising ideas to surface forcing you beyond the crucial point of no return. Your present identity must explode and you will be forced by inner drive to expand, alter and adjust who and what you are.

Therefore, consequently what you can achieve - over time – with enduring perseverance.

I detest being aroused by something ringing. Alarm clocks are the worst, disrupting my natural rhythm of waking up when the body is well rested and chocking my system awake. But this rousting at four o'clock on a leaden November morning is less horrible than most, because before I grasp the phone, I know it's Scott calling from Katmandu.

"I came across a good friend out here and invited him to Climb Everest with us in the spring. It's Anatoli Boukreev, a Russian super climber. Have you seen the James Bond movie Moonraker? Anatoli is a lot like the guy with the metal jaws". Scott is thrilled, his voice bobbling with intoxicating vigor. "You can't ask for a stronger climber than Anatoli to be up there with us. He is probably the most experienced mountaineer in the Himalayas. If we get into trouble, Anatoli will be there to pull of us off the mountain. Who knows what might happen up there?"

"Do you have it?" I interrupt. Scott is in Katmandu for a week - in his role as an executive of Mountain Madness and expedition leader-suffering through the dampening and decisive meetings at the Ministry of Tourism. Get-togethers with the right people in the right ministries are all necessary investments in the scuffle and contest to opt for a climbing permit for Everest via the South Col during the spring 1996 climbing season.

"Do you have it, the permit for Everest?"
"Nah, not yet. But we we'll get it!"

I discern that Scott needs the certainty of having the Everest climbing permit so much more than I do. For year's Scott has worked systematically towards making Everest expeditions the culmination of his business as a professional mountain guide. The future success of his company Mountain Madness will depend on having that permit. His company has arranged almost the entire expedition without knowing whether the promised permit will be issued. I know Scott well enough to acknowledge that his 'But we will get it!' expresses the conviction he needs to make things happen. It's the same kind of confidence I must have to make summiting the highest mountain in the world a reality for me. Anatoli Boukreev and Scott Fischer, like most of the other expedition leaders gathering at Base Camp in the spring, have climbed some of the same mountains.

Before these two magnificent species of masculine representation met face to face, Scott and Anatoli have been amused by anecdotes and entertaining verbal interpretations about each other through their mutual friend, the Russian mountaineer Vladimir Balyberdin. Anatoli; about the gregarious, intrepid American with his gold earring and ponytail, who in 1992 climbed K2 as a member of a Russian-American expedition and Scott Fischer about a maverick climber, who had dodged the draft for the Afghan war to climb mountains instead. Anatoli was becoming legendary for his excessive endurance and extraordinary speed on his high-altitude ascents. In May 1994, the two iconic yet different personalities bumped into each other for the first time.

"We met at a party in Kathmandu where Rob Hall was celebrating the success of his recent triumph on Mount Everest. Scott was celebrating his own victory, as was Neal Biedelman and I" Anatoli shares. Scott had finally - after three attempts -

reached the summit of Everest and immediately after Everest, successfully ascended Lhotse (8,511m). It was a great achievement for Scott, especially because he had summited Everest without the use of supplementary oxygen and additionally became the first American to summit Lhotse. "To me Scott was a Russian's classical ideal of an American. Scott looked like he was from the movies, tall, blond ponytail and handsome in a profound masculine bewitching way. His benevolent, open smile just drew people to him. I thought Scott had great potential as a high altitude climber. I have had the good fortune to climb with many of the world's finest alpinists, and Scott could stand with the best of them.

Although he was not well known, I had for him the respect I had for American Ed Viesturs, whom I had met in 1989", Anatoli contemplates. 1995, pursuing their free spirited lifestyles brought Anatoli and Scott together for the second time in Katmandu mid October 1995. Their unplanned encounter caused Scott to call me with the thrilling news of having secured Anatoli as a guide for our expedition. Scott was mobilizing to create his first huge Everest expedition with a worthwhile amount of paying clients to boost the economy of his company Mountain Madness and Anatoli was struggling to keep his climbing career going after the crumbling of the Soviet Union, as he knew it. In May 1995, Anatoli had guided Henry Todd's successful expedition on the northern side of the Everest. This is the expedition where Michael Knakkergaard became the first Danish male to succeed in scaling the Everest. Henry Todd of Himalayan Guides was eager to corner Anatoli's services for the 1996 season on Everest, where Todd was also planning an expedition from the south side. Scott continued rambling around Katmandu, playing the crucial game with the Ministry of

Tourism to gain one of the 11 permits about to be allotted for the spring 1996 climbing season.

"I was walking down a narrow side street when I saw Scott browsing in the market stalls near the Skala, a Sherpa-owned guesthouse, where I was staying. I thought maybe he wouldn't remember me, so I tapped him on the shoulder and asked him what was happening in America. Immediately he recognized me and broke into a smile."

"Hi Anatoli. How's it going? You have time for a beer?"

"Scott knew the situation in the former Soviet Union. I didn't want to talk so about the hard times, so I told Scott, I'm going to climb Manaslu with a team from Kazakhstan next month. You want to come along?" At first he was silent and then he realized I was serious, and he began to laugh again saying how much he envied me and my extreme adventures. Scott knew, as did I, that no American had ever summited Manaslu. "Oh, Anatoli man, I would love to make that one but I am so incredibly busy. I'm trying to put together this Everest package for May; I've got some stuff going with

Kilimanjaro. Man, I'd love to do it, but I'm just too damn busy."

I tried to get him off his schedule, to do something for himself: to climb. I could see it was hard for him not to accept my invitation. His business was pulling him one way and his love for the mountains another. I understood his dilemma. It is extremely difficult for high-altitude mountaineers to support their climbing without going commercial in some way or another.

"We have a truly strong team, and you would make it even stronger. Join us!"

Scott kept glancing at his watch, wanting to be punctual and properly respectful for his upcoming meeting with the Ministry of Tourism. "Permit politics," he said, "are incredible, and the prices they ask. Fifty thousand for five climbers: ten thousand for each additional climber. Unbelievable!" Scott said he already had some clients signed up and it looked like a "Go" if he could just get the permit. Good relations with the Nepalese bureaucracy are mandatory because nobody climbs without a ticket. Scott asked me if we could meet again the next day. Next morning over second and third cups of coffee, Scott talked a lot about Everest and then we began to discuss high-altitude guiding. He was giving serious thought to a commercial expedition to K2. K2 is only the second highest mountain in the world but is generally regarded as the most dangerous of the 14, 8000 meter peaks. He acknowledged the difficulties of its routes and the tragic stories about the attempts to reach its summit.

    Anatoli knew Scott had his own dramatic history with K2, where Scott's heroic actions had helped save Gary Ball's, Rob Hall's best friends life. Anatoli debated with Scott, "What is true for Everest is also true for K2. You know, you've been on both. There is no room for mistakes. You need good weather and very good luck. You need qualified guides, professional climbers who know high altitude and the mountains. In addition, clients need to be screened carefully; you need people who can carry the responsibilities and challenges of high altitude.

    This is not Mount Rainier. High altitude climbing requires a different set of rules. You have to develop self-reliance in your climbers. It's dangerous to say that Everest can be guided in the same way that Mount McKinley can". Scott listened and then surprised me. "I need a lead climber, somebody with your kind of experience Anatoli. Come with me to Everest and after Everest hey, we'll look at K2 with a Russian guiding team and the Mountains in Kazakhstan. What do you say?" "I already have a tentative offer from Henry Todd and we have an expression in Russian 'You don't change ponies in the middle of the stream' ". Scott laughs, "What is Henry paying you? I will pay you twice as much". Anatoli weighed the prospects. He had confidence in Scott's ability to handle the complexities of compiling an expedition of this magnitude and appreciated Scott's climbing capabilities. Moreover, Neil Beidleman our co-guide was a friend of Anatoli. Anatoli Boukreev had assisted him in his effort to climb Makalu in 1994. Neil Beidleman's endurance was extraordinary, but Neil had no Everest experience. I didn't want to say no, but I didn't feel I could say yes, so instead I asked for USD 5000 more than what Scott was offering, thinking that Todd would understand if it became reality. "No way, no way", Scott shook his head. "Okay, no problem". Honestly, I thought that was the end of our negotiations that I'd be working for Henry Todd as I had the year before. As Scott was leaving, he said, "Let's have breakfast again at Mike's tomorrow, nine? Think about it."

The climbing permit that Scott is pursuing is the all-important key to transforming the media show that I have sparked here in Denmark into a reality on the mountain. Lene Gammelgaard written on that piece of paper will be the permission to set my feet on the Khumbu Icefall in four months and a few letters worth USD 10,000.

Oh! I so intensely hope that everything is progressing as we envision, so I won't make a public fool of myself and loose the sponsors that have committed themselves so far. In each other's company, Scott and I achieve a knife-edge balance of enthusiasm, realism, criticism and mutual encouragement.

We acknowledge that we each have more than a full load to attend to and we see each other through the momentary depressions, connected with pushing ourselves too hard for extended periods to secure the achievement of what we dream about accomplishing. It's an uphill battle for my part that primarily stems from the hard work of fundraising. We find a balance amid the psychic strain of knowing that what we are planning is a dangerous game. When stressed and agitated we attempt to complain and moan, but such behavior is useful only if somebody exists who can fix the world for you. We both recognize that negative exclamations are a sure death for the unending initiatives that are necessary to overcome all hindrances on the path towards our goal. We remind each other: I am responsible for myself in this endeavor.

I want to get to the summit of Everest and safely return!

4

"People of mediocre ability sometimes achieve outstanding success - because they don't know when to quit. Most men succeed because they are determined to."
George E.

Transforming an Everest expedition the size of ours from the vision 'Do you want to climb Everest with me in the spring of 1996?' into the detailed organization of actually being prepared and able to climb the mountain is a tremendous effort, as well as a costly endeavor. From the first attempts of conquering Everest until today, where everyone is online while on the mountain, the media has played a major role in financing our quests. If the mass media catches interest, more sponsors will support us, as beneficiaries more often than not, go for massive media attention to promote themselves via our challenges. In an effort to generate more press for both Mountain Madness and himself, Scott and his loyal female staff aimed for media exposure to promote our 1996 Everest expedition as belligerently as they searched for client climbers to commit to paying the top-ticket of
65,000 USD. Early on, there seemed to be a promising serious opportunity. Precisely, the reverie of breakthrough that fueled the national and international recognition that Scott invested in, was to promote his future grandiose visions for himself, Mountain Madness and the people he wanted to co-create his dreams with. Part of Scott's challenge in launching his expanding expedition business, was his lack of global visibility.

Scott did not have the reputation of many of his fellow mountaineers in high-altitude climbing, who adorned the covers and pages of climbing magazines and equipment advertisements.

"Yeah, I am negotiating with Outside Magazine to secure Jan Krakauer a slot on our trip."

Scott being Scott met Jon Krakauer on several occasions after Scott summited Mount Everest in 1994 and in his usual manner exuberantly shared the splendor of Everest. Jon Krakauer was a Seattle based climber, journalist and bestselling author. Scott's positivity attracted and generally piqued people's interest and seemed to work its magic on Jon Krakauer. He describes their interactions in Into thin Air:"Few weeks after Scott returned victorious from Everest in 1994, I encountered him in Seattle. I didn't know him well, but we had some friends in common and often ran into each other at the crags or at climber's parties. On one occasion Scott buttonholed me to talk about the guided Everest expedition he was planning, "You should come along", he cajoled, "and write an article about the climb for Outside". When I replied that it would be crazy for someone with my limited high-altitude experience to attempt Everest, he said, "Hey, experience is overrated. It's not the altitude that's important; it's your attitude Bro. You'll do fine. You've done some pretty sick climbing stuff that's way harder than Everest. We've got the big E figured out; we've got it totally wired. These days, I'm telling you, we've built a yellow brick road to the summit".

I can almost feel the effect of Scott, when he displays this one-sided version of his métier. Nevertheless, he had ignited a spark in Jon Krakauer and talked up Everest every time they ran into each other in Seattle. Scott was able to take his expertise and natural abilities to perform in the mountains and to share his passion to enable other people's own ambitions. He seemed genuinely motivated through opening his world to others. He was keen on encouraging the opportunity of having a journalist for Outside on his expedition, hoping that it would be the precious promotional media break through needed for making the Mountain Madness Business easier and more profitable in the years to come. Scott bogged down an editor of Outside, Brad Wetzler and for months, the discussions progressed. In exchange for a discounted price for Jon Krakauer, Mountain Madness was lobbying for advertising space and a feature story. Jon Krakauer expressed enthusiasm too, telling one of Scott's associates, that he wanted to climb with Scott's team because Scott's group actually had better climbers and because Scott was a local guy and an interesting character. By January 1996 Outside made a firm commitment to send Jon Krakauer to Everest. This was thanks to Scott's concerted lobbying which is exactly the kind of life expanding influence that was uniquely characteristic for Scott. Scott wanted others to experience the excitement, the inner satisfaction, the gift of what's it like to stand on the summit of Mount Everest and be capable of accomplishing a goal like that. Encountering Scott, you might be on your way to taking on life from a different vantage point as I experienced it in myself and seen it in others. Scott influenced yet another human being to pursue an adventure, which Jon Krakauer might not have been cognizant of pursuing without Scott's special aptitude. He was truly able to spread his love for the high mountains and the excitement about climbing. Outside Magazine, the leading outdoor recreation magazine in the United States, now wanted to sponsor an

Everest slot in the spring season 1996 for a climber-writer, Jon Krakauer, as Wetzler indicated as a member of our team. Outside Magazine was commissioning John Krakauer to write a feature article on the hype connected with the exploding market of commercial expeditions to Everest. Scott's charismatic charm and disarming persistence had convinced Outside Magazine - now wanting to buy a slot for Jon Krakauer - to attempt Everest.

What is the attraction behind charismatic individuals like Scott? What makes Scotts different? Are inspiring personalities shrewder? Do they have more edification? Were they born with some kind of skill or gift that others were not? Did they acquire this demagogic approach?

There are distinctive characteristics that are shared by global icons and successful innovators and none of these "markers" are so exclusive that you can't possess them too. Scott personified the individuals, who perceive the world differently who they look at the bigger picture and see opportunities rather than barriers. They think outside the box of traditional business and look at others as a valuable resource and give back so others can be successful too. They intuitively choose the right environment, finding just the right place at just the right time where their inclinations can thrive. They are willing to shake things up if need be; acknowledging that change can be hard but good. They embrace the global lifestyle, they like people, thrive in diversity cultures and do not harbor feelings of superiority when they invest in building relationships and grow socially responsible projects. They constantly expand their circle of influence by making new contacts and entering new venues. They adapt to their market and improve or create new offers or services in response. They plan for the next life expansion always looking ahead to stay in front because they are mobilized by innovation. They don't wait until the last minute to throw together a plan. They're strategic in their nature making every move count. They don't keep "all of their eggs in one basket"; therefore they don't rely on a single skill set, market or economy for sustainability and growth. They're constantly motivated by seeking new opportunities and are willing to weather the 'downs' while thriving in the 'ups'.

"This can be the press breakthrough that I have been looking for, coverage in a major mass-market magazine reaching trekkers, climbers and wannabees who can afford big-mountain prices. All the visions I have for expanding my business seems to become realized ones we bag the big E with Jon Krakauer on board", Scott was truly fired up. "Recognition was important to Scott", says Jane Brommet-Scott's publicist –who was to accompany us to Base Camp to file Internet Reports for Outside Online. There was a long period where we really thought Jon Krakauer was going to be on our trip. Moreover, Mountain Madness held a slot open for him, still negotiating with Outside Magazine for a combination of advertising and writing a check. One month before we were due to fly to Katmandu, Outside went to Rob Hall instead of finalizing the negotiations with Scott and Mountain Madness and posed the question, 'what will you give "It" to us for?'

John Krakauer got a call from Wetzler informing him that there had been a change of plans. Rob Hall had offered Outside Magazine a significantly better deal than the one Scott was willing to comply to. "I knew and liked Scott Fischer and I didn't know much about Rob Hall, so I was reluctant but after a trusted climbing buddy confirmed Hall's sterling reputation, I enthusiastically agreed to go to Everest with Adventure Consultants", John Krakauer shares in Into thin Air. Recalling the magazines decision to take Hall's offer, a spokesperson from Outside say they did not select Adventure Consultants 'solely for financial reasons' but had also taken into account that Rob Hall had considerable more experience guiding Everest and more of a track record in terms of safety.

"God, It's typical of the media, typical bullshit!" Scott was profoundly infuriated by Outside's decision. He personally called Jon Krakauer to confront him in person, although confrontation, especially with friends, was not something Scott was comfortable with. Scott notoriously avoided upsetting people and wanted everybody to cruise along, leaving it to his female packed back-office to untangle what might be lost in the void between what Scott conveyed to those he wanted to connect with and the real demands from the guardians of the business of Mountain Madness. Scott was fundamentally distraught by Krakauer's shift and on a deep level I assume Scott was not only fuming after being outplayed by the low offer from Rob Hall, but profoundly disappointed that he had inspired the whole deal and the disloyalty obviously displayed by both Wetzler and Jon Krakauer. He had extraordinary sensitive antennas for detecting loyalty and its counterpart, exploitation. He wanted the expanded publicity that only mass media generates but he was not going to sell himself short. In a genuinely altruistic and tender manner, Scott wanted to share his enthusiasm, being in the world to provide what stimulus he could. 'You can do it', 'We can do it', Scott Fischer was a psychic motivator, unselfish and genuinely generating a transformative wake. He was not willing to match Rob Hall's offer to Outside Magazine. Rob Hall agreed to accept only 10,000 USD of his usual fee of 55,000 USD in cash. Advertisement space and the article Jon Krakauer was commissioned to write, would offer Rob Hall the advertising he was strategizing to get access to the American upscale adventurous audience. "Probably eighty or ninety percent of the potential market for guided expeditions to the Everest and the Seven Summits is in the US. After this season, when my mate Scott has established himself as an Everest guide, he'll have a great advantage over Adventure Consultants, simply because he's based in America. To compete with him, we'll have to step up our US advertising significantly", Rob is fundamentally aware of the tactical advantage Scott held.

In 1996 there were at least three expeditions that had focus on serving the growing hunger for dramatic footage from the extreme and dangerous environment of climbing Everest. The most prestigious and complex expedition was the IMAX Film expedition lead by David Breashears ,an entire expedition with massive Sherpa contribution, solely designed and compiled to create an IMAX Film for the world to see. What a media stunt! The film production, with one of the largest budgets ever committed to a documentary about Everest, was to result in a large-format film. David Breashears, in his early forties, is something of a legend in the Himalayas, more than any other climber, except for perhaps Sir Edmund Hillary, who with Tenzing Norgay summited Mount Everest for the first time in 1953. Breashears has been successful in making Everest a source of income, deriving over the years a substantial portion of his revenue from his activities on the mountain.
In 1985, David Breashears had the distinction of guiding Texan businessman and millionaire Dick Bass to the summit. Bass, at fifty-five, became the oldest climber to date to make the top. This accomplishment by many is seen as the pivotal

point in the history of attempts to climb Everest. The adventuresome and the well-to-do took notice. If a fifty-five-year old with motivation and discretionary income could do it, anyone could! Commercial expedition companies were spawned to address the demand thus became stimulated. Rob Hall had Jon Krakauer, a paid journalist writer embedded on Adventure Consultants Everest expedition. Jon Krakauer will climb with the parallel agenda of being commissioned to write articles as well as his own book about this endeavor. As Outside chose Adventure Consultants for Jon Krakauer's climb, Scott and Mountain Madness were able to land an even better branding opportunity. They succeeded in signing on Sandy Hill Pittman, a contributing editor to Allure and to Conde' Nast Traveler. Sandy Pittman is a prize for Mountain Madness and Scott. Sandy, forty years old, very wealthy and soon to become the socialite ex-wife of legendary television businessman Bob Pittman, joined our team in the 11th hour and is acting as a web correspondent for NBC Interactive Media. Sandy Hill Pittman will become the direct eye and mouth to countless audiences, feeding live updates from base camp to the summit via internet. In her first report, she wrote: "I have got as much in the way of computers and electronic hardware as I have in climbing equipment. Two portable microcomputers, a camcorder, three 35 mm cameras, a digital camera, two tape recorders, a CD player, a printer and a sufficient quantity, I hope, of solar panels and batteries to make the whole lot operate. I would not like to leave without taking a blend of coffee from Dean & DeLuca, as well as my espresso machine and because we will be on Everest for Easter, I have also taken four chocolate eggs. Hunting for Easter eggs at 5000 meters should be interesting". Sandy planned a meeting with her friends - including Martha Stewart - at Base Camp and had the latest copies of Vogue and Vanity Fair ferried up to her, while our team acclimatized to the high altitude of the Himalayas.

Excessive wealth often seems to spur expectations of special treatment.

Sandy has climbed the six highest mountains on the continents, but so far, Everest has eluded her. On two previous climbs, one guided by David Breashears of the IMAX team, she turned back before the summit. She has more altitude experience than Jon Krakauer does, and with her agreement with NBC Interactive Media to do a daily feed to their World Wide Web site, Scott has sincere expectations of gaining the recognition he yearned for to sustain and expand his Mountain Madness business. However, Sandy has to get to the top, and Scott knows it. Scott wanted to make sure Sandy could feed news about our progress for the world to follow all the way to the summit. Therefore Lopsang Jangbu Sherpa, leader of our climbing Sherpas', will carry the computer and batteries up the mountain. This is Scott's oneoff chance for media exposure and he invests in making it happen as professionally as possible. If Scott get's Sandy to the top, she'll write about him, she'll talk about him, making him famous in the right circles. If he doesn't, Scott will face a publicity fiasco, jeopardizing access to the well-to-do money loaded circle of acquaintances Sandy socializes with. Utilizing mass media promotion is a two edged sword- Will Rob and Scott push themselves differently with the prospect of future gains connected with successful reports from their respective media representatives? Does the way we conduct ourselves scaling Everest change, when such a massive media spotlight is introduced? What will happen in the extreme that lies ahead of us? Will any of the decisions made on the mountain, especially relating to risk taking and focused concentration on summiting, be influenced by the dimension of on-line presentation to the public? Will it conflict with my private quest? I am also an author as well as a journalist and have my own contract to honor with a daily tabloid newspaper in Denmark- good for self-promotion and securing sponsorships- yet not a major player in the grand scale of global PR that Scoot is yarning for. Does media presence influence what happens on the mountain and off?

    I know that the public commitment I made in Danish media to become the first Scandinavian woman and the second Dane overall to scale Everest, fueled my self-commitment to truly give it my all. Having exposed my grandiose vision onto the public arena, forces me to acknowledge that there is no short cuts, no cowardice way out, because I might feel like giving in to negative self-talk and anxiety. The public commitment propels me to transcend the fear, laziness and socialized giving-up from my previous life.

    Ever since the first mountains were attempted in the Alp's and the Himalayas, securing the funding of this type of explorative adventure has called for finances from various sources. Few are the lucky ones who can pay their own way entirely. Now, as from the outset, most aspirants search for angles to approach sponsors to fund our quest. Therefore, introduction of live media broadcasting is the predictable and foreseeable next step into the modernity that technological improvements introduces, for arm chair interested to gain insights into the remotest regions of our globe. When we arrive at Base Camp Scott no longer harbored any grudges against Jon Krakauer. Bouncing back swiftly from setbacks, Scott welcomed Jon Krakauer to our campsite with his usual bear hug and a mug of Starbucks. I never detected any negativity in Scott after he with his unusual lack of antipathies acknowledged that Jon Krakauer would not climb on our team.

5

"Simplicity is the ultimate sophistication"
Leonardo da Vinci

Scott Fischer's mountaineering passion, launched at the young age of 14 when he participated in a NOLS Adventure Course. His father was an outdoor enthusiast and called Scott in to watch a television program one night at their home in Basking Ridge, New Jersey. The program, Thirty Days to Survival, was about NOLS – National Outdoor Leadership School- and that evening they made a deal: If Scott could raise half the money; his dad would match funds and send him to NOLS. Scott got himself a paper route, managed to scrape the necessary pecuniary investment together to pursue his target, and joined his first NOLS outing. After accomplishing his NOLS course, NOLS founder Paul Petzoldt called the young man into his office and offered to send him right back out into the field as an unpaid assistant on a Wilderness Course. Still only 14, Fischer began his career as a mountain instructor. Back home, his interests switched from playing quarterback to climbing in the Shawangunks of New York. Upon graduation from high school, Scott Fischer thought not of college but of the mountains. He moved to Wyoming and began climbing in earnest. After Scott, a young teenager, went to Wyoming to spend a few weeks as a participant on the wilderness course with the National Outdoor Leadership School (NOLS), his life changed and would never be the same. It became the inauguration for a life full of adventure.

NOLS might justly attribute some of Scott's success to his association with the school: the mentorship of his early teachers like Tom Warren, the opportunities offered by and the inspiration of Paul Petzholdt, and his long career as a respected instructor. Scott Fischer's early start in climbing was initiated through NOLS and pursued with his own drive and determination. As Scott puts it, "I was a tough little fucker".

Now 40, Scott has been living his passion for a couple of decades. He has a reputation for what climber's call 'pushing the edge'. In earlier years, his attitude towards climbing might have best been termed reckless. The first time he lead a NOLS Mountaineering Course, Scott says, "We were climbing everything. One day, I told my co-workers that I was going to take students up three peaks in a day". They said, "No way, you'll never have time". Scott's confident response was, "We'll be back by 5:00". Successful on the peaks but nearing the 5:00pm deadline, Scott stomped fast down the Dinwoody Glacier. Though the glacier is generally very benign, the urgency to prove himself caused Scott to fall into a crevasse where he dislocated his shoulder. The shoulder remained dislocated for three days during the long hike out to a doctor.

Fifteen years later that same shoulder, dislocated on a dare, almost thwarted his efforts on K2 and kept bothering him on Everest in 1996. At 18 Scott met his future wife Jeanie, the instructor fell in love with one of his students. In pursuit of opportunities, Scott and his wife, Jean Price, moved west to Seattle, Washington in 1982, where they had two children, Andy and Katie Rose Fischer-Price. Jeanie became an air pilot, for several years making enough money to support the family of two children Andy and Katie Rose, as well as Scott's fun- and freedom loving lifestyle. Scott's career as a NOLS instructor had allowed him to include his love for the mountains in cutting out a professional lifestyle for himself. Soon though, he came to the realization that the highest peaks were the ones he loved the most. What better way to increase his time in the high peaks than to start a business that took him there. In 1981, Scott and his good friend Wesley Krause founded a company called Mountain Madness.

    The highest summits on each continent - known as the seven summits - were offered by Mountain Madness as were corporate leadership training seminars. The appropriately named company evolved to specialize in taking people to the world's highest summits of the world's highest mountains for fees in the $50,000 range. Supported financially by Jeanie's position at Alaska Airlines, Scott succeeded in confirming his desire for the high mountains, when he himself summited Everest in 1994 climbing with the first American woman Stacey Allison to the top of the world. Successively Scott became the first American to summit 27,940-foot (8,516 m) Lhotse, the fourth highest mountain in the world. Mountain Madness was a low earning enterprise and In 1995 Scott earned about 12.000 USD, still depending heavily on his wife's financial upkeep. Somewhere along their life path, Jeanie seemed to become too fragile to cope soundly with the complexities of her own career complications, as well as their marriage arrangements, shouldering quite some responsibility. What does Scott's wife Jean, think about his Everest endeavor? "I've always known Scott would be a climber, it's what he does. I'd probably have a very different answer for you if Scott was pursuing K2. But one thing that I hadn't anticipated is that Scott's profession could allow him to be such a good father.

    When he's home he has a lot of time for the kids. He's a very participate father, closer to his children than any father I know. Scott spends as much time with us as he can. Time for talking climbing with friends is reserved for late at night, after the children are tucked in". I know Scott truly loves his children. Even in the midst of expedition planning and dreaming of the mountains, Scott's parental passion shows through. He suddenly looks up from route photos and exclaims, "You haven't met my kids, have you? You've got to meet my kids, they're amazing!" But why is he always leaving them for another adventure or PR-option? Out of Andy's nine birthdays, Scott has only been at home and participating in two. Scott's relationship with his wife, who apparently is sometimes mentally fragile, is more opaque. I sense that Scott respects his wife and acknowledges Jeannie as his life companion.

For the majority of his adult life he has depended on her to support his way of living, through her profession as a pilot at Alaska Air, while Scott was exploring the world and being Scott.

In 1991, I met Scott in Nepal in the Khumbu region. Scott and Wesley were conducting Mountain Madness expedition to Baruntse on which five of their nine participating friends reached the summit. I encountered Scott's group on their trek out from Baruntse base-camp. It was impossible for me to escape Scott's charismatic good looks, even though I tried hard for 24 hours. His playful masculinity combined with his genuine insecurity made Scott so very human. He was fun yet elusive to be around back then, charming, boyish, instigating beer drinking and bottle walking contests and generously sharing their stock of Starbucks coffee.

Scott flirted with all women and would evaporate somewhere if any of us as much as attempted to pin him down. Over the years, our friendship formed and on the various occasions where we spent time together in wilderness, I experienced that I was better at finding my way than Scott was, though more prudent and not as physically strong. Therefore, I do not anticipate following him as the leader on our Everest route. Consequently, I have to think strategically and utilize my limited resources carefully. He is still not capable of resting contented within himself. He is less entertaining and sparkling than he was five years ago, yet functioning as coherent as I know him, which is never 100% up to the epitome standard, outsiders projected unto him.

Projections Scott needs, even craves to fill his inner desire to be admired? Loved? Respected? Escaping the negative complexity of his base, with a financing psychically unstable wife and two kids he sees too little? Money in itself is of no interest to Scott, just means to gain recognition for the business aspect of Mountain Madness, as a potential path to untangle himself from the dysfunctional gratitude's he honored towards Jeanie's enduring generosity towards his way of being. I have never experienced Scott discussing his marriage or getting even close to criticizing his domestic set-up. He's never disclosed criticisms regarding his marriage. He was excessively loyal, protective and committed to his wife on profound, deeprooted levels that it would have taken him massive momentum to clarify, if he ever would have considered leaving that part of his existence for good. Scott was not egotistically, obsessively, neurotically pursuing a personal narrow-minded ego promoting climbing career, a path that might have contributed to the recognition he desired to expand his never sufficient income. He was more than a neurotic eremite, pursuing purposeless routes and climbing fame. He was different. Maybe due to his extensive background with NOLS-National Outdoor Leadership School, Scott was a sharer. Intermingled with quite a few charming yet immature character traits, Scott was altruistic and truly opened his adventuresome lifestyle to as many people as possible that he encountered on his travels. Very rarely did Scott climb for the sake of climbing on his own, actually never in the years I knew him. He was a generous human being, unconsciously developing myriads of human beings, through sharing his mannerism and not his caring. Probably he did not even realize the impact he had on people. Scott often guided trips with a charitable angle, and thus gained some of the PR he acknowledged was crucial to expand his business through those channels. He was a charismatic, stoic and hugely attractive male on the outside.

However, in him, there seemed to be an ongoing vulnerable and self doubting process running as a destabilizing current, exposing him to his own doubts and inner conflicts. In sociology and psychology, self-esteem reflects a person's overall emotional evaluation of his or her own worth. It is a judgment of oneself as well as an attitude toward the self. Scott at times often seemed to crave people to fill or escape some hole in him, driving him onwards and in pursuit of new adventures. Developing a strong sense of self-respect can help you fulfill your potential, develop healthy relationships, and make everyone around you perceive you as a person who is worthy of respect. A person with self-respect simply likes her or himself. Self-respect is not reliant on success because there are always failures to contend. Neither is it a result of comparing ourselves with others because there is always someone better. Pursuing successes are tactics usually employed to increase self-esteem. Self-respect, however, is a given. We simply like ourselves or we don't. With self-respect, we like ourselves because of who we are and not because of what we can or cannot do. Scott was probably still struggling with self-esteem issues, prompting him to stretch himself too thin and pursuing the venues he felt would bring him ahead.

    Everyone attempting to summit Everest - one way or the other might be driven by a compulsion to prove oneself. Ambition can be a constructive mobilizing force, propelling you to authentically pursue the utilization of your inherent resources. Ambition can transmute into focused determination and compulsion, driving you towards a fatal outcome. Some individuals establish high personal expectations, causing them to have to prove themselves repeatedly. In order to meet these internalized dogmas, they tend to focus only on the fulfillment of their grandiose project while they take on work overloads. More often than not people who set themselves mountaineering goals, alter their manner in which they interact with their surroundings. From the time they devote the whole shebang to fulfill their ambition; they have no time and energy for anything else. They become excessively focused. Friends, family, eating and sleeping seem unnecessary or unimportant, as they take up the time and energy spent on working towards the fulfillment of their extraordinary vision. Therefore they leave a wake of destroyed relationships behind, having exploited the goodwill of loved ones in their pursuit of whatever it is they connect with, summiting yet another mountain.

    Everyone and everything but the summit dwindles into oblivion until they return to the shambles of their lives, wondering why people are behaving hostile and hurt. The driven, self-focused project- oriented person might become aware that their narrow pursuit and exploitation of their surroundings for furthering their ambition is not entirely right, but a climber planning the next expedition seems unable to comprehend the source of the problem. In this stage, climbers tend to isolate themselves from others and they might begin to be emotionally blunt and intolerant.

Being the person on the outside, you tend to see more aggression and sarcasm. It is not uncommon for mountaineers to blame their increasing problems on time, pressure and all the work that they have to do on whoever is in their proximity. Pursuing an adventure seems fundamentally meaningless for a loved one on the sideline, even more so, when experiencing the destruction that seems an inherent consequence of being single-mindedly obsessed. People, in their immediate social circles are cut off and often at times blamed for whatever does not run according to the focus of the vision-driven individual. Such depersonalization leads to losing contact with themselves and they no longer see themselves or others as valuable. They feel empty inside and to overcome this, they might look for even more activity, as well as sex, alcohol or drugs. Whatever they pursue is often exaggerated, leading to burnout and consequently depression. The single-minded driven person risk becoming exhausted, hopeless, indifferent, and believes that there is nothing for them in the future.

6

"If you never test your limits, how will you know what they are?"
Lene Gammelgaard

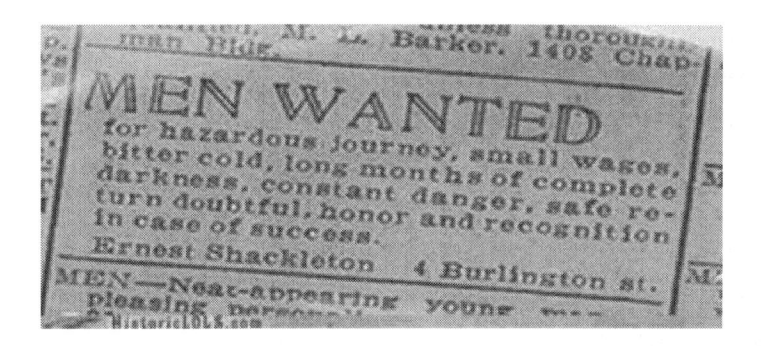

MEN WANTED for hazardous journey, small wages, bitter cold, long months of complete darkness, constant danger, safe return doubtful, honor and recognition in case of success.
Ernest Shackleton 4 Burlington st.

- Realize your unique observation of the world.
- Beware of making assumptions about peoples intentions.
- Our view is subjective, partial and likely to be distorted.
- Explore different perspectives for innovative richer solutions

Who are we - the individuals who thrive better under primitive, harsh circumstances than remaining within the confinements of relative security and expected predictability of everyday life? Who chose to go against sound preserving instincts to pursue high-risk activities? Having the urge - and following the urge to climb Everest is by any standard an unusual act. I have been a seeking soul, driven by some uncontrollable longing to challenge the parameters of the world I know. Fired by the desire of self-actualization, need for authentic achievement, belongingness, eminence, and other subconscious motivations based genetic internalized mental patterns and social influences from an environment and larger world's perceptions of gender based options and warranted conduct. I acknowledge the fact that we don't know the limits until we have given all to test ourselves in reality. I am driven by the desire to know myself. As a young girl I drove my parents crazy - questioning and protesting norms, social conformity, gender roles, religion, destiny itself - yarning for meaning in life. As I grew to adulthood, I suffered a lot of resistance in my immediate environment because of my way of being, my scrutinizing need to confront whatever I condemned as empty values and superficiality. My feelings of being trapped, bored, unfulfilled, frustrated and downright unhappy doubtlessly were compounded by the fact that I was growing up to be a woman. I am socialized in a middleclass conform family in a small Scandinavian country. On the surface, you talk about equality in Denmark, but in partial reality, I discovered a number of invisible blockers that hinder you in piecing together the full picture of your inherent resources. Directly and indirectly, I was molded by being told what I could not or should not do, because I was a woman. I was susceptible to dullness, restlessness in ordinary settings, intolerant of repetition or mind-numbing people's small talk. More times than not, I did what I was not expected to do. Add to that and a lot more that none in my vicinity ever even predicted, like crossing the Atlantic when I was 18 years old absolutely unsupported by my family and societal values. Do women and men differ in their propensity to choose a risky challenge because of innate preferences or because their innate preferences are modified by pressure to conform to gender stereotypes? Research proves that single-sex environments are likely to modify risk-taking preferences in important ways. Results show that girls from singlesex schools are as likely to choose the real-stakes gamble as much as boys from either coed or single sex schools and more likely than coed girls. Moreover, gender differences in preferences for risk-taking are sensitive to the gender mix of a group, with girls being more likely to choose risky outcomes when assigned to all-girl groups. This suggests that observed gender differences in behavior under uncertainty might reflect social learning rather than inherent gender traits. I never felt I had a choice, I could not conform, It is just who I am, who I must be - to be me. Climbing the highest mountain in the world prompts the component of risk taking capacity in women and men to an extreme. Can we understand what complex motivators may be driving someone's behavior and actions? Understanding what truly motivates someone to do something can be very difficult and prone to error, since we are not directly experiencing those motives in ourselves. It's essential to keep a humble mind and collect as much evidence as possible before coming to a firm conclusion as to the cause of someone's conduct. Risk willingness includes both biopsychosocial and environmental factors that can be predisposing factors for risk taking. Whether or not predisposing factors lead to risky choices and behavior depends largely upon the social and cultural context where the choice is made. Socialization is crucial. Risk taking occurs when an inner drive motivates the organism to act in ways that will reduce feelings of tension. In psychology, a motive is generally defined as a state of physiological or psychological arousal, which influences how we behave.

Do we climb Everest because of biological factors? Since we are all living organisms, our biology plays a big role in how we conduct ourselves.

Activity igniting drives, which stem from our biology, are known as "biological drives" and their purpose is to keep us alive and out of danger. The innumerable and complex needs of our body create various biological drives that influence much of our everyday behavior. These drives can act as a source of changing our behavior in some ways. In order to keep the body alive, we need to satisfy our drives at the right time and stop when they are satisfied to an adequate level.

The way the body does this is through a process known as homeostasis, which essentially involves keeping the body in balance. Hormones can have a big influence on regulating our biological drives. Hormones, such as melatonin, can influence when we sleep or how tired we feel throughout the day. It is important to realize that biological drives can be modified, which can result in a drive increasing (up regulate) or decreasing (down regulate). Drive reduction theory states that when we do something that reduces the tension associated with a biological drive (we are in a state of arousal), then that action is einforced. Therefore, whenever we do something which is successful in satisfying a biological drive, that behavior is likely to become reinforced and so we will repeat it time and time again. Like biological drives general, psychological drives are also innate drives. However, they differ from biological drives in that they do not operate on the principle of homeostasis.

Some of the main general drives include the curiosity drive and the activity drive. The activity drive causes us to physically move, when our biological drives are satisfied; for example, humans have a natural urge to be active.

Curiosity is a drive to experience new things, and is vital to the growth and development of the brain. The curiosity drive causes us to seek novel information and experiences from the world around us. The curiosity drive is very important for keeping the brain healthy, as the brain relies on exposure to new stimuli in order to grow and develop. If we were not curious, the brain would not get enough stimulation and would eventually begin to atrophy. The curiosity drive is triggered by a change of stimulation, such as when we are exposed to something, which we have never seen or experienced before in our lifetime. If we are exposed to the same thing over and over, we become bored with it very quickly because familiar things are not good at stimulating the brain sufficiently to feed our curiosity need. Our attention is naturally drawn to things that are strange or unusual. It's almost like the brain is opening up the senses to their maximum capacity, when we are exposed to novelty, so that the brain receives as much information about this fresh stimulus as possible. The need of the brain to be stimulated by information, activity and new experiences is so dramatic, that people with my psychological make-up seek challenges like climbing Everest. Sensation seeking is a personality trait defined by the search for experiences and feelings, that are varied, novel, complex and intense and by the readiness to take physical, social, legal and financial risks for the sake of such experiences. Risk is not an essential part of the trait, as many activities associated with it are not risky. However, risk may be ignored, tolerated, or minimized and may even be considered to add to the excitement of the activity. There are people like me who prefer a strong stimulation and display a behavior that manifests a greater desire for sensations and there are those who prefer a low sensory stimulation. Those who are high sensation seekers require a lot of stimulation to reach their optimal level of arousal. When the stimulation or sensory input is not met, the person finds the experience disagreeable, boring and of no interest. Risk can be defined as the assessed likelihood of a negative outcome for a specific performance. Risk taking behaviors are volitional, purposive, goal oriented and carry potential for harm. This behavior is seldom initiated because of the inherent risks, but because the brain is stimulated the most through certain activities. Thrill and adventure-seeking can be channeled into a desire for outdoor activities involving unusual sensations and risks. Experience-seeking individuals find new sensory or mental experiences through unconventional choices, including social nonconformity and desire to associate with unconventional people. All of these features serve to stimulate the brain by introducing something new to a person's life even when it involves risk-taking behavior,- defined as any sort of behavior that involves unnecessary risk of physical injury.

One possible explanation for risky behaviors such as mountaineering is the curiosity drive in action. Our brains crave extraordinary stimulation to release the chemical reactions that makes us feel a live, excited, fulfilled, content and satisfied. As a result of partaking in an unfamiliar activity, the brain gets a massive dose of stimulation by engaging in a challenge that involves risky behavior, which seems to satisfy the brain for a certain period of time. In modern society, we rarely face physical threats. Challenges are more likely to be mental or emotional. Stress is our body's way of responding to a perceived challenge. Positive stress can be the flare that propels you to act constructively and pursue new venues; negative stress can become debilitating and stop you even before you muster courage to progress.

As you embark on your plans for novel action, you must learn to take control of the negative stress in your system. You will never be able to eliminate either negative or positive stress because we do not inhabit a perfect universe, but successful individuals learn how to minimize the crippling consequences of negative stress and cope with it when it is inevitable. When a sensation prone person gets bored with the regular routine of everyday life, they will often do something out of the ordinary or extreme to make themselves feel alive again. It is interesting because that specific urge literally mobilizes a rush of information to the brain. The brain craves unknown stimulations to release the chemicals that give us satisfaction.

When you actually initiate your action plan, the activities will eliminate a great deal of stress. We feel stressed out when we believe that we're not in control of life and try to control our stress by taking control of events. So following an action plan gives us a feeling of being in control. Individualistic purposeful action releases a feeling of satisfaction, of being alive and present.

An alternative explanation for risk taking behavior may be due to a gradual process of desensitization, whereby a person gradually performs increasingly risky activities and wants to "up" the challenge to feel alive, by doing something a bit more daring. This is a logical explanation, as the brain eventually becomes weakly stimulated by familiar tasks no matter how complex, dangerous or simple they may be consequently developing greater tolerance to uncertainty and ambiguity that is unknown risks. Risk takers greater tolerance for uncertainty and the unfamiliar and an increased desire for and focus on neural rewards probably wires us to explore the unknown. You don't know what you're going to find is the most alluring motivator for experience seeking individuals.

If you are ambiguously tolerant it will enable lust for exploration of the unknown. Any change, encourages experimentation with novel behavior. In other words, it takes some acceptance of uncertainty and comfort with not knowing, in order to learn and to be open to new knowledge. We come into the world with limited awareness about what kind of consequences we will experience after making decisions and also about how likely these different outcomes are. Of course, we want to learn, so tolerance for unknown risks might stem from an underlying biological feature that makes learning about the unknown less unpleasant for some than it is for others. Indeed, some risk taking is considered developmentally appropriate. Whether we are attempting mastery or testing limits, taking risks appears to be a way of gaining self-understanding toward the main developmental tasks of adolescence, forming an identity and developing autonomy.

Although adolescents take a disproportionate number of risks compared to any other population, there is no indication that most are willfully attempting to harm themselves or others. What often looks to others like irrational behavior, risk taking by adolescents can be a rational process. Nevertheless the taking of certain risks can have grave consequences. Unfortunately not all risk-taking is healthy, conducive behavior that supports sound personal development. If the frequency and intensity of risk taking increases, it might no longer serve a positive developmental purpose and becomes problematic.

Gratuitous risk taking, or recklessness, where risk is not minimized and perhaps even consciously exaggerated, when precautions could be taken against it, are particularly tricky. Although some risk taking behaviors are socially sanctioned, such as extreme sports and mountaineering, a challenge lies in distinguishing between those behaviors, which are health enhancing and health compromising. Norms for risk taking behaviors are often culture and gender specific. Men are admired for being strong and courageous while climbing high mountains and women are condemned as irresponsible mothers.

Performing exactly the same acts under identical circumstances -two judgments-a difference based on gender bias. Humans take risks for countless reasons; in defiance of authority, as a commitment to others, as a transforming experience and to define relationships. Sharing risks can result in cohesion, trust, and greater closeness with peers. Since risks vary according to different groups, risk taking can become a badge of social identity. Risks connected with climbing Everest hold a high potential for harm or loss, but also hold great potential for growth and opportunity. The motivation for risk taking expresses the reality that more and more do not see sufficient important roles for themselves in society. Communities do not provide useful roles where inherent energy can be constructively channeled, thus finding meaning in life is difficult. Risk taking includes both bio-psychosocial as well as environmental factors. Whether or not predisposing dynamics leads to risky choices and behavior depends largely upon the social and cultural context where the choice is made. Socialization is crucial to this process.

We humans as a race tend to live longer; therefore I advocate that we must consciously develop a 'young attitude' towards reality. We need to be able to keep adjusting and innovate mentally beyond adolescence. We must condition ourselves to go against the mature brain tendency to make choices based on experience, as a method to keep us safe from harm. With the speed of global development today, we need more flexible brains and an increased ability to deal with the unknown, as we grow older end tends to biologically stagnate. We need to cultivate a certain degree of risk taking to create innovative human beings. Human behavior is fundamentally shaped by our primitive animalistic biological drives; this is why people will often act like animals when they are in danger.

Essentially, our brain puts us into survival mode so that we do whatever is needed to keep our body safe and alive. Everest cannot be interpreted by the generally perceived standard for ethical conduct that we ideally expect is ruling the society we are part of. Everest is an extreme environment, were you can only judge yours and others mode of conduct, if you have been there and experienced high altitude to the core of your being. We human beings are basic biological organisms when put in a survival situation. Very few fellow beings excel as heroes and super humans under such circumstances. But how many of us are truly heroes even under normal conditions?

My belief is that life is meant to be lived fully. You shouldn't wait till some other time to detect and initiate plans to fulfill your innermost aspirations. To find meaning in life, you must drive yourself to pursue defining what your goals might be and have the courage to persevere, even in the face of failure. The ability to learn from fiasco and grow through losses is a necessary part of anyone's endeavor - the fabric of life itself - no matter what your talents and desires might be. You will experience setbacks, disappointments and disasters. When that happens, pick yourself up, dust yourself off, figure out what went wrong, make the necessary adjustments and get on with the journey. Do you know what you dream off and are you willing to transform your desires into reality; to risk change?

For if you never test your limits, how will you know what they are?

7

"Whether you think you can, or you think you can't - you're right."

Henry Ford

- Once you have decided what to place at the center of your life, your next step is to focus on the areas that you can effectively influence.
- Some of what is important to you will be beyond your sphere of influence.
- You will face countless limitations and hindrances that you can do nothing about
- Focus on the possible.

"Maybe I will not go to the summit of Mount Everest this year, but find people to take my role."

"I think that's a brilliant idea."

"We are playing a deadly game. The mountains are supreme - most powerful. I don't want to be dead - I want to be alive.... Don't let me die, Lene. Keep me humble. I am probably not humble, but I need to be. I must be careful...." At 40 Scott is lying flat - tired, deflated, exhausted and burnt out. He has transmuted through a downward spiral in the years I have known him, from the fun loving, engaged, vibrant, boyish and full of life zest. Scott is still displaying the undisturbed fun driven aspects of himself in spells, but more and more exhaustion, tiredness and illness is prevailing. Burnout due to many options, all at ones Scott is at the forefront off, having to push and persevere to accomplish the good, he envisions for himself, Mountain Madness and the number of followers who look up to him. High expectations from too many people, persevering to the point of not allowing himself time for relaxation and socializing, Scott's fundamental distance in close and personal relationships might aid in creating the feeling of burnout. His lifestyle which involves doing too much with too little resources and going beyond human limits is the guaranteed track to burning out. Burnout often involves loss of motivation, ideals, and hope, the very ingredients Scott used to be the bearer of.

Having followed Scott's decay due to too much of the time Scott and I spend together during the winter of 1995 was tainted by Scott's somber doubts about whether it was too late for him to leave the high mountains and find contentment elsewhere. Scott was taking a midlife review. He felt like shaking things up in his personal life and in his role in Mountain Madness. He wanted me to summit Everest and then come to the States and become a part of leading Mountain Madness expeditions. A longstanding dream comes true for me, as I have wanted to settle in the US for a long time.

This opportunity would truly give me the foundation to build a new life for myself: a very intriguing and much desired motivation. When I first lay eyes on Scott in 1995 after departing Nepal in 1991 at our exuberant hotel in Islamabad heading for Concordia, I gasped for air and thought, "This guy is so attractive it's almost a crime." Scott's adventurous flamboyant boyish "Let's make it happen and have fun!" and the fact that he always did make great adventures happen, not to perfection, and certainly not being the serious leader. But he

got a lot done and invited people into audacious realms of the world, life expansions they would not have pursued if not for Scott. He offered them adventures that they grew from, became able to undertake them by themselves, after sharing life with him. I have seen Scott's charisma work wonders time and again. Working because Scott was who and how he was. He was not arrogant and aloof and therefore attracted aspiring adventurous souls who longed for what he personified.
Through encountering Scott, they contracted "it". Spending time with Scott on expeditions exposed the doubting, yet unspoiled self-reflecting and withdrawn side of this extraordinary human being. I do not think Scott ever found inner peace. He was gifted with an impressive outer appearance, truly fabulous looking and very strong: a walking icon of American masculinity. Yet had so far not profoundly wanted or managed to mature and grow up and out of mountain madness. Mountain Madness former general manager, Karen Dickinson, described the company's decision to package expeditions to Everest as "Kind of the ultimate in high-altitude mountaineering. There was a demand from our clients, that we wanted to service or lose them to our competitors. If it goes well, it can be a very lucrative niche, so there was financial motivation. It's a high-stakes game financially." Scott had bargained for years to get the climbing permit for Everest, another adventure about to happen. Scott's long pursued strategy and trips to Nepal was about to pay off. Then Everest happened.

Climbing Mount Everest is a relatively expensive undertaking. Climbing gear required to reach the summit may cost in excess of USD 8,000 and most climbers use bottled oxygen, which adds around USD 3,000. The permit to enter the Everest area from the south via Nepal costs USD 10,000 to USD 25,000 per person, depending on the size of the team. The ascent typically starts from Base Camp at the foot of the mountain, which is approximately 100 kilometers (60 miles) from Kathmandu; transferring one's equipment from the airport to the Base Camp may add as much as USD 2,000. Beyond this point, costs may vary widely. It is technically possible to reach the summit with minimal additional expenses, and there are "budget" travel agencies, which offer logistical support for such trips. However, this is considered dangerous (as illustrated by the case of David Sharp). Many climbers hire "full service" guide companies, which provide a wide spectrum of services, including acquisition of permits, transportation to and from Base Camp, food, tents, fixed ropes, medical assistance while on the mountain, an experienced mountaineer guide and even personal porters to carry one's backpack and cook one's meals. The cost of such a guide service may range from $50,000 to $100,000 per person. Since most equipment is moved by Sherpas, clients of full-service guide companies can often keep their backpack weights under 10 kilograms (22 lb.), or hire a Sherpa to carry their backpack for them. In contrast, climbers attempting less commercialized peaks, like Mount McKinley, have to carry backpacks over 30 kilograms and occasionally, to tow a sled with 35 kilograms (77 lb.) of gear and food.

Until the early 1990's quite a few Everest Expeditions were organized as government or science sponsored projects using tax payer money. The leadership and climbers were frequently inexperienced at high altitude. Some were organized through want ads in climbing journals and notices posted in alpine huts. The majority of Everest Expeditions are commercial in the sense that someone other than the person climbing pays the expenses. Most climbers seek sponsors for at least equipment and supplies and try to secure some kind of funding through writing or reporting about their quest. Beginning of the early 1990's some Everest expeditions were professionally organized by internationally certified mountain guides. Professional mountain guiding has been a trade in the Alps for more than 175 years. As the history of climbing in the Alps, that risk cannot be eliminated even with guides -no matter how much you pay for the most experienced guide and equipment. A guide is just another human being, some are truly risk adverse, and others are close to crazy. Most are still men, socialized to present a macho façade to the world as well as to themselves. Which can be a risk factor in itself, as it is not first priority for men to admit weakness, tiredness, fear or defeat. Individuals willing to venture into the unknown are the explorers who modify the present. Without the psyche to take high risk decisions - and venture into the unfamiliar and uncontrollable - Mount Everest would never have been climbed by anyone at any time. Attempting to climb an 8000-meter peak is dangerous. We who are willing to venture along those life paths - individual psychological impacts mobilizing us to live with those risks - might for whatever reason - set us apart from security loving individuals. A minority of us acknowledges that climbing is excessively dangerous and most deny. Others control their emotions with hashish and pills. Mount Everest takes all kinds from geniuses like Anatoli to the crazy people, displaying their raw bone ends with glowing pride, quiescent in the perception that limbs lost to severe frostbite is a sign of honor. How and why we climb Everest is a testimony of profound personal and cultural imprint. The motivating force to summit Everest is al engulfing. Ordinary perceptions of how climbers and teams conduct themselves, how they are all heroes when it truly counts in that brief snapshot of existence. The ethic impressions that we will abstain from fulfilling vain ambitions in the wake of death are all illusionary, when confronted with the real existential undertakings up high. Surviving over the edge proves who we really are in the now. Mirroring the fundamental zest in humanity to get to know ourselves and the existential conditions of life, because only when looking death and destruction in the eyes, do you encounter your potential for just and ethic ,acting or fail in the eyes of the world and yourself. I have come to learn that our petty drama on Everest, must serve as a sounding board for everyone who takes an interest in our dealings. Probably, our destiny presents a simple and brutal confrontation with existence of how we fantasize we would be dealing with similar challenges. You can die on each climb you undertake, independent of the difficulty. Whether you are a real mountaineer or not, you must be careful, aware, humble, self-responsible and even afraid. By climbing mountains, we are learning how big we were. Additionally we are finding out how breakable, fragile and how full of willpower we are. You can only get this extreme self-knowledge if you expose yourself.

High-altitude alpinism has become mass tourism. The commercial trips to Everest are just as dangerous as any other expedition and even more so as some of the guides and organizers articulate to clients, "Don't worry, it's all organized. Hundreds of Sherpas prepare the route. Extra oxygen is available in all camps, right up to the summit. People will cook for you and lay out your beds." Clients feel safe and might not fully comprehend the risks involved. The less experienced - the more need to trust an experienced guide with your life. Edmund Hillary went on record saying that he has not liked "the commercialization of mountaineering, particularly of Mt.

Everest". Hillary claimed that "Having people pay $65,000 and then be led up the mountain by a couple of experienced guides ... isn't really mountaineering at all", nevertheless noted that he was pleased by the changes brought to Everest area by the Westerners. We bring money into an income scares region. "I don't have any regrets because I worked very hard indeed to improve the conditions for the local people. When we first went in there they didn't have any schools, or medical facilities. All over the years we have established 27 schools, two hospitals and a dozen medical clinics and built bridges over wild mountains, rivers and put in fresh water pipelines in cooperation with the Sherpas".

8

"Let's make it happen and have fun!"
Scott Fischer

- Point of no return.
- There is no turning back - let yourself be engulfed by your vision.
- If you believe - "If this is not working, I'll go back to the way I was before", - then you will always fall back....

Ever since Scott and I met in Nepal in 1991, we have corresponded through letter writing and thus have gotten to know each other. I see Scott the human being, more than I see Scott the "American Hero"- one of the world's strongest climbers. Scott comes from another culture; he is accustomed to strong, competent women in the high mountains, has been with several on expeditions and considers it natural that I can "climb that big thing." I realize that I actually thrive being believed in, backed up; something Americans are good at. However, that specific constructive inclination I was welcomed with back in 1991, is excruciating and fundamentally contrary to the Danish phenomena "The Jantelov"; a cultural diminishing equalizer claiming "You should never believe you are special. And if you do, you have misunderstood something".

I am definitely the less experienced climber compared to Scott. He is a man of vision and has proven by the way he lives his life –"Let's make it happen and have fun!" That he makes dreams come true, for himself as well as the myriads of people, like me, that have their existence expanded through chance encounters with Scott's infectious life attitude. Scott lived and breathed transforming vision into real life adventures, for himself and through his companionable generous personality, also for all the people he invited into his universe by creating never-ending expeditions for likeminded and aspiring individuals to expand their life possibilities. Scott was widely loved and admired; I believe his ego needed his huge audience to feel sustained. A certain frailty and shyness hiding beyond his grand appearance, was probably contributing to his attractiveness, as he never prided himself of his great looks, never displayed even the slightest glimpse of self-importance or distancing himself from less outgoing contemporaries. Sometimes Scott's wishful thinking stretches the bounds of reality. Or, I guess it is more correct to say that what he plans is possible, but typically requires more time than he prophesies. That's why I am appealing for Scott, my patience and endurance, involuntarily cultured through rising from disappointments. If you have patience and endurance and know what you want, a lot is possible.

   I do not believe I can conquer Mount Everest, but I do hope I will be capable of estimating the conditions and come back alive If I am fortunate. My experience in the mountains and as an ocean sailor can't convince me that climbing Everest will be as straightforward and simple as Scott expresses in our detailed plan for the expedition progress. Just how many winters have I spent in the Chamonix Aiguilles, with great plans and aspirations to climb this or that route and winter after winter being rejected by the weather and my inferiority? Gale, snow, whiteout and various cocktails of weather have left many an ambition unfulfilled. I am frightfully aware that if nature rises in all its might, I stand no chance. And no fine day by-day schedule will make any difference then. I discuss with Scott.

We see the world differently Scott and I. I have had numerous setbacks in the mountains, often debating with my own cowardice for turning around, instead of narrowly focusing on the summit. I do tend to turn around if the conditions or my inner fear overtaxes my desire to push upwards. I am probably an overcautious climber. Scott has - for a period of 5 years- had nothing but success on his expeditions. Except, that is, for Mount McKinley in 1995, when profoundly astonished, he wrote to me,

"I am back from Alaska. Guess what? Mount McKinley beat me this time. It was the worst weather I have ever seen, anywhere."

His defeat by the weather up North made me smile and ponder; "So much better if nature teaches you a bit of humbleness." I did not think this out of malice, but because I truly care about Scott and wish him a long life. Scott has already survived longer than I dared believe when we first met in 1991. Back then hiking from Pheriche to Katmandu and partying with Scott, Wesley Krause and his friends - among them Dale Kruse, who was also on the trip in Pakistan and will be on the Everest team as well - I kept my emotional distance to this big, boyish guy who climbed mountains for the fun of it and partied like a mad man. I grew closer to Scott's dark version Wesley Krause, a strong, more mature version of the same grand capacities as Scott displayed. In 1984, climbing partners Wesley Krause and Scott Fischer scaled the Breach Wall Direct on Mount Kilimanjaro in Africa.

As the only other climbed by Reinhold Messner and Konrad Renzler in 1978, this was a significant and notable achievement. Wesley Krause was on Everest together with Scott, when they attempted it the first time. Wesley was based in Tanzania, founding African Environment, leading new routes up Kilimanjaro. My gravitating inclination was towards Wesley, who is a much more composed and inertly secure man than Scott would ever take time to become.

I drank and partied with Scott and formed a lasting bond with Wes, as we abandoned waiting for the weather to clear the long waiting line of stocked up climbers in Lukla, hiking all the way back to the bus depot in Jiri, deserting Scott to fly out. Wes, teaching me about the birds on the trail and how to navigate the huge kite he brought for the fun of it. I had this feeling about Scott after our first encounters, that one day I would receive the message that he had perished in the mountains. It didn't happen. Instead, one letter followed another, Scott's written unfolding of his climbs of peaks around the world. In addition, over time revealing the doubts, self reflections and hopes for the future this fun guy shielded within. Contemplating trouble with his marriage and finances, was it too late in life to settle down and change career path?

Scott's persisting loyalty and ability to build a friendship that I tried to shield myself against, won me open. Scott wanted and pursued bonding year after year with people he held in regard. Somehow, we had made a connection on a deeper level by sharing life back in 1991 trekking through the Khumbu region, getting to know each other by being together 24/7. Scott was lavish yet also very sensitive towards being exploited for his embracing way of being. I remember asking him to buy a bivouac sack and a pair of long john's for me in the US - and he gave me both items as gifts- inquiring if I only upheld the connection with him to get free equipment. His defenselessness made me want to spend more time with him. A chance we both got in the preparation for Everest, where Scott ventured to Denmark to participate in various press conferences, securing the public awareness for my ambition to become the first Scandinavian woman to scale Everest.

Cognizance that was needed for me to gather the huge amount of money that my dream to scale Everest with Scott depended upon. Scott without a doubt was fascinated by me and vice versa. I have a particular photo from the press conference at Park Café in mind, where Scott is caught in an unconscious glare at me. Truly exposing what he might have been feeling: emotions that I will never know if he had intentions to follow through with action. Scott and I had a plan. For years I had wanted to relocate to the US, again and again realizing as David Breashears would state years later, when I were in Boston for a lecture, painting vernissage and documenting a film tour that, "Denmark is just too small for that woman."

Scott has grand visions for Mountain Madness, visions that fit my way of dreaming how life could be. Expanding Mountain Madness adventures globally. When I succeed in becoming the first Scandinavian woman to scale Everest on Scott's team, we will utilize the branding and publicity to promote Mountain Madness in Europe.

Scott appears conscientious of becoming known overseas. After our successful expedition, with as many climbers summiting and no casualties I will move to the States and become part of the Mountain Madness team, leading adventure trips around the world. A dream of future prospects that suited the life Scott and I easily envisioned, feeding it in each other's company.

"Shit, I did not realize it would be this professional," Scott whispers as we are confronted with the massive media array hustling to get a space at the press conference I have announced at Park Café' today. As much as Scott yarns for media recognition, I am not aware if he has developed a professional strategy of how to approach and deal with the phenomena, one's it begins rolling. I have, with my background working with emitting companies to the stock market and background as a journalist. Scott seems truly taken aback and impressed, as I take the lead in answering questions and constructing the impressions and hype I want. No journalist dared ask the question I know many pondered upon, whether Scott and I had an affair or not. But many photographers took pictures of us together, a radiant adventuresome looking twosome. I can detect the surprise in Scott's eyes as this circus starts working to our advantage. Scott is truly bad at relaxing and enjoying himself at dinner at Nyhavn.

Restless from stress and lack of smoking hashish to calm himself I guess. He has not dared to bring any weed into Denmark, realizing that the European drug dogs would have picked up the scent of his favorite substance. At this juncture he has to contend himself with beer.

"I'm tired Lene, am contemplating changing my life. I applied for a leading position at NOLS, but they found someone else. I don't want to die in the mountains, but I get depressed after being home for a while. I'm not as free as you are. I've got obligations, my wife, Jeannie, who I owe a lot, Kathy Rose, Andy and Mountain Madness business. I doubt this is the way I want to continue."

Scott's predicament was the accumulated consequences of Scott being Scott. Some rightly saw him as an accomplished climber, guide, owner of Mountain Madness (the name tells a lot) and photographer, but also a happy go lucky, unserious, slightly immature maverick, always looking to have a party like time- which became more and more difficult over the years I spend time with Scott. The opportunities for fun were plenty, mostly initiated by Scott 'the Man', but more often than not, he seemed to fail at fully enjoying the moment, as the years moved him from youth into getting closer to 40. Scott lived as he used to, being 'Bruce, the Dude', but might have encountered the restlessness, depression, boredom, exhaustion that follows not adapting to the inner and outer changes life consists of. Not taking enough time to fundamentally dig into what he needed to transform and what not, why, how and when. Scott for now continued compiling more of the same, focusing on creating a huge break through the untapped possibilities by organizing this commercial expedition to Everest.

"Mountain Madness will organize most of the details and my people behind the scenes make it possible for us to climb this great mountain. The whole spectacle includes permit, Sherpas, Sirdars', Buddhist Priests, guides, expedition outfitters, cooks, porters, medical doctor, helicopter pilots, oxygen, food, porters, yaks, line fixer, clients to pay for it all and a number of details - but when we're on the mountain - we are just a group of friends, out having fun."

Scott's approach to being the leader of our Everest expedition is one of my whys and wherefores for wanting to join Scott on this adventure. Scott always leaves the team to itself and has his own grand time, doing his thing and never in any way wanting to lead or take the role of being the front figure. I know he would never micro manage and try to tell me what to do and when. He never has. On the contrary, there have been several occasions around the globe, where Scott wanted to cajole me into taking over responsibilities the team members would rightly expect were his to take, if any should. I acknowledge that if I shall stand a chance of accomplishing this mountaineering endeavor, I will have to utilize my limited resources extremely ruthlessly, careful not to wear myself out on anything not conducive to my quest. I therefore must to be climb when I feel strong and rest when I feel the need, to allow my body to acclimatize in its own rhythm instead of following an outer regime. I also know that
the people, who choose to climb with Scott, are people I'll get along with: independent, self-ruling and exclusively anti dictatorial. We are compiled of and attracted by comparable qualities. Scott's characterizations makes for a certain kind of unsavory reputation and rightly so. He does not comply with the kind of image that attracts lucrative Fortune 500 sponsors. Scott is, for that league too dubious and uncontrollable. His nature attracts anarchistic climbers, likeminded individualists, 'Dudes' who has honest insights in to what Scott is and is not and for those very reasons want to climb as part of the Mountain Madness team and none other. Scott truly is a guy

who wants to share his adventures with others and participate in the fun that life expansion offers us.

We who know Scott, never expects him to lead and those who do, become sadly disappointed. Being the authority in front is just not a Scott thing. This makes Scott truly remarkably, in spite of his human flaws. Scott's mannerisms cause my world to explode in growth opportunities. I am having fun! Thanks to Scott's existence. And I have encountered quite a lot of people on my trips with Scott, who has changed the way they live after returning home from one of his treks.

His example and person sparking in us and what we have inherently, but had not mobilized until we encounter him. Igniting fuller lives and courage to pursue what we always dreamt of, but did not dare or master to carry through until Scott crosses our life paths. Life will never be the same after the 'Dude encounter'.

I don't think Scott does it on purpose, he is just one of those sadly rare personalities that inspires, whether he wants to or not. Actually, I guess I rather like that Scott is also timid in spite of his grand looks and attractive, demagogic personality. He would be truly magnificent and potentially hazardous, if he ever becomes grounded enough to strategically manipulate the hordes that cannot help but be attracted to him. Still he is a slightly insecure youngster, periodically touching upon the fundamental questions in existence. "Does the way I live, give meaning?"

I thrive and grow when I move under my own steam, untroubled by the interference of those whose egos and lack of trust in others (and themselves), cause them to overdo the leadership role to an extent where they actually smother the self-reliance and mobilization coming from within. Self-responsibility, self-leadership and courage to make one's own decisions and initiate proportional action are qualities absolutely crucial to dealing with life and death situations in as hostile an environment as Everest truly is.

Scott is tired. Lying on my bed in Østerbro, he is shifting between "Lene don't let me die in the mountains. I need to be humble" to "We will bag the Big E."

Maybe it is just me who's paranoid. Maybe it is possible to indulge in mountaineering and expeditions without being killed. Maybe just maybe you cannot equate climbing with death. A few manage to pull through and create the grandest adventures as well as live a long life, including marriage, children and grandchildren.

Maybe it's possible? I am fueled by the desire to climb Everest, in the company of grand personalities. I have been looking and searching for this constellation since I set out to cross the Atlantic when I was 18: yarning for life and the people in it, not to disappoint me and struggling to find an outlet for me, all of me. Now at 34, I am in the midst of what I dreamt life has to offer. After years of depressing divorce and suffocating life conditions, my inner drive is forcing me to venture into the grandiosity of the unexplored.

A point of no return, as it turns out. Our climbing itinerary fulfills my desire to make the chaos of life manageable. Scott makes the intangible secure by writing up a detailed climbing plan - black print on white paper - and through such a simple and insignificant act, we humans convince ourselves and others, that this is how future reality will unfold. We are in control of what will happen. However, I know that some choose to trust detailed meticulous climbing itineraries developed and presented by expedition leaders and guides to avoid taking complete responsibility of themselves. I want to believe that all is going to run smoothly - and why shouldn't it?

9

***"It does not matter how slowly you go
so long as you do not stop"***
Confucius

- An compelling vision awakens your passions.
- An exciting vision will propel you towards a future so enticing that you will do whatever it takes.
- Your vision should fill you with constructive stress that impels you to change and adapt to move toward your goals.
- Sustaining motivation entails developing a strong reason to pursue your action plan to a successful conclusion.

No Mountain Madness Crew at the airport. I arrive prepared; I know which Hotel our team will be staying at for the few days we are waiting to be assembled before our expedition commences. I recover two bulky 110 liters Lowe expedition duffels, easy to sport with the huge sponsor letters - Netto and Ekstra Bladet sewn onto their sides - yet another way I raised funds, spotting my 70 liter backpack and the 40 liter climbing daypack with all my photo gear, snailing towards me on the squeaking transporting antiquated rubber serpent. Tomorrow I will have to find the cargo storage and waste hours with the Nepalese impenetrable bureaucracy to get my remaining two bags released from customs. Giggling overwhelms me, as I recall the hazels it takes to get an expedition in and out of Nepal. Rupees needed to help the process run smoothly, stacks and copies of neat accurate paperwork that after all the bother, faces a good chance of ending up at the foot of a stairwell serving as a well-deserved feast for the holy cows, who graze at the bottom. A dignified manner of filing paperwork. My feet hurt. Among other stress induced 'infirmities', I suffer from squashed forefeet, as the specialists so thoughtfully brands what I thought was bunions. The strain of raising funds and training extraordinarily hard, parallel with being available for whatever the press invents for my exposure, have presented a whole new palette of quite unexpected disabilities. I dare not ponder how it will be for my body to exhaust itself day after day, week after week on the actual climb ahead, when just getting all details in line for departing from Denmark has taken such a huge toll on my health.

    Waiting in line at Katmandu airport, I try to kick my brain into functioning mode. Do I have to declare my expedition gear? A process domed to take 23 Hours. My money belt contains a great deal more cash than the allowed amount, but following Scott's example - he stuffs enough dollars into his boots and Starbuck Thermos to pay for the whole expedition - I march through, nothing to declare - innocently... No problem! Himalaya - why has it taken me so long to come back? Here where I discovered the peace in humans, the serenity I have unconsciously been seeking on my travels to foreign parts of the world. Here where the land itself seems to radiate peace and tranquility: where the highest mountains in the world do something unfathomable to us.

    I shift from my serene contemplations to the lovable hectic as I arrive at Hotel Manang, in the Thamel, Katmandu's tourist district. The bathroom is quite luxurious by Nepalese standards, but the water from the taps is more turbid than clear. It is a dubious enterprise to clean oneself in Katmandu water, let alone digest it, so from now on, only bottled water for drinking and brushing teeth- four to eight liters for every 24 hours. I respect the violent natural forces on Everest, one uncontrollable risk-generating factor on top of the other. I do not have extensive high altitude experience, but I do have thorough, abundant and longstanding experienced based insights on the hazards connected with the pollution of the water in Nepal. If I get the two-way runs, I might suffer defeat from becoming too weak and losing the extra body weight I have trained and eaten on, to up my chances of surviving Everest. Scott is ill again, he's coughing and has a fever. I feared as much from his recent letters. He is pushing himself to hard and does not rest thoroughly between his big trips. I guess that leaves me to participate in his 'support team', again. We'll have to see what results my cocktail of vitamins can have on the effect and long term consequences of high altitude mountaineering and signs of burn-out due to Scott's success infused lifestyle of constantly being on the go, hike or fly.

    I fundamentally wish my Tai Chi teacher could have worked with Scott more intensely, when he was in Copenhagen. Perhaps Scott could have grasped the necessity of relaxing deeply, allowing his body to fully recover now and again. Scott just spoke on the phone to his wife and two kids, Andy and Kathy Rose back in Seattle. "I miss them", Scott shares. Whenever Scott mentions his kids, his voice alters, a note deeper, profound untainted unconditional love for his offspring just swells through his few words. Undoubtedly, they mean the world to him. However, he never remains at home to be with them for very long and becomes impatient and cranky when he tries- a fact I have touched on in our correspondence over the years.

Working with drug addicts, I know what damage an absent father can do to his kids. What will the long-term consequences be for Scott's children living the reality that their father always chooses the next adventure, the next mountain, the next mistress over sharing their everyday lives? Taught by bitter experience, I know it is beyond my control to change Scott's approach. I have tried to influence him over the years and others have too for that matter. I hold Scott in high regard and truly want him to endure in the longer run. Can I make a difference in other people's lives? Should I? I would truly love to influence Scott because he is worth the effort.

The American climbers on our team who are arriving from the States are delayed. Although the plane not arriving according to plan means a lot of scheduling problems for the expedition, it suits me perfectly, handing me a chance to rest for a couple of days, after the hectic sponsor hunt and the overwhelming attention from the Danish media. I will need all my strength to accomplish what I set out to master, so I carefully consider where to eat lunch today, to minimize the risk of the ever-lurking Katmandu quickstep.
Ingrid Hunt, our expedition doctor and a very serious young woman, states: "About the probability of catching the runs while you're in Nepal, I'd say. You either have it, or you'll get it." Unfortunately, my previous experiences indicate she is dead-on with her predictions. Ingrid and I decide to have lunch in one of Katmandu's green oases, a tropical garden in the midst of noisy, teeming Thamel with its ancient narrow paths, stuffed with colorful items to purchase for fair prices. "I met Dr. Igor Gamow, the man who invented the Gamow Bag, a cigar-shaped, portable

hyperbaric chamber used for the treatment of Acute Mountain Sickness. By increasing air pressure around the patient, the Bag simulates descent of as much as 7,000 feet, thus relieving AMS symptoms in a brilliantly simple system. The altitude-stricken person is placed inside the nylon chamber and air is pumped in with a foot pump. The combination of increased air pressure and oxygen simulates lower altitude." Ingrid shares. Our expedition brings a Gamow Bag, as does Henry Todd's. All teams on Everest will share the two bags. One will be situated at Base Camp; the second at Camp 2.

These orange cigars can be the margin between living and dying as reality should prove true in the not too distant future. Jane Bromet, a tiny energetic example of one of Scott's conquests is officially joining us to Base Camp to promote Scott and Mountain Madness. Jane landed a deal of filing daily reports on the expedition for Outside Online, another attractive media exposing opportunity for Scott. Jane I her hectic upbeat manner she discusses promoting me worldwide via the Internet and I'm thinking: "All I want is the summit. I want to storm onto the international climbing scene and I'm going to do it." Apart from my desire to summit Everest, I know Scott sees me as an asset to the well-being and smooth functioning of the expedition. I don't think Scott knows what it is I do that seems to work on expeditions, but he notices that it makes a difference whether I am there or not. We feed each other's desire for expanded mutually beneficial opportunities in the wake of successfully summiting Everest.

"Lene, this is Anatoli, the Russian climber." Scott spreading out his gorilla arms as we are introduced at our expedition dinner. Ah! This is Anatoli, the strong Russian climber. Anatoli seems unobtrusive, almost shy or timid. He is blond, about five feet ten inches tall. No conspicuous bundle of muscles. He is obviously uneasy about the slightly formal atmosphere - we're all behaving civilly for our Swiss host- another female admirer of Scott. I feel attracted to this tall, slender iconic man. With a humble sparkle in his blue eyes, unconscious dressing code and withdrawn observant manner, I feel calm and at ease in his vicinity. Obviously, Anatoli does not tick by the same kind of attention that Scott craves. More so, Anatoli seems to rest very contently in his own company. A gentle smile just adding to the curve of his mouth.

"Anatoli, weren't you on Dhaulagiri the spring of '91, making the first ascent on the West Wall?"
"How did you know?"
"I recognize you as one of the Russians who donated your vodka to us, the night we spent in bivy bags outside your camp. Don't you recall four women scrambling up the glacier moraine in the early evening? We were hiking out from Dhaulagiri Base Camp. I even have some photos of you."

In 1991 I accompanied my now former husband on his quest as expedition leader to become the first Dane above 8000 meters. Dhaulagiri base camp is in one of the most rugged and inaccessible regions of Nepal. Hidden Wally is a totally remote and uninhabited sphere of ice, snow and the hugest moraines I have ever scrambled. True wilderness that craves detailed planning and carrying of all equipment and food supplies for the entire length of the expedition: there is nothing but wild unspoiled, uninhabitable, harsh natural hazardous surroundings for months there. My husband and I had fought dramatically as he had disappeared himself more and more into his becoming the first Dane above 8000 meters quest, shutting me out from the domain he shared with his climbing buddies. My envy, love, possessiveness, lack of experience in being the waiting wife, never ever accepting that position, we had almost killed ourselves and each other leading up to our departure for Nepal. He did not want me on the expedition, probably with good reason: I lacked experience. And this group would never contemplate inviting a woman on any of their expeditions. Living as a spectator to the tunnel vision my ex-husband, drive activated, being reduced to non-important - a nuisance really - in comparison to a mountain. My envy of his life quest, his risk willingness, creativity and stamina to invent sponsor deals and TV-presence, drove me into realms of my personality that I do not want to acknowledge or admit.

   My ex-husband Søren Smidt is a Danish mountaineer, professional expedition leader, cand.mag in literature and history. He has conducted more than 20 expeditions to Himalayas, Greenland, Africa and Antarctica.
He is a certified mountain leader from Ecole Nationale de Ski et d'Alpinisme, Chamonix, authorized UIAA rock climbing instructor from International
Mountaineering and Climbing Federation. Søren climbed as the first Dane to
Ama Dablam (6856 m) in alpine style. In 1991 Søren was leading the first Danish expedition to Dhaulagiri (8167 m) in Nepal. He reached the summit of Dhaulagiri 14th, May 1991 at 12.30 becoming the first Dane to climb an 8000 meter peak. In 2008 he invented and headed a world record breaking attempt on the Seven Summits: the seven highest peaks on the seven continents.

Danish Businessman Henrik Kristiansen improved the previous record with 20 days, as he accomplished the Seven Summits in 136 days, achieving the new Guinness World Record. Søren Smidt summited Mount Everest (8848 m) in 2008 and became the 9th Dane reaching the summit of the highest mountain in the world. In 1991 he and I had been married for a year. We had been secretly in love since we meet years previously as he was hitchhiking to go climbing on Kullen in Sweden.

I come from a middleclass family background, my parents truly lived life together. I had not been conditioned to husbands taking off on life-risking egocentric adventures without their families; therefore I gave Søren the hardest confrontational non-acceptance of his quest to pursue Dhaulagiri after we got married. I was unconsciously acting on my imagining that married life was a life together. He - being like most mountaineers, never considered changing his lifestyle because of another human being. I then and now still advocate that it is madness to climb mountains, if you have a family. The risk is too high and a summit makes no sense. Our hard battled compromise ended with me accompanying him on his expedition into Dhaulagiri Base Camp, my ego caused me to construct plans of my own - a circumvention of the Dhaulagiri Massif - urging the other accompanying wives to join in, followed by a solo attempt of Island Peak in the Everest region. To test myself, overcome my fear of heights, risk and self-responsibility and gain some of the altitude experience my husband confronted me with that I lacked.

Leaving Søren and my rough marriage behind in the vicinity of avalanche prone Dhaulagiri base-camp, the wives set out to detect the route out of the remote setting at the foot of the massive Dhaulagiri range. I had picked the strongest, tallest porter to carry the food, stove, fuel and simple few provisions to see us through the days to come. The terrain we negotiated is the most demanding I have ever encountered in the Himalayas.

The greatest risk apart from getting lost or dying from lack of food, were the rock falls. We hiked, stumbled, and struggled through huge glaciated moraines and following the occasional riverbed, the flow of the stream confirmed we were at least heading downwards. We eventually ran low on fuel and expected to encounter two Danish trekking groups, headed for Base Camp to greet my husband's expedition team. Evening approached the third day - expecting a cold, exposed night in our bivouac bags with very little food left- we struggled to surpass the left moraine wall, praying to not be hit by the falling rock from the high slope above us to the right. Sticking my sweating head up over the huge rock boulders and spotting a colorful tunnel tent, too big to be the Danish trekking groups mess tent….

Four dirty women, one extraordinarily tall porter approached what turned out to be a Russian climbing camp. None spoke English but the rugged, unshaven men seemed welcoming enough. We managed to understand that they are there as the first expedition to see how many times they could climb to the 8000 meter summit within a specific time span. Lean, smelling, old-fashioned climbing gear, lots of vodka and melancholic guitar tunes: the spitting image of my prejudice induced imaginings of brain-dead vodka drinking Russian climbing robots. We are welcome to remain the night and roll out or bivouac sacks a short distance from their camp. "Hmmmmm!" That meeting obviously left no trace in Anatoli's memory. This trek in 1991 was also when I first meet Scott coming back from my failed attempt of soloing Island Peak, my self-test in solitude in the Himalayas.

Broken, confused, exhilarated and staggering between fear and hope I was desperate, tired, sad and exhausted from realizing while trekking among the giants of the world that I had to divorce Søren: my husband who I still loved. Suddenly a Hercules like appearance and white backpack caught my eyes from a distance, someone fabulous, masculine, exuberating energy, standing aloof in front of a blue tarpaulin covered teahouse with walls constructed out of the local rocks.

I never before or since meet anyone hiking with a white backpack. Scott Fischer. Scott's great looks and gregarious way of attracting adventure seeking personalities like me, disrupted my lonely journey back from the solitude and fatiguing thoughts of being alone in this ice-clad landscape. Little could I discern just how this hormonal encounter would become a turning point in my life matrix. Scott and his team of friends he had worked with as a young guy invited me to join them on their two week trek back to Katmandu and civilization. I declined at first; after all I was still a married woman, sensing their endangerment to my faithfulness, if I spent too much time in the company of these fabulous men. Yet, after a sleepless night in a stone hut, trying to close out some of the sounds as well as smells emerging from the porters and local herdsmen assembled in this one chamber black smothered stone shelter, I came to my senses and raced down the trekking track. Desolation transmuting into mobilizing and igniting strength I had long forgotten on the steep ups and downs of scaling altitude meters on my trekking routes. Yarning to catch up - bump into the Mera Peak group again - exposed and undefended to whatever my choice would involve.

1991's chance encounters became life altering for me. I chanced upon Scott Fischer and Wesley Krause: the blond and the dark personifications of the American hero. Scott and Wesley asked me to join their party all the way back to Katmandu. Welcoming me into a world I'd longed for and hoped existed all along, but had not found in spite of my search around the globe. Human encounters that reinforced my resolve to divorce my husband and find my own way forward through the ruins of shattered dreams and illusions about love and living happily ever after. The man I had longed for and ended up marrying out of pure passion and all-encompassing love had turned out to be a disaster. I did not dare nor desire to fall back into our obsessive, all too dramatic and dysfunctional war-like passion. I wanted to change. I learned valuable life preserving lessons the hard way through my climbing marriage. Never believe you can change a passionate, obsessed mountaineer. No love from a woman will make him choose to stop climbing and transform him into a domesticated mature and responsible husband. Have fun and even affairs with the adventurers, but don't marry them unless your ideal of a marriage is to sit alone with all the mature responsibilities, controlling the pain and fear of him dying while pursuing just another ridiculous mountain and receiving a wasted, drained guy back home. A guy will be contend for only a short while, requesting you to nurture, admire and pamper him. As soon as he restores some life zest, he will turn your lives into hell, through negativity and restlessness, until he dreams up his next vision. He will claim he loves you as he tunes you out, more and more as he gets closer to the realization of his next quest, ending up in hilarious manipulations, as he tries to convince you that climbing mountains is not dangerous in spite of all documented facts that prove the contrary.

My ex-husband in all his harshness was a great tutor. His fundamental confrontations shaped my foundation for surviving

Everest where others did not. You are just as good as your climbing experience and the amount of trips in the Himalayas has molded you. I tried to break my husband, because he would never comply with taking care of me, due to my lack of experience and willingness to risk what he was risking in the mountains. Thanks to my unsuccessful mission, I had to develop my own capabilities. For this, I thank him. You personally, must put in all the hard work, leading climbs, being in the mountains, take risks, develop and invest willpower, courage and self-control. If you want to survive up high - you must develop the full packet that you want others to provide for you.

Chance encounters might just be the ticket to the future you envision, but you must make the choices and live with the consequences. It is not too late - until you are no longer alive. There might be fabulous life opportunities when you break free from habit and socialized limitations. There are grand humans living life entirely different, which can inspire you to develop new aspects of yourself. When I first stumbled across Anatoli and his record pursuing scaling buddies in 1991, I got the impression that Anatoli was a burn out, severely affected by his many ventures above 8000 meters and massive vodka consumption.

As Anatoli's English was extremely limited in 1991, I assumed he was unintelligent and affected by the damages following suffering oxygen deprivation at altitude. The Russian expedition just raced up and down former unclimbed 8000 meter Dhaulagiri routes for the sake of establishing speed records. Anatoli won. Later that season we met again when the Danish Dhaulagiri expedition headed by my former husband celebrated at Rum Doodle. The famous bar in Katmandu, where all expeditions come to write their autographs on big foot shaped

boards that are pinned everywhere on the walls and ceilings. A historic meeting place for the rookies of the world.
You brought a bottle of vodka as a present, and left your address in case you ever had the opportunity to climb Khan Tengri in your home country. Now it turns out that not only do you know Scott, but you are also a good friend of Michael Jørgensen."

Michael was the first Dane to reach the top of Everest, from Tibet in 1995. He died in 1997 trying to summit Makalu. Yes, Michael and I became friends while we climbed Everest last year. He is strong. He will climb on Henry Todd's expedition this year, trying to summit without oxygen from the south side this season, and climb Lhotse after.

"You want to be the first Danish woman to summit Everest? Why do you want to climb? You are a woman!"

I thought to myself. Here I am among the elite of mountaineers - including this thirty-eight year old Russian, who has summited more mountains than any mountaineer, could ever dream of - and he asks me why I feel driven to climb the highest mountain in the world! A gender discriminating code obviously operates in Anatoli's world. I am accustomed to that bias and his type of response. Sometimes I forget my past battles for justice, fighting for fairness and equal opportunities to every odd challenge no matter your gender and the socializations that installs unnecessary limitations and shortcomings. I need not answer. Need not verbally confront Anatoli to prove anything - vocally try to convince him. All I want is to get to the summit of Everest, *"To the summit and safe return."* There will be people who will tell you that you can't accomplish your goals. "It's too hard." "You set your sights too high." "That's not possible." I hate those words! The truly grand personalities make you feel that you, too, can become great. Never allow yourself to be fenced in by the doubts or expectations of others. Sometimes your worst worrywart is yourself. At some point before and during most climbs, I reach a point where I feel overwhelmed by the difficulty of the task and I want to give up and try another time. That's where my commitment to success kicks in and I summon the reserves to continue moving in the direction of my vision. You too will hit those hard patches during your life journey and will think about giving up on your dream. Banish those thoughts from your mind and stay on the path.

Talking about my wish to summit Everest will not get me there. I'll only take energy away if I try to convince another being of my desires and hopes of strength and whatever I need to develop, while climbing into the unknown for me. Only the actual climb will reveal whether I've got it or not. Therefore, I keep my mouth shut. I too, want to find out if I am capable of what, deep inside, I believe I can accomplish. Visions have to be transformed into reality, through strategic planning, loads of hard work combined with the will to carry through no matter what. Otherwise, they are but illusions, self-inflated imaginings. I detest it when people talk and talk, but never execute. I have to be careful not to waste resources by giving in to that intoxicating habit. I stick to the power of my Vision: To the Summit and safe return.

"Now I know who you are," Anatoli utters. "I recognize you now; you competed for the world championship in bodybuilding, correct?"

The guy's got a sense of humor! Anatoli clearly doesn't have a clue that he's already met me several times, but as a professional he has obviously evaluated my bulk. According to his verdict, all my hard training has paid off. Among some of the best mountaineers in the world, I will be scrutinized, evaluated by my performance - my total capacity to climb this thing or the contrary - and nothing else. I will be exposed exactly as I am able to conduct myself on this expedition, day after day. Every shortcoming, weakness, lack of self-discipline etc. will be exposed high on the mountain. Self-control: my ability to control my emotions, behavior, and yearnings in the face of external demands in order to function in extreme situations is essential for my survival.

My self-regulation will be indispensable to achieve my goal and to avoid impulses and reactions that could prove to be negative, when under the pressure and stress that is inevitably connected with being and living on Everest for months. No facade, title or lie, will shower over the brutal reality of what one human being is capable of, at this specific point in time. Constructive action and self-control will count. I will need to regulate my emotions, my ability to respond to the ongoing demands in a manner that is socially tolerable and sufficiently flexible to delay spontaneous reactions as needed. Emotional regulation is a complex process that involves initiating, inhibiting, or modulating my psychological state as well as behavior in a given situation. Functionally I must discipline the tendency to focus my attention to the task and cultivate the ability to suppress inappropriate behavior. Emotional regulation is a highly significant function in making a successful expedition team. We are continually exposed to a wide variety of arousing stimuli, existing under constant pressure on Everest.

Inappropriate, extreme or unchecked emotional reactions often obstruct adequate functioning within the climbing society; therefore, people must engage in some form of emotion regulation almost all of the time. Emotional deregulation is difficult in controlling the influence of emotional arousal and quality of thoughts, actions and interactions. Individuals who are emotionally deregulated exhibit patterns of response in which there is a mismatch between their goals, responses, modes of expression and the demands of the social environment in our small, exposed society of excesses. My pondering is interrupted by Anatoli's mumbled good-bye, as he vanishes from the party, setting out on his own paths in Katmandu. Existence has hammered out a man without pretension, gentle, though impossible for me to ignore. A tall slender man, Anatoli moves with the grace of something untamed. In my life, I have encountered human beings who emanate the peculiar unmistaken forte of the wild three times: for the first time in 1991 I encountered a few of the inhabitants that come from the narrow land strip between Kag Beni in Nepal and Upper Mustang. Wild in the most profound awe-inspiring materialization of a human being that has never adapted to the restraints of domesticating civilization:

    Anatoli and the third, a huge young man from the Russian planes. He escaped his void upbringing by dog sledding to Finland, then wandering through Europe until he became semi adopted by a Swiss Businessman and mountaineer. When I meet him, I was almost blown off my feet, instinctively detecting true strength in a human being who is still in touch with some fundamentals that we seem to loose, when we are domesticated to inhabit limited space without killing each other. Anatoli's composure is at once cautious and open. Humble - aloof, subdued interest lightening his blue eyes. Keeping to himself and in the outskirts of our group and yet attracting my desire to give in to this self-contained man. I would have allowed myself to love him; if I had still been naïve enough to believe Anatoli could ever live and be content elsewhere.

The rough wilderness and fair play of high altitude is the only true place for grand personalities like Anatoli. He is free. Unpretentiously, Anatoli only truly existed in the mountains, driven by the certainty that mountaineering cultures the human psyche, expressing ethics that might almost be lost in the present. In this harsh environment, that most people find restrictive and intimidating, Anatoli could express his genius. Anywhere else, within any job function, civilization with all its routine and mediocre pettiness would have been an intolerable confinement for this man. It is a rare woman or man who faces the existential paradox of meaning of life, ethics and morality as relentlessly as the mountaineer does. Anatoli's resources and life events allowed him to experience a great measure of what is possible for a human being to accomplish in a lifespan. He is the only human being I have encountered where I had to learn that he belongs in the mountains. I instinctively like him and must admit his English has improved considerably since our last encounter, when I judged him 'indoctrinated, unintelligent and inarticulate'. I do enjoy when life teaches me that I can be mentally arrogant, critical and forms judgments based on very little information, verdicts that have little foundation in reality. Serves me right not having a clue about the truth! P.B Thapa, our fabulous trekking agent and dear friend of Scott's, winds up the evening at his house by revealing a vision he's had a few nights ago.

"You will reach the summit. You are strong."

10

"It's not altitude; It's attitude"
Scott Fischer

- There is an inertia in our lives that tends to keep us in the habits we are used to until we encounter a strong enough substantial reason, to change direction.
- Upgrade your self-rating.
- An exhilarating vision is not an impossible fantasy if you alter the way you unconsciously rate yourself.
- If the vision excites you, you can achieve it. If it is beyond your reach, it won't enliven you.

"Our goal is to get as many climbers as we can as safely as possibly to the summit of Everest. To summit the highest mountain in the world will stretch the limits of our physiques and psyches to the utmost. To reach the top of Mount Everest is one of the greatest athletic challenges in the world. Correct training will be crucial so that we arrive well prepared for this extreme challenge. On Everest, attitude and mental toughness will determine who reaches the summit." I read in Scott's preparation letters to our team. Every time I mention my goal, think about my venture, train to achieve it or talk about it, I drill myself mentally,

"To the summit and safe return."

Programming my subconscious, constructing and installing trust in myself and my ability to succeed. Expanding and exploding previous limitations in my self-perception and opinions of what is doable in life for me. I am convinced that specialized mental training can make a difference in the way we cope with life and set ourselves up for either success, or the contrary. In order to accomplish great initiatives in life, you need a visionary plan. A passionate vision that truly compels you to move beyond what you have accomplished in your past, which creates and installs a blueprint in your psyche that drives you through all obstacles. You may want to make adjustments along the approach, but stick to the overall strategic plan. If your vision is truly unleashing some deep felt aspirations in you, there will be no hindrances you cannot find a solution to overcome.

Often people share exciting ideas, but never transform them into executable action plans. Often, the person mistakes an intriguing vision for an impossible delusion. We go through an unconscious self-evaluation process when we are seizing up the hindrances between where we are now and where we dream about being. We compare the task with our present capabilities, realistic or the contrary. If we sense the task is bigger than our present self-rating, we become discouraged and never take the first step towards realizing the idea. If we believe the target is beneath our capacities or a mere repetition, we're bored by it, we surpass it and the energy dwindles. If we feel the goal matches our self-perceptions and the capacities we impersonate, we're likely to be fired up and mobilize. Sometimes it is best to focus just on the short-term goals so you are not overwhelmed with the enormity of the task. For example, when I climb, I often just think about getting to the next rock or ice wall up the mountain, and I focus on that as a short-term goal. Then, when I reach that rock or ice wall, I find another landmark and set that as my next target. Step by step, literally, I make my way up the mountain and eventually I stand on the summit. Plainly putting one foot in front of the other - ten paces at the time and then taking a break to gasp for air - is what should get me to the summit of Everest. Just move your feet, ten steps at a time over and over and over again. Mental strength can be developed and conditioned by a distinctive kind of "adversity training" - instigated through practice that prepares you for upcoming ordeals.

Mental strength training and resilience encoding, involves learning and conditioning cerebral skills that toughen your ability to control your thoughts, emotions and cope with enduring performance.
If there are certain thoughts that tend to cause you nervousness, an experienced climber will know what those thoughts are, be able to recognize them, be able to get them out of their mind and instead insert opposite considerations. The result of your mental disciplining must be a sensation more ideally suited to optimize extraordinary performance. Self regulation encompasses an individual's capacity to adapt the self as circumstances prove necessary, to meet the demands of the environment you have to cope soundly with. Patience, impulse-control, endurance, self-control and willpower are all traits involved in the complexity of self regulation. Self-control is imperative for people who want to be successful in all areas of life and is absolutely crucial to survive on Everest. Sometimes even the simplest progress craves so much more than we can fathom and desire to invest while pursuing our dreams and sometimes you need to slog away - for years - before achieving your goals.

Short-term goals are important stepping-stones to achieve your long term goals. Endurance and continuous persistence in goal-directed behaviors are crucial for overcoming the inertia existence exposes us to. It is human to desire results as fast as possible and delayed gratification isn't easy to cope with and often times deflates the crucial momentum you need to keep wanting something specific, more than other trivial actions. Having practical, manageable goals that give you measureable results along the way will sustain you and keep you from giving up.

Define the steps you need to take to achieve your goals. Knowing what your goals are, will not be enough to help you attain them. You must also condition a clear understanding of the path that will get you where you want to go. Break your goals into short-term and long-term and ask yourself, "What specific measures do I need to instigate right now to reach my longer-term objectives? What specific steps do I need to take today, in the coming months or years to reach what I aim for?" In 1996 I want to become the first Nordic woman to scale Mount Everest. Years spent absorbed in psychological research papers, my education as a therapist, hands-on experiences with drug-addicts and practical work with leaders and the human psyche have revealed to me that humans are a bit like computers.

Through our upbringing, culture, gender, religion, genetic pole combined with life experiences - we are programmed and program ourselves - in certain ways. Being aware of our potential for reprogramming and the fact, that scientist now can prove that our genome can change when exposed to certain impact; we truly hold the potential of shaping ourselves differently for the future. We can indoctrinate ourselves to a certain degree, if there is something we fundamentally desire. I therefore attempt to program my brain - perceiving it and utilizing it as a bio computer -by installing a soft ware packet to facilitate my sole purpose of summiting Everest and survive to tell the tale.

Almost anything is possible if you are mentally committed to succeed through hard work. Your endeavor might require short-term sacrifice for long-term gains. I tell myself, never indulge in the inclination to give up and lower your expectations. If you are determined, work hard keep practicing and sacrifice some laziness in the short term and you will enjoy long-lasting fulfillment and gratification in the longer run. Based on my conviction and the latest research, I implement my self-programming strategy in my mental preparation for ascending Everest. I initiate my success pursuing strategy and my self-invented subconscious indoctrination with simply stated the following imperatives and action:

- Gain knowledge of our route by studying expedition reports.
- Talk to and learn from those who have been high on Everest.
- Think "To the summit and safe return" while climbing, swimming, jogging and practicing Tai Chi.
- Improve my mountaineering skills through mountaineering.
- Expand my subconscious capacity to cope with risk through spending as much time as possible mountaineering during the winter season and spend time in snowstorms as high as possible in the Alps

I leave nothing to chance this time and am about to turn into a control freak, as I realize that above 7300 meters I trespass the "Zero tolerance for mishaps treasure". I prepare myself for each passage up the mountain from the route descriptions I have collected and concoct myself for the climb to the summit by overloading my brain with information of what it is like for the system to be depleted of oxygen. Selectively, I study the accounts of successful expeditions and communicate with people who have a playful, positive attitude toward mountaineering, based on more experience than I have myself. My incentive is to encrypt my mind with sufficient affirmative input to overrule my own healthy skepticism and to forget the stories I myself have gathered over the years as arguments against my former husband's desire for climbing mountains. Arguments I have made frequent use of with others I either envied or did not want to lose, or as justification for all the times I know I have turned around in the mountains, wanting the reason to be intelligence based and not the coward bailing out.

Getting psyched up and ready to climb the highest mountain in the world - mental preparation is equally important to physical preparation. A constructive mental approach gets me past those tough times when the demons from my past befriended with exhaustion of the present, sit on my shoulder and nag me to give up. I am a profound advocate for that this strategic technique works for the furtherance of all extraordinary goals we set for ourselves in life. If you want to achieve those objectives, it is critical that you mentally commit yourself to attain what you set out to undertake and believe that you will make it. An important part of mental preparation is to visualize your success. Just beyond the South Summit of Mt. Everest there is a knife-edge ridge called the Cornice Traverse. It is also known as the "Death Traverse" because the fall on one side of the ridge is 8,000 feet into

Nepal and the fall on the other side of the ridge is 10,000 feet into Tibet. One misstep and the climber takes what mountaineers call the "big ride."

When I first saw the Cornice Traverse, I visualized a safe and successful crossing in my mind and I kept that mindset until I safely made the ascent. You should do the same when inherent fear of failure tries to overcome your commitment to success. I prepare myself to win this time! My focused strategy is based on the latest research of how the brain functions and the fact that if I visualize the different phases of the route again and again and again, my brain cannot determine whether I have actually been up high in reality or not.

By mentally programming numerous, detailed information into the subconscious, my brain is developing new roadmaps, newfangled synthesis connections. So, when I actually set foot on the mountain for the first time in the real world my brain will not need as much processing energy to absorb the first impressions, as it would, had I not mobilized and implemented this focused effort to prepare mentally in advance. I hope my self-experiment with my neural system will influence my brain to react as if it's already familiar with the surroundings, the route, the oxygen deprivation and thus saving life important energy: resources I need to succeed climbing high. I hope to program myself to succeed in achieving this extraordinary accomplishment in spite of my all too human frailness. I aim to utilize my limited resources to the margin and only then will I be able to cope with and master, what I have never previously dared to attempt! I consume what I pick out to be necessary literature about the medical hazards of high-altitude climbing such as acute mountain sickness (AMS) and pulmonary and cerebral edema.

I study sufficiently to diagnose the symptoms, to know what to do under the given circumstances and choose not to go deeper. I decide to avoid centering deeply upon the health risks inevitably connected with the oxygen deprivation that comes with the territory on 8000-meter peaks. Logically it is not conducive for the human brain or the body to function on too little oxygen for a sustained period of time, so I discontinue all thoughts about the negative consequences of my venture.

I discipline my mental self-censure to sustain my motivation for the unknown that awaits me in a not too distant future. I enroll myself in a self inflicted human experiment. I am fundamentally determined to use myself as a Guinea pig to test my research and hands-on findings for mobilizing high performance in individuals the willpower and stamina to carry through to completion no matter what hindrances inner or outer that might occur in the complex and taxing process of aiming for an almost unfathomable expansion of the self. I condition and train myself with the purpose of becoming frighteningly goal-oriented, narrow-minded cynically yet humbly and excessively focused. Because I am convinced, that focused self-programming is what it takes to implement and carry through my vision of surviving Everest with my limited resources.

My vision is all-consuming. Never in my entire life have I experienced anything equivalent. A revitalizing cellular explosion, mobilizing yet untapped inner powers that propel me into tremendous quanta jump high performance growth: a barrier exploding, mobilizing tsunami pushing me forward in a developmental process of humongous proportions. I have limited time available to raise fund, to prepare mentally and physically for the most demanding and riskiest challenge of my life to date. The way I have been thus far, is surprisingly forced to give way to whatever I need to learn to master as well as become, to take on the challenge of summiting the highest mountain on earth. Because I authentically want Everest so much I must invent and carry through whatever it takes to get ready. To act, to endure and to deliver...With this profound commitment, it becomes impossible to complain about any of the small irritating, time stealing stuff in everyday living that might normally snip lifetime away, because the vision of what awaits me puts any difficulty and hindrance into perspective.

    No problem!

11

"Depression is not a sign of weakness, it means you have been strong for far too long"

- Knowing what your goals are is one thing.
- Develop and decide on a strategy to attain your goal.
- Learn to direct your efforts systematically. Focus.

Scott and I are indulging ourselves in Katmandu's most delicious brunch selection at Mike's Breakfast, a secluded exuberant garden that has been a meeting paradise for trekkers and climbers for decades. We enjoy the invigorating presence of Henry Todd from Edinburgh, the leader of a mixed commercial expedition on which my fellow Dane, Michael Knakkergaard Jørgensen will climb. Henry Todd is the main oxygen supplier for most Everest expeditions this year - the link between a Russian manufacturer of bottled oxygen and our expedition. He is tall, full-bearded and resembles a British author more than a mountaineer.

For several years, he has supervised the individuals who want to summit with his outfit from Base Camp. Henry's sophisticated, eloquent use of language amuses me. He is grilling me inquisitively; probing to discern what drives and compels me. He starts talking about Alison Hargreaves, whom he knew for more than ten years. "It had to happen - her climbing careerism. I couldn't really get in touch with her in the end. During the ten years I knew her, I was able to hug her only once. We all knew she was going to die in that race." Alison Hargreaves was driven to her death by "Summit fever", according to Peter Hillary, son of Sir Edmund, the first man to conquer Everest. Peter Hillary survived the tragedy on K2, where high winds blew several climbers right off the mountain, as Scott was observing unable to assist from Broad Peak base camp. Bleeding from sun baked lips and weeping, two climbers spoke of the night the K2 took six of their friends in blizzards that left no trace of disaster except an unidentified body and Alison Hargreaves's boots, flower decorated jacket and climbing harness. A Pakistani army officer disclosed that he had begged Allison Hargreaves not to make her assault on K2, warning her that because of the weather conditions, to do so would be "suicide".

Alison Hargreaves was missing her husband and children greatly and had appeared to relent, but then her passion "gripped her again" and she set out on her last climb never to be seen again. Henry Todd is an outspoken advocate for using supplemental oxygen. "It will do the trick when you're lying up there at 8000 meters and a storm is beating through the South Col. Your legs are in the air to keep the tent poles from collapsing. You're freezing your ass off and are about to give in, but then you grab you oxygen mask and warmth spreads through your body the uncontrollable shiver of your carcass subsides and you are in heaven."

The fact that human beings are capable of surviving and functioning at 18,000 feet and that a few have the physiology to endure 29,028 feet without the use of supplemental oxygen - altitudes at which unacclimatized individuals would lose consciousness and die - proves how adaptable the human organism is. If you acclimatize properly, your body responds by increasing the respiratory rate, lung artery activity, heartbeat and production of red blood cells and hemoglobin, allowing the blood to carry more oxygen. At the same time, alterations in the body's tissue allow it to function under lower oxygen pressure. I am trying to talk Scott into climbing with oxygen, to preserve whatever strength he has. Although he basically is a no O2 kind of guy, Scott is the expedition leader and ought to be on top of the situation. He has summited previously without O2 and consequently his ego knows he can do it. It would definitely be better for his brain to be spared this time.

"I don't know, Lene. It's an ego thing," Scott says, grinning.

Yes! The remaining American members of our expedition are finally arriving. So we are booked on the helicopter, heaving us out of the hustle of Katmandu to the Sherpa Capital, Namche Bazar, early morning, March 29. The unified Sagarmartha Environmental Expedition is gathering in the hotel lobby this morning. Gazing at each other, trying to access-we are a strong team - no doubt about that.

Scott introduces me to Pete and Klev Schoening first, "They are a major contribution to our team, don't you think?" Scott is very proud and happy about their partaking. Pete is 69 years old, with a few fingers missing due to frostbite, lost through his legendary career in the high mountains. Scott being the maverick in the big boys climbing club, boyish and not altogether serious, probably feels a blue stamp recognition, as the Schoenings' has chosen to climb with him. They all come from Seattle. Klev and Pete are definitely in another league when it comes to seriousness and obligation to decency than Scott has lived before this expedition. There are thousands of famous climbs that stand out throughout the history of mountaineering, but maybe only one truly famous belay: Pete Schoening's on the American K2 expedition in 1953.

The eight-man American team had established Camp at 25,200 feet on K2's Abruzzi Ridge, in place to set up one more camp to position two climbers for the summit bid, when Art Gilkey developed thrombophlebitis. Gilkey had blood clots in his calf muscle and if they moved to his lungs, they would kill him. The team knew a rescue of Gilkey was next to impossible, considering the terrain, the altitude and the weather - a storm had moved in. They decided to attempt to lower him down the mountain anyway, wrapped in a sleeping bag and tent.

Everyone in the group knew the rescue would endanger their own lives. On the descent, the climbers reached a 45-degree slope ending in a massive cliff, thousands of feet high. They started to work to pendulum Gilkey
across the steep slope. The 26-year-old Pete Schoening drove his wooden handled ice axe behind a rock, frozen in the ice and he was roped to Gilkey, the rope running around the big rock and down to Gilkey 60 feet below. The rest of the team waited 40 feet straight across from Gilkey, starting to seek out an anchor to pull him across. Dee Molenaar had taken a rope from Gilkey and tied it around his waist. Then George Bell, roped to Tony Streather, suddenly lost his footing and fell. The rope pulled Streather off his feet, and both men started to hurtle towards a drop of thousand feet. Streather hit the rope between Charlie Houston and Bob Bates, knocking them both off their feet, and sending them toward the edge. Then they hit the rope between Molenaar and Gilkey and Molenaar flew down the slope. Pete Schoening put all his weight onto his ice

axe and the five men slowed and stopped and did not fall to their deaths.

This incident has become widely known as "The Belay." The men gathered themselves and anchored Gilkey to the slope, as they set up an emergency camp nearby. When they returned, his body was gone: the slope had been swept by an avalanche. Some of the group members would later speculate that Gilkey, knowing the danger his rescue posed to his friends, somehow wriggled himself free and fell to his death. In 2006, 53 years later, the descendants' of those men got together in a sort of celebration, calling themselves "The Children of 'The Belay.'" At that time, there were 28 children and grandchildren, who would have never been born, if it were not for Pete Schoening and his ice axe high on K2. "The Belay" is far from Pete Schoening's only notable deed in the mountains. Schoening and Andy Kauffman completed the first ascent of Gasherbrum I in 1958, becoming the first Americans to stand on top of an 8,000-meter peak. Gasherbrum is the only 8,000-meter peak first climbed by Americans. Schoening also was one of several men, who made the first ascent of Vinson Massif, the highest peak in Antarctica, in 1966. In 1974, he went on the first American expedition to the Pamirs, which were at that time in the Soviet Union. At age 68, Pete climbed Aconcagua and Kilimanjaro and joined our Everest expedition. As our expedition progresses Pete is not part of our summit bid, as he has not been able to sleep without bottled oxygen - even at Base Camp. We did not know about his medical predicament at the time of our climb, but I am convinced Pete knew and therefore chose to attempt climbing Everest. What did he have to loose - living fully to his last breath? It turned out; he dealt a long battle with blood cancer, but remained active up until his death in 2004. Three weeks before he died, he went hiking with his longtime friend Tom

Hornbein. In his 2004 obituary in the Los Angeles Times, Dennis McLellan wrote, "The characteristically humble Schoening always downplayed his lifesaving actions on K2, "I'm surprised that it attracts interest, frankly,'" was Pete's comment."

Standing in front and below Klev, almost at navels height, gazing up trying to find the end of Klev and speaking to both Schoenings', I'm convinced they truly are added value. Their serious, humble and composed demeanor reminds me more of my inner attitude towards our near future than Scott's playfulness: a remarkable pair, these powerful gentlemen of the mountains. Meeting Klev and Pete reminds me of my "pettiness". These guys are stronger than all the training in the world can ever make me.

Mixing with the elite as I am now, I feel a touch of insecurity. I know from Scott that Pete, who belongs to a different era of mountaineering, is skeptical of having women on our expedition. During the preparations for this adventure, I was, for a long time, the only woman, but within the last few months, Charlotte and Sandy joined in to expand our minority presence. In light of his skepticism, I discern no disapproval from Pete. I enjoy an exquisite dinner with Pete and Klev Schoening: A rare privilege sharing the presence of two decent stoic gentlemen. We mention neither mountaineering nor our impending trip to Everest - the sole reason for us to be here- but talk instead of life, Pete's experiences as a businessman and Klev's solid family network.

Being true to their old-school maleness, the two-some insist of taking care of the bill and I felt very much like a woman. It's out of the question I can ever carry as much weight, for as far a distance, as they can. Nature sets its limitations. Now I am looking forward to meeting Charlotte Fox and Sandy Hill

Pittman. We might team up, to kind of equalize the physical aspects of our gender. Charlotte turns out to be slightly taller than I am and if's she's put on weight for improving her odds on Everest, I dare not picture what her normal shape is. Her friend Tim Madsen is a little guy. Charlotte grins and states, "There's no way I could allow myself to weigh more than my boyfriend." Tim decided to come at the last minute. He has no high altitude experience, but is an all-round top athlete. Sandy has summited the highest mountains on six of the seven continents.

There are two distinct measurable records climbers might pursue: climbing the 14 peaks above 8000 meters. All women who have attempted this quest until this day have died in the process. Then there's the 7 seven summits on the seven continents. Sandy has spent hours at bodybuilding. I recognize her distinct rounded musculature. She's got dark hair and I am soon to discover that her assertive attitude sometimes makes my mind slip and think to myself "pit bull" instead of "Pittman. Sandy is divorcing Bill Pitmann, who is about to marry David Breashears former wife. Rumor has it, that the two spouses meet when Sandy and David tried to climb Everest in 1994. Ed Visteurs and Scoot scaled K2, this year Ed climbs with the IMAX team. Rob Hall, Scott and Ed have been on K2 together and now they are here, climbing on three different expeditions: as colleagues or friends? Not necessarily competitors, but realistically they probably are somewhat affected by the presence of their strong climbing buddies.

Sandy definitely displays an exaggerated sense of self-importance. Underpinned by humongous wealth, that sets her apart from what I have experience with. Whether her attitudes stems from a dysfunctional personality or the position that great wealth sometimes constructs, is questionable. Fact being, excessively wealthy people might never be confronted with what people truly think of them. Interactions are always infused by an unspoken difference; rich people are treated as superior even without achievements that warrant it. Because wealth is a dissimilarity, that allocates the type of power money can buy, richness over years might change the way you perceive yourself.

Wealth opens doors, grants opportunities you might not otherwise deserve, gets your invitations by important people who needs the mirroring or your money or who want you to pay their way through life. The fact that we value money exceedingly sets wealthy and unwealthy people apart. If you thrive in a money supported lifestyle, it might lead you to require constant admiration, as well as expressing a sense of entitlement, expecting special favors and unquestioning compliance with your expectations and taking advantage of others to get what you want. Behaving in an arrogant or haughty manner, crossing the border of healthy confidence into thinking so highly of yourself that you put yourself on a pedestal valuing yourself more than you value others and displaying an inability or unwillingness to recognize the needs and feelings of others. "If you don't mind, please step outside so I can shoot some photos for my diary on the Internet, and if you could briefly introduce yourself on this tape recorder, I'll have my secretary type it up." Red light, full stop! "Sandy, the letter you distributed to us about your media project said we could participate if we wanted to. And I am not sure I want to be a part of it."

Sandy seems unable to relate to others as live human beings; it is as if we are actors she has the right and power to orchestrate to her likings. It will be interesting to learn how I will manage the delicate balance of harboring my true private observations without jeopardizing the necessary conducive atmosphere desired on a trip of our magnitude. Martin Adam's does not attract my attention at the beginning, and it is going to take me quite some days before I manage to get his and Tim's names right. Initially all I can remember is that the two not-so-tall guys are Tim and Martin, but who is Tim and who is Martin? In the crowd of extraordinary masculine and bulky looking male mountaineers, these two men at first drown completely. Neal Beidleman is absent. He's the unfortunate one whose duffel bag disappeared during the plane delay and among other important items and his high-altitude down suit is missing. Neal decides to stay behind in Katmandu until his gear shows up. He's got a cough similar to Scott's and claims that it's got nothing to do with the consequences of high-altitude climbing. Dale Kruse I know from several previous trips- we met up again this winter in Ouray, Colorado, where Scott, Dale and I amongst more friends had a fantastic training week, scaling frozen waterfalls and hot tubing together. Dale is a strong climber, exquisite at ice climbing, huge and very strong, with loads of wilderness experience. I also know from close observation that Dale is not able to adjust to altitude. I like Dale and have become great friends with his wife Terry on our trek to Pakistan in 1991 and from the times I climbed ice with them in the US I know Dale will be at peril as soon as we leave the helicopter. Every single time he ventures above 3500 meters, he is in real life-threatening trouble. Kind of unintelligent to be the first to pay for the full climb - characteristic for friends of Scott - for Scott to be able to begin financing the Everest adventure. Scott and Dale are well aware that Dale has never been able to climb high. I am happy, happy to be here, happy to be part of this strong team.

"Thanks Scott, for giving me this opportunity!"

12

"If you are going through hell, keep going." Winston Churchill

Charlotte, Sandy and I gather, tittering and discussing our "increased body mass,": typical women. Sandy had her secretary purchase the most outrageous bikinis for the team ladies to pose for NBC – online intended for "before" and "after" pictures at Base Camp. It feels great to have a thorough laugh and to get rid of all the accumulated tension. Jokes are well suited for the lunacy we're headed for. Gregarious upbeat by the prospects of partaking in something truly spectacular and carried by the hope than is inherent in all vision carried desires. Hope is an optimistic attitude of the mind, based on an expectation of desired positive outcomes related to events and circumstances in one's life. Hope is to "expect with confidence" and "to cherish a desire with anticipation". Hope also derives from focusing on a person or vision in which expectations are centered. It rises with looking forward to something in the near future with desire and reasonable confidence. Hope is to believe, desire, or trust. To feel that something sought after may happen. To want something to happen or to be true and usually have a good reason to think that it might.

"Abstain from eating anything with meat for your lunch," advices Doctor Ingrid as we are about to order in the sun outside a small teahouse on one of the terraces at Namche Bazar. However, contrary to sound advice from a true professional, I am compelled to order mixed momo's, Nepali-style miniature spring rolls, which contain yak meat and local vegetables. Charlotte orders a club sandwich; she is excessively courageous to dare anything that exotic under these remote conditions. She goes down big time soon after. "It comes out of both ends, and fast," is Tim's accurate description, when we empathetically inquire how his sweet heart is doing. It is custom that mountaineers as well as backpackers place postcard with their names and destination written upon them on the walls of the teahouses we pass on our trek onwards towards base camp. I spot familiar names on one, Henrik Jessen Hansen, Bo Belvedere, Jan Mathorne and Kim Sejberg. Some of the climbing friends my ex-husband formed the first Danish Dhaulagiri expedition with back in 1991, when I ventured to Nepal for the first time. My ex was the expedition leader. He is a tough and headstrong mountaineer and absolutely the best qualified and the most driven for that specific task. But his uncompromising personality and rivalry between big egos in their group founded hatred in some of the guys that never healed. I had rather little to do with Henrik and Bo on Dhaulagiri, but it seemed that the grudges they probably rightly held towards my husband, transferred unto me. They detested him and therefore they detest me.

Rather primitive and unreflected.

Now we are all headed to Everest Base Camp with one sole purpose in mind, Summiting Everest. I am climbing with Scott, Michael with Henry Todd; the other Danish guys bought a slot on Mal Duff's permit, actually a pretty impressive gathering from Denmark this season. As far as I know, no

Dane has challenged Everest from the Nepalese side since Claus Becker Larsen's adventurous and illegal attempt entering the area without a permit. Now six Danes are aiming for the summit.

Doctor Ingrid's prophecy has caught up with me and herself, with whom I share a room in the lodge, owned by our Sherpa Sirdar's family. Our direct jump from Katmandu to 11,300 feet requires three to four days of rest, with minimal activity, before we can start working hard at gaining altitude on the trek. I am aware that the risk of altitude sickness is huge, flying in as we did, is pushing our luck. High altitude cerebral edema (or HACE) is a severe and sometimes fatal stage of altitude sickness, that results from capillary fluid leakage due to the effects of hypoxia, the reduced oxygen content on the mitochondria-rich cells of the blood-brain barrier, caused by high altitude. Symptoms can include headache, loss of coordination (ataxia), weakness, disorientation, memory loss, psychotic symptoms (hallucinations and delusions) and coma.

HACE generally occurs after a week or more at high altitude. If not treated quickly, severe cases can result in death. Immediate descent by 2,000 - 4,000 feet is a crucial life-saving measure. Medications such as Dexamethasone can be prescribed for treatment up high, but proper training in their use is required. Anyone suffering from HACE should be evacuated to a medical facility for proper follow-up treatment. The Gamow bag can sometimes be used to stabilize the sufferer before transport or emergency descent. she can provide for his ambitious visions? Jane sure is trying her very best to give Scott the public recognition his ego and future vision for Mountain Madness is hungering for.

I seek solitude to reconnect with the inner peace I know is the crucial foundation for my summit attempt. I trust that the altitude problems I suffer through now, will improve as my body acclimatizes. I also realize that for the next months at high altitude, I will expose my system to extreme stress and be pressing myself towards and probably beyond the utmost brink. Therefore, I must restore my serenity. Every time I take a close look at Scott, I truly want to fall in love with him. He is the most attractive looking man I have ever encountered. His combination of boyish "machoness" and at the same time insecurity, vulnerability and his apparent fatigue and openness about his doubts concerning his way of living, makes Scott excessively magnetic. I want to spend more time with him, I want to get closer to what's truly going on beyond his outward actions, I want to protect Scott against himself and his ego that's obviously causing him to say yea and yes and yep to every opportunity that he creates due to who he is and what he accomplishes. However, I witness how huge a toll his predominately "one gear forward" is taking him. Scott is as close to burning out, as I have ever perceived. I truly yarn to make him stop, take a rest, adapt himself to the fact that he has exceeded his limitations and ought to learn to say no to make conscious decisions about what to pursue and what not. Not based on visionary, wishful thinking and ambition and the experience of what he has been able to pull through in his earlier years, but based on his actual mental and physical state. Scott is successful in promoting himself and he has every right to enjoy the well deserved abundance of options offered to him, but no one can go on and on and on without paying a price. I comprehend Scott's fundamental tiredness - why will he not listen? What can I do about it? If I could, I would convince him to rest and rest and rest, and confront the mess he is avoiding to deal with at various levels of his life, by always keeping active and moving forward, maybe without consciously deciding if that's the most constructive course of action.

Scott seems to be unaware of the price he pays with long-lasting fatigue and reduced strength forestalling the burnout process; I have seen transpiring in Scott over years.

In 1993 Scott Fischer guided a climb for Care on Mount McKinley (locally called Denali - 20,320 feet) in Alaska. Organized by eight students at Princeton University, this expedition raised $280,000 for the American Foundation for AIDS Research. As the climbing leaders of the 1994 Sagarmatha Environmental Expedition, Scott Fischer and Rob Hess both summited Mt. Everest without supplemental oxygen. This expedition removed 5000 pounds of trash and 150 discarded oxygen bottles from Everest, and led to a bottle recovery plan to which every expedition must now follow as per Nepal's government. The expedition not only paid Sherpas to carry gear up the mountain to be cached at higher camps for later use, but also paid the Sherpas a bounty to carry trash, old climbing and camping gear and empty oxygen bottles down the mountain. This summit accomplishment also meant that Scott Fischer had climbed to the top of the highest peaks on six of the seven continents, the exception being Mount Vinson in Antarctica. That same year, the American Alpine Club awarded the David Brower Conservation Award, "an annual award recognizing leadership and commitment to preserving mountain regions worldwide," to all members of Scott's expedition. After his successful Broad Peak expedition in Pakistan in 1995, Scott began focusing on the potential of the big rewards and prospects of an easier future that could come from organizing a successful guided Everest expedition: always expeditioning and pondering how to attract the media and sponsors to continue the lifestyle, which is intertwined with his identity and ego. Now and then wanting to leave the climbing scene, questioning what to make of himself instead of pursuing mountaineering and leading expeditions, applying for a leading position at NOLS, but being turned down, smoking pot and popping pills to keep going and follow the only pattern he knows. In January 1996, Scott and Mountain Madness guided a fundraising ascent of Mount Kilimanjaro (19,341 feet / 5,895 m) in Africa. Named the "Climb for CARE", it celebrated the 50th Anniversary of the founding of the international relief organization and raised nearly a million dollars.

Six weeks after returning from the charity climb of Mount Kilimanjaro in Africa, Scott left Seattle and travelled to the Himalayas in Nepal.
Approaching 40, additionally Scott is burdened by speculations of financial concerns, the magnitude of "Bagging the big E" catching up with Scott the youngster, dealing with the whole kit and caboodle by smoking hash and taking uppers and downers in a colorful cocktail. Always concocting a new female in tow - one for every trip and adding the spice of a trip by getting involved with one of the female possibilities. On our voyage the chosen one is - Jane Bromet.

13

"Mountains have the power to call us into their realms"
Anatoli Boukreev

- Focus on detecting opportunities.

- You'll make more headway by exploiting opportunities than you will by solving problems.

"Why do you want to climb? You are a woman. If you want to climb Everest - you must have the will to suffer." Anatoli programs me after posing his initial question. He gently joins our group on the trek into base camp and I try to get a deeper sense of whom this slender guy is. Scott has a very extrovert side to his personality. A gregarious charisma that attracts hordes of people and at the same time keeps him apart from the more serious and mature, who keep a distance due to Scott's "go getter" boyishness and what follows. Anatoli is so much more the introvert and expresses his sensitivity through his romantic descriptions of the size and fragrance of the strawberries in his home region Almaty, complementing the beauty of the women from Scandinavia but remaining faithful to his notion that the loveliest females in the world are Russian: unbelievable competition.

I like Anatoli's withdrawn magnetism. What a contrast to Scott's need to attract admirers attention and in the long run leaving them starved and wanting more of what he initially fascinated them by. "Don't waste energy, humbly respect the mountain and endure more hardships than you ever imagined in your worst nightmare. In addition, when it is time to rest - you rest! Climb high, exhaust yourself, push yourself some more and then sleep and rest low." Anatoli's tough self-discipline and his phenomenal endurance, determines his ethical behavior and the invaluable lessons he would teach me on Everest. He is the toughest and most experienced mountaineer I have ever shared life with as well as the most intelligent and humble human being. He seems politically, genuinely individualistic, molded by and adapted to the unpretentious demands coupled with venturing high. On the surface, Scott offers himself on a plate, but I doubt many of his admirers truly get to know Scott. Behind his outer laid-back, wide-open appearance, he is actually a hard guy to get close to an intimate with. Anatoli seems to offer what he is. Not in any way trying to gather an audience, even though, he has a life and manner that attracts. Simply speaking I am of the conviction that Scott thrives best, when everyone is fond of him. His self-worth to some degree seems dependent on being liked. I do not think Anatoli needs anybody, to be at ease with himself in the world. He appears to rest contentedly within himself and that I find truly attractive. His solidity - his inner peace - especially as I step by step discover that Anatoli is no way near the impression I formed and I doomed him by, back in 1991 when our adventures caused our paths to cross. I am discovering an ethic, deeply philosophical, authentic and profoundly intelligent human being who happens to be one of our times most experienced high altitude mountaineers. Anatoli Boukreev is a rare, yet authentic multifaceted genius with a unique wit and serene inner strength. He enchants me with his narratives in broken English about the beauty of the Russian women and the sweetness of the giant strawberries from his home region in Almaty and leaves me with a profound love and veneration for the Russian soul. Causing me to choose a Russian Fertility clinic for having my twins when I wanted to provide my oldest adopted daughter with siblings. I am a single mother by choice. When Anatoli sat with his guitar, turning his attention inwards -he sang, venerating the essential - the universal in human existence, love, grief, beauty and loss. He was a stoic romantic, who was fundamentally present in the here and now, taking serious pleasure in simple things and grateful behaviors. Genius of the Mountains Anatoli Boukreev - the strong and ethical man from Caucasus, who became my friend - personified the proper purist mountaineer. Is decency, ethic, moral, honest behavior, showing kindness, caring about the feelings or problems of other human beings and approaches that express respect an inherent genetic trait? Anatoli came from a different culture, demanding on levels westerners are too spoiled to expose themselves to and as tough as the mountains he loved. Straight and uncorrupted he was also a tender man with a philosopher's soul. He never pampered people, but would exhaust himself to come to your rescue if you were in real trouble.

For those of us who took time to get to know him, we were rewarded by his fine qualities, which were abundant. To me he became a valuable and highly respected tutor in the most profound sense. Not that he ever wanted that predicate, but his decency and humble integrity, combined with his grueling experience in the mountains, compelled me to learn from his example. Commercialization and Anatoli Boukreev are fundamental contradictions. In 1991 when the Soviet Union collapsed, generations of Russians were left in the shambles of their country. While western alpinists of extraordinary caliber, such as Reinhold Messner became famous icons, Anatoli's bent for individual accomplishments made him an anomaly in the USSR. When he was 33, the collapse of the Soviet Union shattered the fabric of his life. At the peak of his physical potential, political instability and economic chaos opened like a great crevasse, destroying opportunity and shattering the ethic and financial system that supported his athleticism. His role as an Honored Master Athlete and his income in the Soviet society evaporated. The idealism and inner strength that Anatoli possessed endured. He salvaged what was positive from his culture, funneling the bewildering political and social contradictions into something exemplary, something uniquely Anatoli.

    He prepared for the pitfalls of capitalism but unwilling to give up a quest that had charted his course of life since the age of sixteen, Anatoli´s inner drive for pristineness and fundamental earnest simplicity found an outlet in the mountains. His grand fundamental personality would probably not have been able to exist anywhere but in the high mountains. His urge for climbing revealed a rich interior world with a core of philosophical idealism. Anatoli seemed to be a renaissance man - more so than a product of an era. Deprived of the political system that had created his opportunities in Soviet society, he ventured out in the world, leading him to America, to the Karakoram, to the Himalaya's, K2, yet always returning to Almaty. He never mistook accumulation of objects for wealth or freedom. 15 years of hard won experience, secured him a position as climbing guide in an emerging global market place; the world's 8000-meter peaks. Anatoli couldn't but refine demanding physical experience into the meaning of life. Anatoli's reserve might also have been shyness, combined with his imperfect English. On Everest, he was careful socially, never seeking the center of attention - in all probability genuinely respecting Scott for his embracing charm- a trait Anatoli most likely would have worked on internalizing and conveying in himself, had he been granted more years.

He upheld a refined sensitivity and groundedness that were not fundamentally shaken by any of the myriads of mediocrity and less than respectable human behavior on Everest, as well as in the aftermath.

After Anatoli died on Annapurna in 1997, I learned a lot more about his background and the magnitude of his accomplishments, than I had access to, when I shared life with him in 1991 and 1996. He was a unique uncompromising human being, the most impressive person I have ever encountered. He seemed driven by a pure unpolluted, uncompromising and very pristinely inspiring quest for life. The world would be a grander place, if more of us had the capacity and courage to be as true to simplicity and decency as Anatoli was. He lived the complex challenges and high risks in the soaring mountains.

When Anatoli died on the slopes of Annapuna on December 25, 1997 the world lost one of the greatest mountaineers of our time: a fine man with authentic integrity and a seldom humbleness. A man few people really knew, man who became altered by the media's power to distort reality. A man every human being could have been inspired by. In hindsight, I can somehow be comforted that Anatoli did not have to find a way and come to grips with the commercialization of the high mountains that was his life.

Having lived without sharing life with Anatoli since he perished on Anna Purna, I have come to realize that some people truly are greater than death. To me meaning ,that their way of conducting themselves in the world, when they were alive, have an inspiring impact long after they are gone. Like art, a contemporary generation might not be able to predict what will endure for generations to come.

Anatoli was one of the rare humans that truly live on in me, due to who he was. I recall listening - being spellbound by the song and guitar that emerged from Anatoli's marguerite covered cotton tent in the vicinity of base camp - simplicity, tenderness, melancholy and longing. Anatoli seemed to personify the essence of the superlative qualities a human can display. To uphold oneself to consistently moral and ethical standards is a personal choice. He impersonated integrity - the quality of honesty- emanating "wholeness" deriving from his consistency of character. He presented a composed reserve; he was an intensely private man. He appreciated life deeply.

Sharing life at Camp 3 before our summit bid - I saw a very philosophical and humorous side of him - when he with an amused grin inquired into the vastness of the oncoming nightfall,

"Who am I?"
"Who am I?"

Without Anatoli my experience climbing and surviving Everest, would have been less grand, less determining for who I am and what I choose to pursue at present. Mountaineers like Anatoli are a breed apart.

Anatoli Boukreev and Lene Gammelgaard   Everest Base Camp 1996

14

*"As long as you are alive - you have choices
and live with the consequences"*
Lene Gammelgaard

- Prepare mentally - you will be able to stay focused for the duration, if you think everything through before you start executing your detailed action plan.
- You must always have a plan B.
- Plan B must take you toward the goal you set for plan A.
- Anticipate what might go wrong and develop strategies to deal with it, to counter energy consumption and de-motivation caused by debilitating surprises.

Our ascent via the Southeast Ridge begins with the trek to Base Camp at 5,380 m (17,700 ft.) on the south side of Everest in Nepal. Expeditions usually fly into Lukla (2,860 m) or Namche Bazar, the Sherpa Capital from Kathmandu. We then hike to Base Camp, which usually takes six to eight days, allowing for proper altitude acclimatization in order to prevent altitude sickness. A sea-level dweller exposed to the atmospheric conditions at the altitude above 8,500 m (27,900 ft.) would without acclimatization, likely lose consciousness within 2 to 3 minutes. Achieving the necessary level of physiological performance requires prolonged altitude acclimatization, which takes 40-60 days on a typical expedition like ours.

The human body is able to exist within an amazing range of environments; however, the necessary habituation processes to adapt to an out of the ordinary milieu usually requires time. When climbing, it is advisable to adopt a "climb high, sleep low" strategy. On expedition-style climbs like ours, mountaineers will often climb as high as we safely can during the day, sleep high for one night and then return to a much lower elevation to regenerate, sleep and allow our bodies to adjust to the elevation we just came down from. Increasing the sleeping elevation by only 350m (1,150ft) per 24 hours greatly reduces the probabilities of the potentially deadly altitude-related conditions (AMS, HACE & HAPE). Every 1000m (3,280ft), climbers should plot in a rest day, in order to get fully accustomed to the novel and low atmospheric pressure.

One side effect of low oxygen levels in the blood due to the changed atmospheric pressure is a vastly increased breathing rate, often 80-90 breaths per minute as opposed to a more typical 20-30. Exhaustion can occur merely by attempting to breathe. By conservatively implementing well-known acclimatization practices, you should stay relatively safe regarding altitude-related illness. When acclimatized, the clue is to get up Everest and back down as speedily as possible. We have to be self sustained for the 40-60 days our expedition will last. Yaks, dzopkyos, yakcow hybrids, and human porters carry all our climbing equipment and supplies to Base Camp. When Hillary and Tenzing climbed Everest in 1953, the British expedition consisted of more than 400 climbers, porters and Sherpas and started from the Kathmandu Valley, as there were no roads further east back in those days. Sherpas are the indigenous people who live in the northeastern part of Nepal, in the valleys of the Himalaya Mountains. There are about 40,000 Sherpas, many of who live near Mount Everest in the high rugged regions at the foot of the world's highest mountain. The Sherpas probably came to Nepal from Tibet in the early part of the 16th century. They still have many customs and traditions of the Tibetan people and dress in Tibetan clothes.

Most Sherpas are Tibetan Buddhists. They have no written language and worship the mountains around them, which they view as the home of their gods. Mount Everest, for example, is called Chomolungma: Mother Goddess of the Earth. Some people glorify the Sherpas as pure, natural and mystical gods of the nature. Others view them as low-caste inhabitants of the third world. The truth is of course that the Sherpas are just like the rest of us; some are good, some are bad and most are somewhere in between. Sherpas are the sole inhabitants of the Khumbu-valley, the national park surrounding Everest. Living at altitude for generations, they have developed a genetic natural allowance for it. If you are well trained yourself, you might find that in Kathmandu the Sherpas do substantially fewer push-ups than you might.

Don't get too excited. Once you go above 3000 meters/10000 ft. most of them will easily outrun you. Their natural advantage is strongest up to 8000-meters/23000 ft., there after they too will face problems.

Most Sherpas will consequently require oxygen above Camp 4 in order to perform at their best. They are usually happy and easy going. They take great pride in their mountaineering heritage, just as another famous people of Nepal, the Gurkhas, who take pride in their warrior skills. Since Sherpas are stronger than we are at altitude, they are very well suited for alpine style expeditions in the Himalayas. They are a valuable aid to us because we are not genetically adapted to altitude by birth. Be grateful for their advantages, as you will need them to carry the oxygen, the gear and as a safety precaution on the summit push.

Many "solo" climbers actually bring Sherpas' with them all the way to the summit. The Himalayas are still inaccessible and just 80 years ago, the world did not know very much about the Sherpas'. They lived alone in their villages, traded goods and grew corn and potatoes. When the British started mountain climbing expeditions in the 20th Century, they used Sherpas' as guides. With the help of yaks, Sherpas' helped mountaineers bring their heavy loads into great heights. Over the years, Sherpas' have been admired for their physical strength. They have been existed in higher altitudes for generations and are genetically adapted to cope better with the unforgiving environment. Only the strong survive and live to adulthood under these conditions. The Sherpas' generally function better than we do, coping more efficient with the reduced oxygen level and are used to working hard at high attitudes and in thin air. Even today, Sherpas' rely on walking to move around. In the more remote parts of Nepal where Everest is situated, there are no roads, no cars or other vehicles. The only means of transportation in most parts of Nepal is walking. In 1953 Sherpa Tenzing Norgay and Edmund Hillary- mountaineers from New Zealand- became the first people to get to the top of Mount Everest.

This year Tenzing Norgay's son Jamling Norgay will attempt climbing Everest, participating on the IMAX Film expedition. While mountain climbers pay around $ 60,000 for an expedition, Sherpas' earn 2,000 USD on a trip. 2,000 USD is the equivalent of two years average income here, which of course makes it attractive to become part of an expedition in spite of the risks involved. Helping tourists get to the top of high mountains has become a great source of income in this region. Some Sherpas' have started their own business, operating hotels and lodges for trekkers and tourists. Even though Sherpas' know the region and the weather patterns better than we do, they too risk their lives assisting our desire to expedition.

About a third of the people who have died trying to conquer Mount Everest have been Sherpas'. In the last few decades many international organizations have helped them improve their life. A foundation set up by Sir Edmund Hillary has brought health care and modern medicine to remote villages. Water power plants and hospitals have also been set up. The tourist industry has made life easier for most Sherpas'. Many have adapted to a more western way of life, even though some still live as their ancestors did many centuries ago. The Sherpas' are not our servants. They speak broken English and are usually not so schooled, but they can think very well for themselves and have their own respect-demanding modus operandi. We spend a couple of weeks in Base Camp, acclimatizing to the altitude. During that time, Sherpas' and some of the stronger expedition guides fix ropes and fasten aluminum ladders in the treacherous Khumbu
Icefall.
"Hey, Ngima, do you have an idea when my remaining duffels could arrive. I'm still missing one of my tents and will have a hard time getting settled properly at Base Camp and begin my focused process of acclimatization, until I can pitch my igloo shaped mobile home."
"Maybe late today, but we have one runaway yak. Pemba is searching for it."

Our remaining tons of expedition equipment, oxygen tanks, food, etc. are still being ferried into base camp by delayed porters and yaks. Our refugee yak accentuates that our carefully planned expedition can still be thrown off course by a multitude of factors, including porter strikes, weather and snow conditions so "ongoing calculation" of any change in our situation is vital. A lot of the stimulation of mountaineering is about the logistics and strategic side of things as opposed to just the climbing. Climbing is the easy part, if you get any of the other aspects wrong you'll fail in the quest to reach the summit. As common in the Himalaya's, our expedition ran into small disturbances of our well laid out trekking schedule. The snowfall has been extraordinary this spring and our entire logistic has been held up due to deep snow from Gorak Sheep and in to base camp.

A porter, also called a bearer, is a person who makes a living from carrying objects for others. We hire porters to carry our heavy burdens in to base camp. The porter's hard work yields the foundation for our multimonth mountaineering expedition. The use of humans to transport cargo dates back to the ancient world, prior to domesticating animals and development of the wheel. Historically it remained prevalent in areas where slavery was permitted, porters were commonly used as beasts of burden in the ancient world, when labor was generally cheap and slavery widespread and still exists today where modern forms of mechanical conveyance are rare or impractical. Human adaptability and flexibility led to the early use of humans for transporting gear in mountainous regions. Over time slavery diminished and technology advanced, but the role of porters for specialized transporting services remains strong in the 21st century. Porters are still paid to shift burdens in many third-world countries, where motorized transport is impractical, often alongside pack animals. Nepalese porters may be the world's most efficient haulers. Porters here are legendary for their load-carrying abilities. If you've ever watched Nepalese porters in action, you might think they have superhuman strength. How else to explain their ability to carry loads weighing more than 100 pounds (45 kilograms), mile after arduous mile over steep Himalaya terrain? They use less energy than other people would require for the same work: scientists' states. A typical Nepalese porter carries a load nearly as heavy as he is. When he does, the porter burns less energy per pound than we would need to shoulder about half the same weight: research found. That remarkable ability helps porters earn a living, carting goods great distances in the Mount Everest region. On route, the porters traverse more than 60 miles (100 kilometers) along rugged footpaths. During the journey, they can climb around five vertical miles (8 kilometers) and descend about 4 miles (6.5 kilometers). On average, the men and women respectively carry 93 percent and 66 percent of their body weight- researchers report. A porter's gear is simple but effective. The bulky and often heavy load goes into an oversized basket, or Doko, which rests against the back of the porter. A strap runs underneath the Doko and over the crown of the head, which bears most of the weight. Each porter also carries a T-shaped walking stick called a Tokma. When on the move, porters sometimes pause more than they walk. On a steep incline, they'll walk for as little as 15 seconds and rest for 45. At each stop, they use their Tokma to support their load, which allows a standing rest

Due to the deep snow our porters strike and refuse to move further upwards towards Everest Base Camp unless they get a pay raise. It is to be expected that porters at some point refuses to move any higher on the agreed route, stressing the whole set-up, comprehensively gambling for more money. Which is exactly what played itself out a week ago around Gorak Sheep, the last semi inhabited dump before venturing unto the flat sections of the Khumbu Glacier itself. The yaks were not able to progress because the snow is too deep. Try to imagine a 600 kg ox with 200 kg equipment strapped on its back, sink into bottomless snow. There is a natural limit to the progress of the yaks, as well as for our human pack animals. Therefore, our hauling gear into Base Camp comes to an unwelcome stop, until the snow melts and new wages has been agreed upon. We always bring extra gear, boots, snow goggles and down jackets to distribute among our Sherpas and porters, as they are not likely to be able to afford the quality of equipment we take for granted. It is not uncommon to see hordes of porters carrying up till 45 kilos on their backs in the headband around their sterns, traversing snow and ice fields in flip-flops. This is a different universe entirely.

No problem. I'll just continue clearing away rock and chopping ice at the glaciated platform I have chosen in the outskirts of base camp for my home base for the next months. Various tents containing my team are scattered over the glacier. We are forming an artificial colorful village, where we are within seeing and hearing range of each other. I have selected a glacier hillock, slightly removed from the main camp, because of its view of the Khumbu Icefall and because I do not want to be disturbed by the noise from the other adventure prone human beings settling in for the dream of their lives. It is tough work to shape a platform the size of my tent's ground sheet hacking away on the glaciated bottom with my ice axe, doing my best to stay clear of big pieces of rock in my progress to claim my homestead lot for the near future. The glacier that momentarily lies silent beneath me is constantly on the move, inaudibly moaning, creeping downwards under its own steam, melting and refreezing with the rhythm of the temperature swings of any particular day. To reduce the hazards of this thawing frozen environment, we will begin our ascent well before dawn, when the freezing temperatures glue ice blocks in place. Eventually the rocks that are now imbedded in what seems to be solid ice, maybe they'll tumble over - preferably not on top of me. I enjoy the workout, investing in improving my form to climb Everest.

Anatoli Boukreev   Everest Trek 1996

"Strong Danish woman." I gaze across towards Anatoli, smiling, sprawled on his sunbathing rock. Dressed in shorts and his characteristic whitish pointed woolen hat, symbolic for his never relenting romanticized love for his home region, Almaty in Caucasus, anyone but Anatoli would make a ridiculous, almost naked figure. He is engulfed in his experience based self preparing program of getting as fit as possible for what lies ahead. Sticking strictly to his tested program of climbing high, work even harder, sleep low and do absolutely nothing during the rest periods. "Climb High - rest low." Keep still offering the whole system sufficient time and calm to thoroughly recuperate before the next grueling passage up the mountain. Anatoli's square, blue cotton tent, sprinkled with white daffodils, truly brightens this barren place where nothing can live. A bouquet of flowers in a sterile space underscores the difference between the countries and cultures we originate from. The rest of our expedition tents are the absolute latest in high-tech expedition gear.

15

"On the mountain we are all equal"
Lene Gammelgaard

- Gear your life to the concept of rapid change.
- Old skills won't suffice, adapt to what's required.
- Learn from the future as it happens - comply.

"Wouldn't it be great if we could have this expedition over and done with, without any injuries or major accidents?" Scott asks over a mug of Starbucks Coffee, basking in the April spring sunrays outside our mess tent at Everest Base Camp. I do not answer. We both know that what happens - happens. Scott's ambition is to get as many of us to the summit of Everest and safely back down as possible. He might be a happy go lucky guy, but he is aware of the objective risks of our adventure. Even if he in spells seems to lose the helicopter perspective and submerge himself in stuff that takes tolls on his already fully stretched resources. It is my first climb above 7300 meters. I have been climbing for 10 years and before I shifted my need for nature's grand, demanding adventures from ocean sailing to the mountains, I have been crossing the Atlantic and the Biscay; endeavors that most sailors aspire to test themselves in, during their lives with water focus. Through various close-call encounters, I have learned that "I am best when it counts'. Being in storms, capsizing, equipment failure or breakage, I can harbor a lot of doubt beforehand, but when reality truly exposes its brutality, I take action - often where others freeze and become incapacitated by fear. I am confident with this experience-based self- knowledge. I have also learned that I must be able to assume 100% responsibility for myself - no matter how dramatically the situation evolves.

Through my ex-husband, I became confronted with my lack of willingness to work hard enough, risk sufficiently, strengthen and discipline myself to climb higher by climbing higher. I detested him, as the tough, necessary learning process became apparent and attempted absolutely every averting mechanism to circumvent following his hard won recipe for becoming a virtuous mountaineer.

Scott Fischer   Everest Base Camp 1996

Oh, would I have preferred that I could have produced a sparkling tear flow and had him drag me over the passages and crux's I badly wanted to be able to master, but was too inexperienced and scared to bridge in real life. I learned - step by step by step, year by year by year - through investing in doing, what he confronted me with was indispensable. When I arrived at Everest Base Camp, I was ready to assume full responsibility for myself - not expecting anybody to assist me - and hopefully not end up in a situation where I will require help to survive. Climbing the highest mountain in the world is a lonely gamble. You must not trust anybody but yourself. If you unconsciously need a leader, guide or team comrade to do for you, what you are not experienced enough or tough enough to accomplish on your own - it might be a deadly interdependence. I like climbing with Scott because he never tries to be the boss, never interferes with my climbing. I know I will have to climb Everest on my own, paying inward attention to utilize my resources to the utmost, if I shall stand any chance of succeeding in my endeavor and live to tell the tale. I know Scott and therefore have realistic prospects of what to anticipate: never expecting Scott, Anatoli or anyone else to help me.

"Once we are on the mountain, we are just a group of friends out having fun!" It is good to be back in Nepal. I feel at home and at ease with myself. Today, sitting in Base Camp with Scott, contemplating the web of experiences that has brought me back to Everest - I am happy. Collected, at ease and at peace with myself, I do not want to have "this thing over with". I am aware of the uniqueness of my good fortune of preparing to climb the highest mountain in the world, in company with some truly grand personalities and alpinists. This is a once in a lifetime opportunity, and I have a great feeling about our team. It is relatively rare to be part of a truly great and functioning climbers group and here I am. It feels as if everything that I ever rummaged for across the globe is coming together here - this spring. Great companions, truly extraordinary individuals and this magnificent opportunity to instigate the grandest adventure ever: I am happy, relishing every tiny fragment of the aforementioned. I acknowledge that Scott is engulfed in a much more complex web than my pure unobstructed focus of, "To the summit and safe return". Adventure is intrinsic to our nature. Modern climbers continue the ancient legacy of exploring the unknown. We explore and test our limits in different ways, each of us have our own Everest to contend. High altitude is equally fair to all. In the most profound sense Everest is a nondiscriminatory place, where you can find out what you and your fellow beings are capable of or the contrary. Gender, color, religion, status, wealth, ethnicity, etc. do not play a role in how you deal with the struggle of surpassing yourself and others, once you have accomplished to get everything lined up to actually be on the mountain. The highest mountain in the world offers an unblemished mirror that reflects exactly who and what you are at this specific time pocket. Talking, charming, yelling, manipulating, competing or whatever we might utilize to get through existence at sea level, do not count when dealing with Everest. Here it is pure strength, risk willingness, luck, nature's forces, will and resources to carry on and endure, that determines what you are capable of. Mount Everest equals justice. Justice is the moderation or mean between selfishness and selflessness - between having more and having less than one's fair share. Climbing Mount Everest is the supreme symbol of man's personal phenomenal struggle to achieve. As a metaphor, Everest is simple and pure, man versus nature.

It approaches a universal understanding of our primal desire to master ourselves and will eternally stand as a symbol for triumph and failure. As long as Everest and man exist, it will draw adventurers without mercy, leaving neither culture nor people untouched. Being at the verge of what any human being can survive, you also get to learn how you treat your fellow man in the face of ambition and death. After four days of climbing on Everest, I recognize a feature in Sandy that I have spent the last 10 years disciplining out of myself. If you want to survive Everest, you must have conditioned total self-reliance. Truly and thoroughly never, ever expect anyone to save you or do for you, what you must be able to do under your own steam, when confronted with the worst possible scenarios. Sandy is a strong climber. However, she does not seem to have profoundly grasped that Everest is not an American movie. It is as if she unconsciously expects someone to take care of her, when things get really rough. I know from hard over won battles against this specific weakness within myself, that lack of mountaineering maturity can be very hazardous to be in the vicinity of, so I begin looking to climb in the footsteps of Anatoli, who to the utmost personalized the exact opposite matrix. The way you conduct yourself is exposed for all to see on the slopes up high and in addition wide-open to the world through live coverage. Mount Everest is the highest mountain in the world and hence attracts considerable attention as well as climbing attempts by highly experienced mountaineers, capable climbers, grandiose neurotics, weirdoes and wealthy people willing to hire professional guides. Over several decades a set of climbing routes has been established on Everest. There are two main routes, one approaching the summit from the southeast in Nepal, known as the standard route via South Col and the other from the north in Tibet. While not posing substantial technical climbing challenges on the standard route,

Everest presents dangers such as altitude sickness, weather, wind as well as significant objective hazards from avalanches and the Khumbu Icefall. While the overwhelming majority of climbers use bottled oxygen in order to reach the top, some climbers have summited Everest without supplemental oxygen. The summit of Everest is the point at which Earth's surface reaches the greatest distance above sea level. Mount Everest, also known in Nepal as Sagarmāthā and in Tibet as Chomolungma, is the Earth's highest mountain. Its peak is 8,848 meters (29,029 ft.) above sea level and is the fifth furthest summit from the center of Earth. The snow and ice thickness on the mountain varies over time, making a definitive height of the snowcap impossible to determine.

The international border between China and Nepal runs across the precise summit point. The first recorded efforts to reach Everest's summit were by British mountaineers in the early 1920s. With Nepal not allowing foreigners into the country at the time, the British initiated several attempts on the north ridge route from the Tibetan side. After the first reconnaissance expedition, the British in 1921 reached 7,000 m (22,970 ft.) on the North Col. A 1922 expedition pushed the North ridge route up to 8,320 m (27,300 ft.) marking the first time a human had climbed above 8,000 m (26,247 ft.) Tragedy struck on the descent from the North Col when seven porters were killed in an avalanche.

The 1924 expedition resulted in the greatest mystery on Everest to this day. George Mallory and Andrew Irvine made a final summit attempt on June 8, but never returned, sparking debate as to whether they were the first to reach the top. They had been spotted high on the mountain that day, but disappeared in the clouds, never to be seen again. In May 1999, a search expedition located the body of George Mallory on Mt. Everest (8848 m). Mallory was found at an altitude of approximately 8200 m on the north face of the mountain, 75 years after he had last been seen alive. Mallory was frozen in a position of self-arrest at the bottom of a scree slope, having obvious signs of a broken leg and an injury to his head, because of a fall. The search team buried his body under the abundant rocky debris found nearby. Tenzing Norgay and Edmund Hillary made the first official ascent of Everest in 1953 using the southeast ridge route. Tenzing reached 8,595 m (28,199 ft.) the previous year as a member of the 1952 Swiss expedition. Edmund Hillary was knighted and Tenzing Norgay more or less forgotten by Westerners in our odd way of disregarding the triumphs of those with other ethnic backgrounds. Is a Sherpa's risk of climbing Everest different from ours? Why are they generally considered less heroic than we who arrive from the western world? Why don't we even make the effort of speaking about and remembering the names of the Sherpas' who were also on the mountain during May 10 1996?

In 1996 the meteorological conditions around the summit of Mount Everest had not been extensively studied, although weather is recognized as a significant risk for climbers on the mountain. Scientific interest in Mount Everest had largely focused on the physiology of hypoxia caused by the summit's low barometric pressure. When we breathe in air at sea level, the atmospheric pressure of about 14.7 pounds per square inch (1.04 kg. per cm.2) causes oxygen to easily pass through selectively permeable lung membranes into the blood, at high altitudes, the lower air pressure makes it more difficult for oxygen to enter our vascular systems. The result is hypoxia or oxygen deprivation. Hypoxia usually begins with the inability to exert normal physical activities, such as climbing a short flight of ice without fatigue. Other early symptoms of "high altitude sickness" include a lack of appetite, vomiting, headache, distorted vision, fatigue, and difficulty with memorizing and thinking clearly. In serious cases of high altitude sickness, pneumonia-like symptoms - pulmonary edema, due to hemorrhaging in the lungs and an abnormal accumulation of fluid around the brain, cerebral edema - develop. Pulmonary and cerebral edema usually results in death within a few days, if we do not a return to normal air pressure levels. This is where the Gamow Bag - our portable pressure chamber comes in handy.

When we travel to high mountain regions, our bodies initially pose inefficient physiological responses. We face an increased risk of heart failure due to the added stress placed on the lungs, heart and arteries at altitude. Breathing and heart rates increase to as much as double, even when we are resting. Pulse rate and blood pressure rises severely as our hearts pump harder to get more oxygen to the cells. These are stressful changes, especially for people with weak hearts. Later, a more efficient response normally develops as acclimatization takes place. Additional red blood cells are produced to carry more oxygen round our bodies. Our lungs increase in size to facilitate the osmosis of oxygen and carbon dioxide. There is also an increase in the vascular network of muscles. However, successful acclimatization rarely results in the same level of physical and mental fitness that is usual of altitudes close to sea level. Strenuous exercise and memorization tasks remain more difficult. Added dangers include hypothermia, which occurs from extreme exposure to cold. Hypothermia is defined as a body core temperature below 35.0 °C (95.0 °F). Symptoms depend on the temperature. In mild hypothermia, there is shivering and mental confusion, in moderate hypothermia shivering stops and confusion increases. In severe hypothermia there may be paradoxical undressing, the affected individual removes their clothing. Apparently, our bodies react to long exposure to cold environment by boiling us from the inside, as well as an increased risk of the heart stopping. Everest is so high the jet stream hit the elevated sections. Jet streams are fast flowing, narrow air currents found in the atmosphere Earth. The main jet streams are located near the altitude of the tropopause. The strongest jet streams are the polar jets, at around 9-12 km (30,000-39,000 ft.) above sea level. Jet streams are formed by a combination of a planet's rotation on its axis and atmospheric heating by solar radiation. The wind speeds vary according to the temperature, exceeding 92 km/h (57 mph), speeds of over 398 km/h (247 mph) have been measured.

Most of the year, the summit on Everest is battered by winds of over 100 miles per hour that will kill a climber in minutes or even hurtle them into the void. It is only during the onset of the Asian Monsoon that these winds die down and allow us climbers a diminutive seven to 10-days window to scale the mountain. We might be challenged with airstreams beyond 200 mph when the weather pattern changes. Due to the extreme height of the Himalayas, unpredictable shifts in weather enhances the risks of being here. Unsurprisingly, there is no way around the fact, that if we pursue the summit of Everest, we climb into jet stream prone altitudes. The highest recorded wind speed at the summit of Everest was a 175 mph in February 2004. For reference, a Category 5 hurricane has sustained wind speeds of at least 157 mph, throughout the winter; hurricane-force winds pummel the summit for three days out of four. The two windows, in which those harsh winds die down, may happen in May and September. However, snow falls during the September calm, so fresh snowdrifts counterpoise the break from the wind. That is why so many pursue to ascent in May. In May the jet stream shifts north, providing periods of relative still on the mountain. "The weather window" is the one week period of calm, we focus our entire energy and strategy towards for months, as we are preparing, acclimatizing, building up high camps, stocking oxygen etc, a few days of tranquil weather, which normally settles the extreme meteorological conditions around and on Everest a week or two into May and lasts for 5-10 days at best. The "weather window" is what we all acclimatize and wait for, to be ready to utilize to gain access to the pinnacle of our dreams. The whole idea about waiting to summit until mid-May is meticulously timed to take advantage of this well-documented change in the weather pattern up high. We position ourselves, lurking like sharks wired for attack - to be ready to scale the mountain when the "weather window" stabilizes and the Jet stream storms up above. Bear in mind - no one - in their right mind - would have attempted the climb on May 10 if we had access to weather forecasts predicting storm.

16

"A winner is just a loser who tried one more time"

- Keep focusing on the "summit" not to become distracted by "small stuff".

- You can't do it all - Utilize your limited resources.

- Make conscientious choises.

It is quite a get-together of exciting men at Base Camp this season, Big Boys network, Scott Fischer and Rob Hall, 1996 is Rob's eighth Everest expedition. Rob is considered an excellent mountaineer and high altitude expedition leader by all who are assembled this season, David Breashers. Anatoli Boukreev, Ed Visteurs, Henry Todd - an impressive handful of accomplished mountaineers of this decade. All above average looking and charismatic as well, guys who know each other from participating in adventurous climbing expeditions across the Himalayas. All assembled here with the same purpose - summiting Everest - no casualties. I am curious about whom and how Rob Hall is and invite myself for a cup of tea in the Adventure Consultant mess tent, to say hello to the people gathered for the same reason as we.

Rob Hall was born in Christchurch in 1961, the last of nine children in a Roman Catholic family of modest means. Perhaps because of that background, initiative, enterprise and self-reliance characterized his life from an early age. Rob Hall was only 19, when he reached his first Himalayan summit, the 6,856-metre Ama Dablam in Solo Khumbu - the Sherpa region of Nepal where he would later become so well known and liked. The following year he climbed another Himalayan peak, Numbur (6,954 metres), but it was at home, in the New Zealand Alps, that he really caused a stir, making the first winter ascent, with Steve Lassher, of the Caroline Face of Mt Cook. The altitude here is not extreme, but the scale is vast. It took the pair just eight and a half hours to climb this one-and-a-half mile-high face, which had taken most previous parties about 22 hours in summer. Rob Hall made a name for himself in mountaineering when, in 1990, two young and motivated New Zealand mountaineers Gary Ball and Rob Hall decided that it would be a good idea to climb the Seven Summits on the seven continents in seven months.

    Exactly seven months later, Rob and Gary completed their odyssey when they reached the summit of Vinson Massif, the highest mountain in the interior of Antarctica. Gary Ball was the raconteur - the grinning bloke with a sharp tongue and a glint in his eye. He was someone with an innate ability to break down people's barriers and soon have them in fits of laughter and usually at their own expense! Gary Ball sported long blonde hair and oftentimes a bushy beard causing people to pigeonhole him as some sort of hippy, yet were soon taken aback by his quick wit and private school intellectualism. Their quest became a public spectacle and gained national attention when they reached the summit with Sir Edmund Hillary's son Peter, broadcasting on the radio, direct from the top of the world to every home in New Zealand. On their return home, they were greeted by public parades. Corporate sponsorship that would fund the remainder of their Seven Summit quest soon followed.

    Rob has a very dry, laconic sense of humor. You first meet him and you think, "This guy's all business." Rob would have everything organized; he'd be trying to make sure everything was going well. He wasn't the sort of character who would stand up and just order everybody around; he always gave a lot back. There was always a lot of fun, lots of smiles and a lot of subtle wry jokes that you had to know him for a little while before you'd get the hang of. Some people found his character and his methodical approach a little too serious in some ways, until they got to know him a bit better and realized that, yeah sure, Rob was all business, when it came to organizing things, but he liked to let loose when everything was completed the way he wanted it. He loved to have a laugh and a couple of beers with the team. Buoyed by their successes and enjoying their corroboration and the mutual respect they had for each other's abilities, Rob Hall and Gary Ball felt a desire to utilize their skills as expedition climbers and recognized that their combined abilities gave them the insight into how to run successful and well-appointed expeditions.

    With Gary's extensive guiding background and Rob's entrepreneurial streak they formed a company in early 1991 called 'Hall and Ball Adventure Consultants' and established their base in the city of Christchurch in New Zealand's mountainous South Island. Seeing no reason to start small, they immediately set about planning an expedition to Mount Everest the following year. Promoting their new venture, they approached their collective and extensive list of contacts to enlist clients on their first 'real' commercially guided expedition.

While they felt that their leadership on the 1990 expedition qualified as a commercial expedition, 1992 was to be their first real guided trip, where they advertised for people to take up the available positions. They launched their worldwide mountain guiding careers, which was extraordinarily successful, with Ball's positive attitude and flair and Hall's meticulous organization.

To many expeditioners the whole concept of instant, marketable adventure was anathema, but for Rob Hall such purist doubts smacked of elitism, the mountains were for everyone and if clients wanted to pay for expert leadership, he would provide it, complementing Ball's PR skills with his own intuitive business flair. The company quickly built up a base of loyal clients, with a remarkable success rate on the world's most prestigious peaks, particularly Everest. Rob Hall also used the logistics base and the acclimatization from commercial trips to support his own ambitions; in one 14-month period, he reached the summits of five of the world's six highest peaks, concluding with Makalu (8,463 meters) in October 1995. Afterwards he wrote, "Fortune had smiled on me. I gazed across to Everest where we had stood on the south summit just 11 days before. What a fantastic planet we live on and how privileged I am to journey across its mountains. These words suggest that, for all the commercial hard-headedness, he had not lost a sense of wonder. With clients, he was rigorous about timing, leading to his decision to turn back from the South Summit of Everest in 1995. On that occasion, despite good weather and the pleas of clients, he insisted that it was too late in the day to continue safely; Rob also felt compelled to help the French climber, Chantal Mauduit, who was suffering from cerebral edema, even though he was not directly responsible for her. It was to Rob Hall that everyone looked for leadership. Colleagues and competitors were all acknowledging the meticulous professionalism of Rob Hall's outfit.

Contrary to popular misconception, his "guided" expeditions were far more competently run than many a traditional amateur venture and his clients were not necessarily tycoons with more money than mountain experience.

In 1992 Scott and Ed Viesturs, who are now climbing with the IMAX team planned to climb K2 together, but their journey to the summit had been riddled with setbacks and difficulties, which began when Ed Viesturs and Scott failed to raise the money necessary to finance their own K2 expedition. Owing to none other than pure persistence and force of will, they raised enough money for both to join a large, Russian-organized expedition. Scott made the trip even more lucrative by tacking a bit of business on the front end. As owner and director of Mountain Madness, he launched a very successful visit by a group of backpacking supporters, for whom his company organized a trekking expedition to Concordia, the confluence of five major Karakoram glaciers, and K2 base camp. By the time the large and heavily loaded Russian expedition arrived, Scott and Ed Viesturs had already established Camp I.

The team proceeded to lead the way in establishing all the rest of the camps up K2 because, as Scott says, "They couldn't keep up with us." Their speed and effectiveness on the Abruzzi Ridge came not from cutting corners and taking risks, but from an efficiency that comes from experience and readiness for the climb. They played it safe and did not dally. "We were the only team that roped up on the lower glacier or on the upper slopes. We stayed roped together right to the summit." That tactic paid off twice. In the convoluted Godwin-Austin glacier, Scott punched through the ice and into a crevasse below, severely dislocating his weak shoulder. On the other end of the rope, Ed Viesturs was able to help stop the fall and then aid Scott in getting himself out of the crevasse.

The base camp doctor who reset Scott's shoulder gave him a disheartening prognosis: "For you, the climb is over." Hearing news of the accident back home in Seattle, Fischer's wife, Jean, and son, Andy, assumed the same and became anxious for the return of an injured husband and father. However, Scott's deep desire to climb K2 found him back on the hill within two weeks. His wife, Jean, put her feelings mildly: "It was a difficult summer for Andy and me." Scott refused to leave Base Camp and spent two weeks trying to recover. Scott then asked his climbing partner Ed Viesturs to tape his shoulder and tether it to his waist, so it would not continue to dislocate, and then resumed the climb for another month using only his left arm.

Ed Viesturs and Scott Fischer, whose relationship before this expedition was that of two mountain guides competing for the same Pacific Northwest clientele, now began to hit their stride as a team. They continued to climb in a style, which they considered appropriate for the terrain although other expeditions on the mountain were employing riskier tactics. They remained roped together when others did not, wore helmets on most of the route to protect against rockfall, and always stayed near one another to offer aid if necessary. At camp three (24,500 feet) on their first summit bid the team received a radio call for help from above. On their first summit bid, Scott and Ed abandoned their attempt at Camp 3 to rescue Aleskei Nikiforov, Thor Keiser, and the French woman climber Chantal Mauduit, who were extremely ill from altitude sickness. The French woman at camp four, the highest camp at 26,000 feet, was snow-blind and exhausted and could not make it down. Scott Fischer and Ed Viesturs immediately abandoned their summit bid in order to perform the rescue.

Conditions were bad and the snow deep. As they made progress upwards, they noted that the avalanche hazard was high. Again, the rope served its purpose. As Fischer led up a steepening in the slope, Ed Viesturs, ever wary, feared an avalanche and dug a small hole. His plan was to dive into the hole and duck under any snow slide that came his way. "He saved my life," Scott says. "I was suddenly tumbling in the avalanche. I felt a sharp jerk at my waist as Ed stopped my fall long enough for the snow to slide on by and off the South Face. Then he must have been pulled out of his hole and we slid some more but we finally were able to stop. I imagine that if he had not dug that hole we'd have both died." The climbers returned to their rescue effort and spent the next two days laboring to help the French climber down over two vertical miles of the Abruzzi Ridge. Once back in base camp they found that, their Russian partners planned to leave. "There is no more possibility of climbing K2," the leader said. After resting at Base Camp, Scott and Ed Viesturs decided to give K2 one more go and again began climbing to the summit without supplemental oxygen. Knowing that the windows of good weather were brief, Scott and Viesturs made their way back up to camp three in one day. There they spent three days waiting for a storm to clear. Conventional wisdom has come out of the long history of attempt on the world's 8000-meter peaks that it is unwise to stay at a high camp for very long. The hypoxia eats away at one's reserves and judgment, making it ever more difficult to stay hydrated, warm, or to react to any of the potential disasters that may befall the mountaineer.

"We planned to leave at 1:30 A.M. on our third night at high camp but Ed got restless and started the stove at midnight." Scott said. "Before I knew it he was dressed and out of the tent and I thought, my partner's ready so I'd better get going! We were on our way by 1:00 A.M. and summited at noon. The clouds chased us up the entire way and I could tell that Ed was always evaluating the weather and considering retreat. I didn't even think about turning around. We marked our way with wands in the snow so that we could find the way down if it whited out." Scott and Ed were at camp four where Charley Mace, perched for a summit bid, joined them. Without bottled oxygen, Scott led slowly up the infamous Bottleneck Couloir, the crux pitch on K2's Abruzzi Ridge. "Charlie caught us and we all roped together right to the summit. We knew we were pushing our luck and so we stayed on the summit for only a few moments". The three men summited and began their descent in bad weather. They climbed back to high camp in snowy conditions. There they found two New Zealand climbers, Rob Hall and Gary Ball, ailing from the altitude after trying to follow the Americans to the summit. Rob Hall and Gary Ball made successful guided trips to Everest in 1992 and 1993, and used the money from the guiding to make a number of private expeditions, including returning to K2. Rob only succeeded on the notoriously risky summit of K2 on his fourth attempt. The pair, who were using bottled oxygen to aid their ascent, had been stricken with high altitude pulmonary edema at the Abruzzi in blizzard conditions. Scott Fischer, Ed Viesturs, and Charley Mace spent the next three days lowering the New Zealanders down in snowy conditions. Rob Hall's health improved with the descent, but Gary Ball's worsened.

The four men - Scott Fischer with a seriously injured shoulder - were all critical in lowering Ball off the mountain and thus saving his life. With their last steps onto the summit, Scott and his partners Ed Viesturs and Charlie Mace represented one third of the Americans to climb this beautiful peak, the second highest on Earth. In recent years, the significance of summiting K2 has gained widespread acclaim. Contrasted with the taller Mount Everest, K2 attracts far fewer summiteers. Whether it is the world's largest or second highest mountain, no one questions that K2 is the hardest and steepest; the challenge climbers take most pride in having overcome. Gary Ball, who pioneered guided tours of Mount Everest, developed altitude sickness while climbing on Mt Dhaulagiri in the Himalayas, an expedition that cost Gary Ball his life. Rob Hall immediately began to climb back down, assisting his best friend Gary Ball, who despite medical treatment, died within 24 hours at a lower camp on the mountain. Rob Hall wrapped Gary's body in a sleeping bag and lowered it into a crevasse.

The tragedy probably influenced Rob Hall's decision to use supplementary oxygen while guiding the highest peaks. After losing his climbing companion Rob Hall brought Ed Viesturs into the Everest guiding business to help with the Everest guiding, and they repeated their success in 1994, but had to turn clients back at the South Summit in 1995. News of Scott Fischer's achievement on K2 quickly made its way back to the States. Stacy Allison, the first American woman to climb Mount Everest, called the Fischer home in hopes of gaining information for her own upcoming attempt on K2. Five year old Andy answered the phone: "My Dad just climbed K2 and he rescued three people. If my Dad hadn't been there those people would have DIED!" Stacy Allison climbed with Scott on Everest in 1987, a trip that restored her broken confidence.

Years before Stacy had married a fellow climber, once they wed, his temper flared often. Allison found herself on the receiving end of violent blows, yet was unable to tear herself away because she felt so bound to him in the good times.

The peaks and valleys of their marriage continued for almost two years, until she discovered her husband was involved in a long-term affair and had promised the other woman he would leave Allison. When she confronted him about it, he produced divorce papers the next day.

However, even after the papers were signed and the split finalized, Allison had trouble eliminating his influence from her life. "That's the cruelest irony of abuse - it's so shameful, it becomes a secret that only spouses share," she writes. "It stays tucked away, putting on weight and adding gravity until it pulls you away from the rest of the world." She moved back to Oregon in an attempt to right her life. What got her through the aftermath of her divorce was her spot on a team going to Mt. Everest in 1987. Scott Fischer led the team that year, a group that ended up fracturing into sub-groups, vying against each other for the summit. After spending weeks laying the route up the difficult North Face, Scott granted Stacy Allison a position on his first summit team, with its promise of making her the first U.S. woman to ascend the peak.

The team made it within 4,000 feet of the summit, but a violent snowstorm forced them to retreat to a snow cave at 23,500 feet for five days. Crawling out of the cave once the storm had subsided, the climbers observed a white plume coming off the summit. The jet stream had descended and was raking the upper reaches of the mountain with 150 mile-an-hour winds that would rip them off the peak if they tried to ascend. "That's the ball game," Scott observed bleakly. The expedition packed up and went home. When I prepared mentally for our Everest trip, Scott gave me the book Stacy

Allison's wrote about her Everest climb. As I opened it, I found Scott's dedication to me on one of the first pages.

"You are tougher than her anyway."   Love Scott

I did ask myself, what is it that keeps Scott from becoming one of those nasty Himalayan statistics himself? How can he continue to go to what so many have called the "death zone" (terrain above 8000 meters or 26,000 feet) and not only return safely, but also rescue others who without his aid might have died on the upper reaches of the mountain. Extensive experience as a climber and as a guide at high altitude has certainly contributed to Scott's success. But it is not just experience that makes Scott successful. Scott has a special drive and determination.

All through the years, his most fervent goal was to climb Mount Everest. "It almost seems as if, talking with him, that he can climb mountains purely by force of will. His next trip to Everest, in the Spring of 1996, is fraught with difficulties including a peak fee that may be in excess of $50,000. I'm a member of that team and when discouraged, all I need do is call Scott". "We'll get the permit for ten grand," he says, "If we don't, we'll pay the fifty and find the money somewhere... if that doesn't work we'll go to Tibet and climb it from the North. I have a line on a permit there. Listen, these are just details, we are going to climb Everest in '96." This is but a few real life stories among numerous that we, who through our own experiences held Scott in high esteem might narrate. I knew from Scott that Rob is held in high esteem within the climbing community.

Rob Hall is 35 years old, but looks and appears older then Scott with his full beard and serious appearance. A man you would immediately tend to trust as his mature and slightly authoritarian manners installs the feeling - that here is a man who knows what he is talking about. I am sure Scott respects Rob for being serious in a way that is not conducive with Scott's boyish incitement. Rob has the best record of success on the mountain, if you measure success in the number of climbers reaching the top, whilst climbing with you. Impressive - 39 climbers from 39 nationalities - No casualties. Rob holds the non-Sherpa record for having summited Everest four times. Rob is well established in running his specialized expedition company Adventure Consultants. Utilizing his flair for professionally branding himself through his accomplishments, with the record of summiteers to back up the advertisement for choosing his company if you are seeking a guided expedition to Everest, almost guaranteeing 100% success in summiting if you elect to climb on his expedition. These male comrades all make their living promoting, organizing and conducting professional alpine expeditions. Attracting climbing, paying clients are crucial for their life quests.

It is predictable that Rob, Scott and most of the guys are on the lookout for profile-raising exposure in the mass media, in their simultaneous endeavor to fertilize their future visions. My dealings with Scott gave me insight in how he tried to coerce Jon Krakauer from Outside Magazine to participate on our expedition, to secure the branding of Mountain Madness as THE Everest Guiding Company. When that strategy failed, because Jon transferred his participation on Scott's Everest expedition to Rob Hall's trip, Scott was thrilled to have Sandy Hill Pitmann becoming part of our team. Not only did Sandy have respectable climbing experience, but she also came with a huge media and promoting set-up.

Sandy and her husband Bob Pittman were separating; her husband divorcing her to marry David Brashears soon-to-be ex-wife. Scott truly believed Sandy's profile, wealth and personality was his ticket to a future stream of full paying high society clients. For Rob Hall to form an alliance with a national outdoor magazine to actually entrench a writer in the climbing team was something both Scott and Rob pursued for positioning themselves advantageously for accomplishing profitable strategies in the future. Jon Krakauer became imbedded in the Rob Hall team specifically due to a financial alliance between Rob Hall and Outside Magazine. A deal that Scott failed to match shortly before we flew to Katmandu. Those who knew the wheeling's and dealings of how Jon's spot was secured on Rob's expedition also had to deal with the fact, that Jon had not specifically chosen to be on their expedition. Outside Magazine had been shopping around for the best low-cost financial opportunity. Rob Hall was casual about the issue and explicated, "Jon is only going to climb Everest and write a story about his experience." That sounded simple enough, but it didn't fool anybody.

Rob's clients and Jon's teammates were acquainted with that Rob viewed Jon as paid help to crank up publicity for Rob and his expedition business. In the alliance with Outside Magazine, Rob fronted most of the cash in exchange for Jon's story and discounted future ad space. Splitting ones focus as a leader between the taxing and complex endeavor to realize the actual climb and at the same time consider best possible promotion through the conduct of one's group might have consequences. Jon's presence and purpose for being on any expedition might have created performance pressures and therefore added risk. Mixing branding opportunities with the safety interest of the climbing participants could deviate from the safest course.

In addition to being a journalist on the assignment for Outside Magazine to share first hand - how it is to attempt climbing Everest, Jon Krakauer was also a mountaineering fiction writer - present on Everest to nail a story, readers would gulp with thrilled excitement. Some claim that Jon Krakauer's purpose had a different dimension than the other members on Rob's expedition. Having a climber as teammate, who was climbing as part of his job and to advance his career as an adventure writer might embroil impacts, differing from the interests of the rest of the team.

17

*"To live is the rarest thing in the world.
Most people exist, that is all."*
                                Oscar Wilde

What is the purpose of life? Why do we get up in the morning to deal with all the practicalities and energy consuming tasks that threaten to drown most people in the never ending process of making ends meet? How do we motivate ourselves to carry on - when the ultimate end-station after all - is death? Why bother with the stress, depressions, problems, choices and sometimes hard decisions that make up life? It seems to be an inherent genetic trait that the human race strives for something additional to what they have already achieved.

We seem to be susceptible to continuously think, dream and project ahead, moving towards something defined or undefined that we hope and believe will give fulfillment and happiness in the times to come. Humans if they live in the pampered part of the world – where they indeed have options - often set goals for themselves throughout their lives. We achieve some and soon after, unable to cherish the now, begins to look for the next venture. What is a goal anyway? The well-balanced, experienced human being strives not only to achieve goals, but lives life fully in the flow of existence, because every expression in the process is equally important.

What people, who fulfill some of their life wishes have in common, is that their quest is important to them and they're committed to being the best that they can be, within the scope of their limitations, competing life commitments, finances, time and their natural ability. They set high, realistic goals for themselves, practice and play hard. They are successful because they are pursuing their objectives and enjoy what they do. Their commitment enriches their lives and they believe that what they get back is worth what they put into their pursuits. There are specific mental skills that contribute to this type of life success and contentment with existence. These strategic skills can be learned by most and improved with self discipline and practice. I believe that implementing psychological strategies is worthwhile because, the mental abilities I experimented with and used in achieving success in climbing, surviving and turning Everest into my professional volition, can be aroused and mobilized through self responsibility, to achieve success in most areas in life. Existence is about appreciating and enjoying - if we are among the fortunate well-fed population in the privileged part of the world - the journey of our life span. Stop and analyze the western world's inclination to always be going somewhere else and instead validate the here and now, because right now is actually all we have. Now and now is truly what life consists of. We ought to purify the ability to be present in every minute of life, while it lasts, selecting as much sublimity as possible. Why not? You only live once. You are responsible for your thoughts, emotions and actions.

Mental skills constitute a broad base for attaining the long-term goal of contentment through knowledge and sustained daily practice. To utilize your brain's capacity for alteration, you need to struggle with your own socialization on a day-by-day basis for long periods, often months and years. You have it within your control to choose and maintain a constructive attitude.

    Disciplined mental skills are necessary for performing well at 8000 meter as well as in non-climbing situations and processes where you dream of achieving something specific, as well as out of your ordinary. You should set high, realistic goals and maintain profound self-motivation. Deal effectively with people, so you do not bind energy in ruminating over unsolved conflicts etc. Use encouraging mental imagery and positive self-talk. Learn to manage anxiety effectively and be able to alter your emotions proficiently. Maintain concentration and focus. Remain resolved and the force of habit will take care of the rest. Through experience, successful people realize that attitude is a choice. They choose an outlook that is predominately constructive.

    They consciously discern their ventures as an opportunity to strive and learn about real life versus illusions, through their accomplishments and disappointments. People with life success pursue excellence, not perfection and realize that they, as well as leaders, teammates, spouses, friends, children, officials and others are not perfect. They strive to maintain balance and perspective between their desired activity and the rest of their lives. Likewise they are aware of the rewards and benefits that they expect to experience through their participation in attempting to shape life according to their desires. They become able to persist through difficult tasks and problematic times, even when rewards and benefits are not immediately forthcoming: realizing that many of the compensations come from their involvement, not the outcome. They set long-term and short-term goals that are realistic, measurable and time-oriented. They are aware of their current performance levels and are able to develop specific, detailed plans for attaining their invigorating goals. They are highly committed to their objectives and to carrying out the daily demands of their agendas. They realize that they are part of a larger system that includes their families, friends, teammates, coaches and others. When appropriate they communicate their thoughts, feelings and needs to specific individuals and listen to them as well. They have learned effective skills for dealing with conflict, difficult opponents and people when they are negative or oppositional.

Through discipline, they learn to maintain their self-confidence during difficult times, with realistic positive self-talk. They use self-talk to regulate thoughts, feelings and behaviors. They talk to themselves the way they would talk to their own best friend. They prepare themselves for the next activity by imagining themselves performing well, through creating and using mental images that are detailed, specific and realistic. They use imagery during struggles to prepare for action and recover from errors and poor performances. They accept anxiety and realize that some degree of fretfulness can help them perform well. They know how to reduce nervousness when it becomes too strong, without losing their intensity. They accept strong emotions such as excitement, anger and disappointment as part of the experience of venturing into unknown territory. They are able to use these emotions to improve, rather than to interfere with high-level performance. They know what they must pay attention to. They've learned how to maintain focus and resist distractions, whether they come from the environment or from within themselves and are able to regain their focus when concentration is lost. Life satisfied individuals have learned how to be in the "here-and-now", without regard to either past or anticipated future events. For the first time in my 34-years long life, I determine that Everest is worthwhile to initiate the tough battle of changing myself. I realize I have to alter quite a few unconstructive habitual thoughts and behavioral schemes to become capable, able and worthwhile to chip in as team player on our team. I shut out, consciously and with effort all doubts, all thoughts of death, frostbite and turning around. I want and need to be best when it counts. I want Everest so fundamentally, that I am willing to change whatever Everest takes, leaving the old Lene behind and discover what's necessary to add and cultivate in me. To deliver whatever it takes…To the summit and safe return! With my impulsive YES to Everest, I have chosen obsession. Or have I? What determines why we act in one way or the other in our lives, or abstain from choosing and performing? I have profoundly chosen to let-go and submerge myself in my all-encompassing desire because I want to climb Everest. I acknowledge that, at any point, I can make an alternative choice. Any day and any minute, I can decide whether I'm still willing to pay the price for the route to the summit. I realize that my choices - also deciding to bail out at this point - have consequences. This time, I aim to win. I train to win, to win over myself and to get to the top of the world.

In the past, I didn't think and act as I do now. I was more timid, flexible, more compromising, anxiety controlled and not totally driven. I wanted to tread an even path and I guess I succeeded. What has this challenge ignited in me? Am I a gambling risk taker, who ticks only when this much is at stake? Or is it simply the right circumstances coming together at the right time? Are the opportunities in this vision grand enough to provoke every pettiness and laziness in me and to win? Is this my opportunity to 5 minutes of fame and whatever might follow, in the wake of exposing myself to climbing high? Normally I try to find answers to questions like this. I intellectually analyze. Perhaps I have finally achieved a state of just living without pondering too much about it. To the summit and safe return!

My self-programming mantra is intended to fuel my body in the thin air above 8000 meters. I anticipate that all motivation and resolve will be sucked out of me as I climb upwards. Oxygen deprivation causes nausea, extreme headaches and debilitates the will and ability to think charged with, *"To the summit and safe return"*. My presumption is that dexterous will power and disciplined over months will drive me up the mountain and back down, even when my brain and deepest rooted survival instincts states that I am exhausted and ought to head down. How can we determine whether our grandiose aspirations are unrealistic or an expression of untapped possibilities? How can we determine the quintessence of mobilization that brings the human race forward and creates innovation for the future? Ambition is an earnest desire for achievement or distinction, power, honor, fame, or wealth and the willingness to strive for its attainment.

The hazard of my innovative human self-experiment is that by focusing narrowly on the summit, victory becomes all-encompassing. The disciplined urge, may be so powerful a motive that I will become incapable of turning around before I accomplish climbing to the summit; at the cost of my health or my life? Sometimes the true victory is to let go and to be capable of turning around in due time without a feeling of defeat; to stay alive. I have practiced this for five years.

Have I mastered it?

18

"Maybe everyone can live beyond what they're capable of"
Markus Zusak

I am serenely happy about my new home of frost, ice and snow. I stare up at the Khumbu Icefall. I gaze around from the rock I am sitting on, in front of my igloo expedition tent and appreciate the different outlandish features of one of the most famous places on earth. Numerous individuals have been at this juncture in the past. We are driven by inner motives that might not be clearly discernable, for the outside spectator. Are we propelled by comparable psychological profiles or are we as individualistic as we might tend to convince ourselves? No matter how many visualizing athletes and grandiose eccentrics' that have survived to live and tell their own tales, this is my first time to test myself against the highest mountain in the world.

The Khumbu Icefall stretches way out of sight, from top to bottom snaking its icy core down between the rock and ice walls of Everest and Nuptse. A gigantic, jigsaw mass of a deep-frozen waterfall, blue ice, white ice towers and crevasses 200 meters deep where some of them are hidden below a treacherous innocent appearing fresh snow cover. I cannot see our entire intended route from my present vantage point. It would be somewhat comforting to at least survey what awaits me, from this safe distance. Nevertheless, I almost trust the experience I have gained through my struggles in the European Alps that I must approach even impossible steep and hazardous appearing obstacles, instead of being scared to take the first step by the immense overwhelming inaccessibility of the challenge stretching and intimidating before me. As long as I approach the seemingly insurmountable hurdle, there will be a possibility for detecting the next few steps upwards and after that, another small section of the route onwards will reveal itself. I just have to set in motion and never let my feelings of fear and doubt gain control over my goal-orientedness.

This majestic sensory impression of great natural beauty, unsullied monumental high altitude splendor can only be found in the remoteness of the wild. Sitting here inactive and quietly, impressions from within are activated. I recall that the Inland Ice of Greenland offers a silence unparalleled to anywhere else I have explored on our planet. An intimidating, serene vast stillness that confronts you with the fact of how difficult it is to truly find quietness and tranquility of the mind and ear in an urbanized lifestyle. Everest is never quiet though. From the mountain walls surrounding my fragile resting place, rocks falling, avalanches of snow, ice and debris roars and echoes, always reminding you of the hazards you are in the middle of.

Even under my orange brown base camp tent, there are sounds of the Khumbu Glacier cracking, moving and groaning, as the glacial snow and ice I pitched my tent on, slowly slides down the Khumbu Valley, till it reaches its melting edge. The same gravity induced movements make The Khumbu Icefall objectively most dangerous passage, on our entire climbing route. The frozen gigantic ice mass, winds its way downwards in a never relenting grinding stream, not caring who or what gets demolished in the process of obeying the rules of Mother Nature. I commit to memory of previous periods in the Himalayas and profound concealed perceptions awakened by the smoke and crackling noises from the juniper branches ignited at the Buddhist stone Altar. Their perfumed scent accompanies you on most treks in Buddhist Territory and unlocks memories long stored away. Isn't it fascinating how reminiscences long curbed, becomes activated by some odd sensory stimulus? When I trek in the Himalayas, protracted disremembered incidences springs to the forefront of my consciousness, enriching my here and now and offering a connection with who I was, what I have pursued and why I am where I choose to be right now. Like a string of beads, offering a whole out of fragments.

I feel I will never tire of being here. It is so majestically beautiful and I am complete and at ease. I cannot fathom leaving this place again in barely two months. Existence here is the fulfillment of my most grandiose expectations to life, as well as my most ambitious adventure so far. My adventuresome life path began with crossing the Atlantic in a sailing boat when I was 18 and fresh out of high school: a psychological pattern breaker that changed how I perceive my life possibilities. I have the ability to dream up what I feel will be fulfilling and I have the risk willingness as well as perseverance to break out of the security giving ordinary life styles we mostly get trapped by. I am capable of acting out my visions if I choose to live with the consequences. A conscious life style I have pursued and practiced ever since.

Adventure, fulfill the next dream and then return to Denmark to recuperated, make some money and wait for the next inner desire to interrupt the occasional monotony other people call everyday living. Climbing Everest is about your willingness to take on extraordinary challenges, uncontrollable risk and the human struggle to physically and psychologically endure the extreme altitude that almost reaches outer space. *"It's a matter of attitude as well as altitude."*

Everest is so tall, that it juts into the upper reaches of the earth's atmosphere, where there are considerably lower concentrations of oxygen than at sea level. Consequently, our bodies get less oxygen from each breath we take while climbing. However, our brains and muscles require the same amount of oxygen to perform, as they would at sea level.

The altitude and the lack of oxygen available make it especially tough to scale Everest. Try to imagine what it feels like to scramble up a strenuous mountain; you get dizzy, your nose, fingers and feet get numb and tingly and your heart thunders in your chest trying furiously to keep up with the muscles' demand for oxygen. Coughing never lets you breathe undisrupted. You feel sleepy, confused and downright lethargic as your brain struggles to function on limited oxygen. Moreover, you think you are functioning normally and feel absolutely capable of making wise decisions. Each step you take is extremely slow and plodding, requiring every scrap of will you have and then some more, taking one step about every one minute. Nausea accompanies your every single movement. Hour after hour, hours turning into days, day after day, week after week and month after month...Climbing Everest is about continuous perseverance in spite of huge difficulties as well as your brains advice to quit as you get higher and more and more exposed to the lack of oxygen. Oxygen deprivation, exhaustion, extreme cold, human error and the inherent hazards of mountaineering all contribute to the death toll on Everest.

An injured person who cannot move unassisted is in serious trouble: rescue and carrying an incapacitated person off the mountain will lead to potential death of those trying. Evacuation by helicopter is generally impossible above 6000 meters and is not yet a standard procedure even on the lower slopes of the mountain. The women and men who die during the climb of their dreams are typically left behind. It is not uncommon to find corpses adjoining the standard climbing routes. Over 250 people have died trying and of those, at least 170 bodies have never been recovered. They are still to be found on the mountain. A popular belief in the non-climbing community is that climbing Everest is a very team oriented and life lasting bonding experience and that climbing the highest mountain in the world validates you as a climber. Some of the world's most skilled climbers have not and cannot climb Everest, not because they lack courage, risk willingness and the will to carry through or expertise. It's purely because their bodies lack the genetic ability to acclimatize to altitude. An inherent feature you can do absolutely nothing to alter. I seem to have the chromosomal matrix well suited for high altitude mountaineering, a genetic disposition that makes me vividly alive and serene as I climb higher; a strike of luck with my present ambition.

The most dangerous stretch on our chosen route-the passage that claims most lives when you study fatality statistics for Everest- is the Khumbu Icefall. When I first encountered the Khumbu Icefall in 1991, I deemed it impossible to ascent unless you were under the spell of some odd death wish. Silently I acknowledge the depressing fact that I did not have the courage it would take; the courage those who climbed through personified. Therefore, I had to condemn the ones doing it, as being inferior and self destructive. Elisabeth Hailey, a British woman, who for whatever reason follows every fatality on Everest and meticulously perpetuates exactly as possible when, why and if possible, where climbers lost their lives.

Consequently there is detailed and sufficient knowledge to study the death hazard, if you so wish. When I peep out of my tent door at Base Camp, I am reminded of the randomness of these 2,000 feet of vertical towering, ice pinnacles and blocks the size of mansions. As snow falls and builds itself up on the mountain season after season, the pressure turns it to solid ice. It glaciates. The weight of the ice mass combined with gravity causes the glaciated snow mass to flow down the mountain valley as a huge frozen waterfall: a turbulent river consisting of blue rock hard ice formations. For about two miles, the Khumbu Glacier flows down this side of Everest forming the relatively level Western Cvm. At about 5,800 meters, the ice river breaks and brutally falls over a steep wall in the bedrock to 3,600 meters-the elevation of our Base Camp. Here again its foundation becomes more horizontal and the frozen snake keeps its movement out of the broad Khumbu valley until it reaches Gorak Sheep, where the temperatures does it in. For months, I will be living, eating, resting and existing with nothing but ice and rock underneath me. An environment unsuited for sustaining life and excessively well carved out for sustaining my dream. I love it, the intense simplicity of being here. To the summit and safe return! The risks of climbing the Icefall are extreme, because the 2,000-foot high and 400 foot wide ice mass is constantly plunging its way downwards. Each time we venture into its death trap - natural forces alter our route, crushing the aluminum ladders we use for our protected passageway and rework the inherent risk. The distance the ice flows each day varies with the weight, caused by how much snow is accumulating, the heat from the sun and the various temperatures.

Some days the mighty ice colossi do not seem to move. Other days it travels a centimeter. Most days it moves considerable more. On average, the icefall slides one meter pr. 24 hours moving unstable apartment blocks of frozen ice over rugged terrain. The motion forces the smother surface in the Western Cwm. to crack open, ice towers to tumble, crevasses to close and swallow aluminum ladders supposed to escort us as safely as possible to the other side and to the next of the 77 ladders, we use to create a passable gateway through this majestic hindrance. Seracs - gigantic sculptures of blue ice- collapse without warning, sending thousands of tons of ice crashing down. A cracking noise, then the next louder crack and then another. The glacier beneath my resting place moans. I will have to adjust my tent poles in a few days because of the melting caused by rising temperatures that stretches the ice field I have turned into my abode for now.

During the day, I have my private small washbasin, melted by the heating sunrays, a clear glacier pond that turns to solid ice as soon as the sunset transforms the unrelenting burn into a deep freezer within 30 minutes. The decrease in temperature, as soon as the sun sets is extreme, as everything else surrounding me. I detect a disturbing shaking, massive dry crack from above to the left. A spine-thrilling reminder of one natural hazard I estimate as being totally beyond my control no matter what I do. Mechanically perceiving a slight shift in the snowline up high on the section of the wall of Everest, I can see from where I dwell. Just barely imagining a perforated line in the snowfield, then a roaring thunder caused by the force of a barrier of air pushed in front of the avalanche released, resembling an explosion with smoke and blurred visibility due to the loose powder snow swirling from the surface of the snowfield no longer attached to the rock wall. Pooh...Close call, dusting off the cold reminder of the uncontrollability of the environment I fell so much at peace in, I have faith in that my ability to "conquer" Mount Everest depends on my mental state. So I alter the common saying "It's not attitude, its altitude" to "It's all about altitude and attitude." I am convinced that my chances of summiting Everest and surviving this adventure depend on my ability to remain composed, serene, calm and unruffled no matter what happens. I used to react emotionally when I were confronted with first-hand and perceived dangerous situations in the mountains. Fear, exhaustion, anger, rage, cowardice, self-blame and defeat are frozen in anxiety attacks, whenever I climbed beyond my limit, which I did a lot, learning the tough lessons of leading routes as lead climber.

I would do whatever: whine, yell, cry, blame and throw my climbing helmet in a rage fit, to avoid the brutal confrontation that I was not yet good enough, risk willing enough, disciplined, courageous enough to actually be the climber I so desperately wanted to be. I truly learned the hard way and now I know that it is all-important for my safety and that of my teammates, to have myself under control at all times. Guess what, I also have my secret weapons to bring me into the proper psychological state and to compose myself. That is, when I have the self-discipline to utilize them.

Practicing Tai Chi since my divorce in 199, the world as I knew it evaporated, yet another time and I have wired my brain differently and more efficient, when it comes to focusing. Climbing Everest is very much about narrow and persistent focus on the task at hand and not much else. I must take responsibility for having no "bad days". Here is no room for energy draining conflicts, inner or outer and foul moods and doubts are something I simply cannot afford to waste energy on. I want to ascent Everest and my focus shapes the alteration of my habitual personality to become fit for this single-minded pursuit. I calm myself, whenever the outer world seems too impenetrable or does not comply with my wishful thinking. I am certain that my "success" to a certain degree depends on my inner equilibrium. To utilize my limited resources fully I need to take control, refocus and re-establish a peaceful state of mind, whenever some influence threatens to misplace my bearings.

Serenity is my responsibility as I decipher how my mind reacts to outside happenings, disruptions as well as internal mood swings which I must control using self-discipline. "Concentrate on the summit, focus my energies and remove myself from whatever is draining my resources." "Did you hear that 11 expedition permits were issued this year?" Scott appears slightly more relaxed now that we have arrived at Base Camp. He seems to have the situation reasonably under control. In the previous decade, the Nepalese government limited the number of annual permits for spring and fall openings to three or four. Nepal's issuance of a higher number of permits is a response to the upcoming of professional expeditions. Outside influx connected with Everest creates a completely new venue of income for this poor country. Big money is desperately needed and welcomed in the harsh corners of this rugged land. Expeditions fuel a strong economy and higher standards of living for the Sherpa community in the Solo Khumbu region.

We are 11 white climbers in our group and for each of us we probably support 5-10 locals during the expedition process. Yak herders, porters, Base Camp Sherpas', High Camp Sherpas' and climbing Sherpas'. We buy as much food as possible locally which is much cheaper than hauling it from overseas, apart from extra luxurious food items to be consumed to keep us fit for climbing.

Our kitchen staff constructs a stone house, roofed with blue tarpaulin and it has become the center for Sherpa social life in camp. Ngima, our Base Camp Sirdar, is a clever, competent leader. I haven't quite gotten down the names of the individual kitchen Sherpas' yet, but their grinning faces confirm my past yearning to return to Nepal, it wasn't something I've romanticized- the Sherpa People have something .Our invigorating mess tent is assembled. Anatoli is the source of introducing our Russian tunnel tent in three shades of mauve. One table at the end is permanently stuffed with candy bars, Gatorade, nuts, dried meat etc. little extras to stimulate the lust to consume calories in this altitude where appetite vanes the longer we remain. A change of altitude affects your metabolism. You lose your appetite and your body begins to burn your muscles, as it takes less energy to extract vital energy from your muscles than it does to alter consumed food into indispensable nutrients. In addition, your body is less efficient at sending oxygen from the lungs into the blood at higher altitudes due to lower barometric pressure. Your breathing rate speeds up to compensate, working the diaphragm muscles harder.

Both blood and muscles become more acidic and you burn more carbs than fat for fuel. Your basal metabolic rate increases to stabilize basic body functions. Therefore it is crucial to tempt yourself into eating something or anything really. Behind our mess tent is the communications center, a whole tent propped with NBC equipment provided for Sandy to be able to broadcast her daily reports from our upper-region settlement and transmit interviews and the like for nbc.com website. I wonder how many extra porters she paid for, to carry the forefront of the modern world of sharing via satellite up here. Dr. Ingrid's medical clinic takes up one-fifth of the space allocated for technology. I have mixed emotions about the media circus

Sandy seems engulfed by, but without the Danish Press, I would not be here.

Our world is to an alarming extent controlled by the media and the sponsor money mobilized, when the backers feel assured that the media are investing their attention in your endeavor. As for myself, I have arranged that no one can contact me except by ordinary post and for a letter to be delivered at my temporary address, takes at least three weeks. I came here to be among the highest mountains on earth. To be at peace and attain detachment from everything that moves too fast and superficial in the modern world. I thrive on long patches of time with no pre-scheduled activities crammed in. I find energy and recuperate by doing nothing in nature. I become stronger and more composed when I am not dealing with daily disruptions of routine and civilization created unauthentic dynamics. Next to the kitchen is our storage tent, containing all the expedition food and paraphernalia. Italian delicatessen, sausages, crackers, rice, pasta, smoked cheese, muesli, beef jerky, turkey jerky, deer jerky, hot chili jerky, smoked jerky and an orgy of sliced dried meats; our main calorie intake here at Base Camp and perhaps at Camp 2.

Above 6500 meters, we will consume mostly liquid nourishment and (the protein in our muscles) - Gatorade, Reload and Power Bars. Here are climbing ropes, snow stakes and oxygen containers, sleeping bags for high camps, the Gamow bag and Jane, who has ferreted out a cozy, warm hollow among the duffels for an afternoon snooze. Jane seems to be suffering the effects of being this high for the first time. I still want to be naïve and remain in my preferred belief that she is only here for professional promotional reasons. Jane is truly petit and very skinny. She radiates a high-strung energy. I detect that I keep her and the implications of her presence at a certain distance. Not in the mode I interact with her, but inwardly. Biding time, trying to figure out what is going on between Scott and her. Why is she here? I assume Scott fell for the promotion she might be able to add to his hunt for PR, as well as her upbeat energetic bouncing femaleness. Is he investing some stolen romantic moments in this year's infatuation, before he shifts his attention to yet another target? Business as usual...

19

"Let's make it happen - and have fun!"
Scott Fischer

Summit fever is the apparent callousness that drives alpinists to focus single-mindedly on summiting Everest, no matter the consequences. The propelling drive causes mountaineers to disregard all ethics and personal values on their Everest ascents, oftentimes literally climbing over dead bodies to reach their goals. "Summit fever" develops through the sheer number of us, as we come together from various parts of the world, united by our individual purpose of climbing high. Because of our personalities, the challenges connected with living Everest and the exhilarating atmosphere of being on the same wavelength, we risk becoming fixed and solely focused on summiting.

An intoxicating chemistry spreads causing climbers to go for the summit no matter what we are all driving each other on, by being in a crowd, within view, following in the footsteps of the one in front. This focused flow is one of the strengths of pursuing the extraordinary with likeminded people. However, the inherent risk is that there might not be careful awareness in the cluster and the most dangerous about the force of group dynamics is that everyone hands over responsibility for herself or himself to someone else. It means that no one is taking responsibility. There can be a false sense of strength in numbers, but it doesn't matter how big your group is, you can have 1,000 people and the mountain will still kill. I acknowledge the phenomenon "summit fever", because I felt it's surge help me to summit. My attitude toward climbing now is the same as when I decided to risk the challenge of testing myself on Everest. You must learn to take responsibility for yourself. Personal value is an individual's absolute of relative and ethical ideals. Some values are physiologically determined and are normally considered objective, such as a desire to avoid physical pain or to seek pleasure. Other values are considered subjective, vary across individuals and cultures and are in many ways aligned with conviction and belief systems. It is debated whether some values that are not clearly physiologically determined, such as altruism, are intrinsic.

Our personal values provide an internal reference for what we define as good, beneficial, important, useful, beautiful, desirable, constructive, etc. Values generate behavior and help solve common human problems of survival by comparative rankings, the results of which provide answers to questions of why people do what they do and in what order they choose to do them. Values can be defined as broad preferences concerning our appropriate courses of action. They reflect a person's sense of right and wrong or what "ought" to be. Our values tend to influence our attitudes and behavior. But whatever values we organize our daily lives among our fellow beings according to the fundamental frame when climbing Everest might crave a different set of ethics. Perhaps it is not simply ruthless determination that makes someone on Everest abandon her or his team mates and yet, still have the energy to summit. In such alien conditions, utterly hostile to human life, climbers might face their own mortality. Under the specter of pure, unadulterated fear, they must realize that they are beyond help as well as beyond helping anyone else. If they don't, they fall among those who never leave, abandoned on Everest.

The world's highest mountain showed me my true capacity and I am fortunate enough to have outlived several contemporary mountaineers. The world's highest mountain is an excellent learning lab, when it comes to confronting lack of self-responsibility. Above 8,000 meters in what we call the "death-zone" you truly have to know, face and profoundly accept that "climbing high" is a survival gamble. It can be an extraordinary and deeply rewarding life altering and future shaping experience, but there is no escaping the fact that you can die. The real lesson we ultimately have to cope with is that nature cannot be controlled. You cannot and for your own safety must not expect anybody to help you, once you are up there. Your fate is entirely in your own hands and at the mercy of the majestic forces of nature, which truly rules here no matter how skilled and prepared we are. There might be unwritten codes of mountaineering conduct and spectacular rescues do occur, but everything you do or do not do is ultimately your own decision and you and others affected by you may be influenced by the consequences. I am a passionate promoter of self responsibility as a climber and as an adult. Stresses the importance to train flexibility to be able to respond and function efficiently; also when things do not turn out as planned and you are in the middle of the unexpected. You are responsible for yourself.

And isn't that ultimately the lesson of life anywhere?

20

"Life's under no obligation to give us what we expect."
Margaret Mitchell

Scott and Anatoli fundamentally hold each other in high regard. Both feel at ease in the company of a fellow climber and man, representing character traits they mutually want to internalize. Scott openly respects Anatoli's supremeness as a mountaineer, his aestheticism, serenity founded in self knowledge and contentedness. Scott represents a boyish, open and people loving embrace, that I in hindsight believe Anatoli practiced making his own, after Scott was no longer among us. Anatoli is a profound authentic individual, wise beyond his years. He is self-contained, with fundamental insight in the mountains and what it takes to survive at high altitude. Anatoli is a true genius in the mountains and the only mountaineer I have ever encountered that humbly acknowledge and express the fact that climbing high might be deadly.

Most climbers deny the truth that we can die trying to outlive our dreams. I learnt that Anatoli answered the question "What are your plans after summiting Everest?" with the plain "First I must survive this mountain then I will plan." All this strength and experience is the main reason why Scott wanted Anatoli here. Scott never directly tells people what to do. Scott being Scott, most people consciously and unconsciously wants to excel and fill in the gaps Scott exposes that need attention. Everyone sort of assumes the roles needed to make this entire organism work. Actually, Scott is the least racist, sexist or hierarchical human I know. Anatoli being Russian and therefore a former enemy of the American folk soul, by some is not regarded for what he is and his less than perfect English, makes quite a few dispel him as not being highly intelligent and eloquent. I know Scott respects and admires Anatoli and truly acknowledges that Anatoli is a hugely experienced and skilled high-altitude mountaineer.

Scott was pleased when he secured Sandy, as the replacement for the media-exposing contributor to our expedition instead of Jon Krakauer, which is understandable. Yet Sandy comes across as conceited, boastful, pretentious, trying to monopolize conversations, expressing a sense of entitlement and when she doesn't receive special treatment, she consults Scott. Sandy's need to have the attention of everybody causes her to complain to Scott about Anatoli's lack of socializing and small talking with her while at base-camp. Scott's hunger for the publicity and drippings of Sandy's high society circles, with the imagined prospects of future social climbing opportunities, lead him to the fundamentally distorted action of ordering Anatoli to fulfill Sandy's need for veneration.

Towards our final summit bid, Scott at times articulated, in a less than respectful way to Anatoli, that he expected him to "entertain Sandy" and pressured out of his ordinary modus operandi he seemed to fail to recall that Anatoli was his strongest card for succeeding the quest of "bagging the big E" with clients and Anatoli never opposed.

Anatoli did not speak much. Talking is wasting energy and will not get you to the summit of Everest or down alive. Anatoli was cautious and did not ponder to charm or socialize superficially. In relations to other people, he appreciates modesty and honesty, his word being his bond. He is serenely obstinately individualistic with an iron discipline that serves his phenomenal endurance and experience with altitude: an ethical character. Anatoli knows exactly what climbing Everest entails. I have never observed
Scott be critical or demeaning to anyone on our previous trips. Somehow Scott's way of holding himself, extracted the utmost performance in his surroundings, causing people to outdo themselves in their attempt to live up to him, as they perceived him.

So for Scott to almost order Anatoli to charm Sandy into contentedness, which was absolutely without reach for Anatoli, and rightly so might substantiate how stressed he was on Everest. Maybe Scott was also falling prey to the unconscious pressure of having several potential competitors closely scrutinizing our style of organizing and acclimatizing scrambles up and down the mountain.

I never heard Scott talk about feeling pressured by the presence of Rob, Todd, David and Ed, the comrades he used to climb with in the past. Scott was the newcomer among Rob Hall and David Breashears, all expedition leaders and male ego's. This are great guys who know each other from other climbs and are now assembled to pursue the same goal -summiting the highest mountain in the world. Were they affected by awareness of the future potential competition for the same client pool - if they displayed the success of getting as many climbing clients to the summit as possible - with no casualties?

Scott adapting himself to the power of money and position and complying with Sandy's offbeat personality whims, made me disrespect him one inch more. Trying to order Anatoli to comply with this dysfunctional egocentric drama, just underscored to me how far off Scott was at this point.

I became very angry and upset. I was angry at Scott for betraying himself, unsettled as I realized and forced to acknowledge his swaying towards an uncharacteristic superficial back-liking conduct, which I could not respect. In addition, even though Scott, at times was a very strong climber he was incomparable to Anatoli's skills, endurance and untainted professionalism. A mountaineer and not a media addict. It seemed Scott transmuted like a chameleon to please the latest whims of our spoiled socialite team member. The leaders' words or actions send a clear signal as to how they expect people to behave. How we interact demonstrates what impact, the perceptions and beliefs we hold of others through subtle signals, actions, and signs, have. I am convinced Scott's behavior deeply unsettled Anatoli. Not Anatoli's ego, but feeding a growing doubt, confronted with the mere fact that Scott obscured reality.

Little by little we began to question his capacity to honorably deal with the complexities involved in an expedition of this magnitude, suspicious of to what extent Scott were on top of the situation and realizing that it didn't seem possible for us who truly cared to get through to Scott. I have tried for the past half year to influence Scott to rest sufficiently to recuperate and potentially regain some of his former strength and stamina. It appears Anatoli detected similar signs of fatigue and lack of his original life zest when he tried to talk Scott into joining him on the Manaslu trip exclusively for Scott's own sake and for the fun of it. Dale Kruse also tried to talk to Scott about his deteriorating health at Base Camp. We pooled together love and care efforts to no avail. Anatoli graciously withdrew into himself and continued doing what he was the best at and the main reason he was here; analyzing, climbing surviving the mountain and preparing the route for a victorious climb for the rest of us. Just the way Scott needed it. Trying to make Anatoli a Sandy pleaser just weakened the fine bond of mutual high regard these guy's had for each other.

Just fathoming that Sandy was so self-centered and out of touch with reality as to demand of Scott, that Anatoli waste life preserving resources by stroking her grandiose ego. And for Scott not to ward off her weird needs for attention? Sandy one more time exposed her strange persona, where it was obvious that her ability to connect on equal terms were close to non-existing. Others where seemingly regarded as marionettes in her schema. I do not think she did it on purpose or consciously aimed at disregarding us. She probably just behaved the way she normally did.

Transitorily I could almost feel sorry for her.

Scott seemed to be losing focus of the fundamentals for summiting Everest realistic and self-assessment. The truth probably is that every extraordinary endeavor stretches our capacities beyond where we are able to react with composure and therefore displays the less than desirable versions of our characters. On Everest, you must be able to evaluate your strengths and weaknesses not to get yourself and others into life threatening trouble. I withdrew myself from Scott even more after the incident with Anatoli. How can I respect him, when he to this ridiculous degree, tries to satisfy Sandy's unfulfillable self-centered prerequisites on the expense of the most distinguished, uncorrupted humble climber on the entire mountain? This was a severe bad judgment call, nauseating even to learn that Scott is now for sale for PR. This episode might seem insignificant, but it is precisely *"points of no return"* like this occurrence that osmoses through an entire team.

    Based on someone's actions - we form our opinions and judgments. I decided to leave Scott to his own troubled inner conflicts after the confrontation that had nothing to do with me. Consequently, I gravitated more profoundly towards Anatoli. Not that he ever discussed any frustration about this obscure demand for socialite socializing with me. Nevertheless, I sensed that he was puzzled by Scott's attitude and probably withdrew into minding his climbing business, as much as I did. Anatoli's responsibilities were so much heavier than mine. Scott's disclosure probably had profound subtle impact on the expedition. The more Scott dissolved his self-contentedness and acted his stress out, the more I let-go of my want to reach out to him.

    Compelled to realize he was out of my influence sphere mentally giving up and leaving him to whomever he preferred to strategically socialize with for whatever reasons. I came to this conclusion having learned from the *12 Step drug-treatment program* that I cannot control another human being and that I must let go. In discussions on behavior and morality, an individual possess the virtue of integrity if the individual's actions are based upon an internally consistent framework of principles. These principles should uniformly adhere to sound logical truisms. One can describe a person as having ethical integrity when the individual's actions, beliefs, methods, measures and principles derive from a single core group of values. An individual must be flexible and willing to adjust values in order to maintain consistency when these values are challenged. Scott was acting out - exhaustion, worry, stress, what I know as the myriads of complexities influencing Scott on Everest - causing him to act out of character and pushing his most profound allies away. Scott's ego, burn-out and strong desire for media generating exposure, distanced him from some of us who truly loved him and would have done everything to try to make him preserve himself, had not shunned us through his blurring focus.

These are the choices that might have contributed to Scotts death on Everest.

21

"Blessed is he who expects nothing, for he shall never be disappointed."
Alexander Pope

The Western Cwm is a flat, gently rising glacial valley, marked by huge lateral crevasses, which prevent direct access to the upper reaches of the Cwm. Climbers are forced to cross on the far right near the base of Nuptse to a small passageway known as the "Nuptse corner". The Western Cwm is also called the "Valley of Silence" as the topography of the area generally cuts off wind from our route. No wind is a plus but the elevation and a clear, windless day can make the Western Cwm unbearably hot. When you first arrive after the taxing ordeal of climbing through the Khumbu Icefall in one piece, Western Cwm. appears gentle and a lot less risky than any other section on our climbing route, but it takes forever to slide through the endless white beauty, systematically moving your crampon clad plastic boots step by step.

Departing from Camp I at 5,800 meters, we spend 5-7 hours scrambling up the Western Cwm to the base of the Lhotse face, where our expedition Sherpas has established Camp 2 at 6,100 m (21,300 ft.) Continuously coping with not knowing whether you have hundreds of meters of solid ice under you crampons or whether you are balancing delicately on one of the myriads of hidden snow bridges: thin ramps spanning freezing death traps hidden below an innocent and assumingly solid cover of snow crystals. It is crucial and mandatory that you keep your mouth shut while wheezing for air, otherwise the inside of your palate might become sun scolded by the reflections of the harsh sunrays. I breathe a sigh of relief every time I feel the solidity of the pebbles of the moraine where Camp 2 is situated on top. Unfortunately, it is so damn taxing to scale the steep moraine bank to arrive at the relative tranquil safe haven of Camp 2.

With our extraordinary Gyalzen waiting to greet us with a steaming bowl of Rara Noodles, preferable with a slight touch of chili to add some spice to my life up high. From Camp 2, we ascend the Lhotse face on fixed ropes up to Camp 3. Our yellow miniature high altitude storm tents are located on a small ledge at 7,370 m (24,500 ft.). The upper regions of Lhotse are an unforgiving place: giant downwards sliding ice staircases, quite avalanche prone and the best option for a much-required rest. There are no horizontal plateaus for the placement of Camp 3. We seek out a nudge quite high on the steep Lhotse Ice Wall and do our utmost to chop out enough almost horizontal ground to merely fit one of our tents onto.

When we arrive at Camp 3, it is no longer possible for our organism to recuperate through sleep. When you fall asleep at 7,300 meters, your slumbering body attempts to strike some balance between oxygen and carbon dioxide levels; therefore it falls victim to periodic breathing causing your exhausted body to fall asleep as normal, only to be woken abruptly by life sustaining signaling from your brain. You snooze for some minutes then you startle, only to fall asleep anew and awaken all through any night.

Periodic breathing is a cycle of decreased breathing, followed by a complete absence of breathing (from three to 15 seconds). Your breathing resumes once carbon dioxide has sufficiently built up in your bloodstream to prompt your brain. Periodic breathing is common at higher altitudes and is not itself a sign of altitude sickness, but it often leaves afflicted individuals feeling worn out upon waking. Then we have to climb for two additional days and nights before we can hope to have the summit of Everest in sight.

From Camp 3 and all the way to the summit and safe return, there are no more possibilities for sleeping or eating properly and sufficiently.

    Sherpas determination and focused willpower are the main ingredients that make a difference up here. From Camp 3, it is another 500 altitude meters and approximately 11 hours of mixed scrambling to Camp 4 on the South Col at 7.920 m (26,000 ft.) From Camp 3 to Camp 4, we are faced with additional challenges: The Yellow Band. The Yellow Band is a section of interlayered marble, phyllite and semi schist, which requires about 100 meters of rope fixed unto the rock for traversing it as safely as possibly. Even though we are scaling a mere 500 altitude meter to reach Camp 4, it takes from approximately 6 o'clock in the morning until 3 o'clock in the afternoon to cover the stretch of miscellaneous climbing between the two camps. In the mountains, we never measure distance in normal terms - only in hours and altitude gained. I am setting crampons sturdily in the snowclad Lhotse Face narrow-mindedly approaching the weird yellow rock for the first time in my life, scrambling upwards according to our expedition plan. Estimated time of arrival at Camp 4 is 15.00 this afternoon May 9.

    The weather has deteriorated – wind and foggy condition- as if the atmosphere is saturated by moisture and contours begin to fade. What a difference from the summer temperatures and false lure of "innocence" of just a few minutes ago. Indeed, Everest now shows her teeth, the small thrilling gusts of wind remind me of the seriousness of our meaningless mission. Sherpas' are scrambling upwards in front of me, hunching, as if to gain forward momentum, Klev - green down suit, blue backpack - and Rob on the Yellow band - red down suit - are about to negotiate another long traverse on slippery snow covered ground. I lift my eyes, which are fixed in position to find safe footing and gaze upwards and see climbers from our and Rob Hall's team - a string of tiny colored blobs - ascending an enormous wall that seems to go on forever. I've been working my butt off since 5 o'clock this morning, hours and hours of moving one foot in front of the other, step by step by step for 10 minutes, then halting for a two minutes break to catch my oxygen deprived breath. What is going on? Obviously, there is trouble with the client Rob is trying to cohere up over the yellow rock. 150 meters in front of me, the down clad figure abetted by Rob fumbles and fiddles. Is it anxiety attack or altitude sickness? Delaying us who await to ascend. The Fumbler ignites my fantasy in the wrong direction. If that strong guy is having problems, the traverse must be taxing: too taxing for me? Old inferiority complexes die hard. Could it be that I am simply more capable and fitted to cope with the lack of oxygen? An almost Taboo ridden reflection - originating from a woman, especially a Danish one of the species. Half an hour is squandered, when the Fumbler finally, heavily assisted by Rob scrambles up the yellow band. As it turns out, I am observing the first massive signs, that Dough Scott is suffering dramatically already at this altitude. In addition, I realize that Rob obviously is determined to assist him up, instead of down. Every single time I start plugging upwards after a breathing pause, my brain cheats me, giving me the impression that I am now well rested and able to push upwards faster, with less exertion.

What a bummer, after one step, I am back where I was before the breathing break, climbing on sheer will power and the steam from my mantra "To the summit and safe return." I feel exhausted and there is still a long, long way ahead, just to get myself to the unimposing shelter of Camp 4 at 8,000 meters. The South Col must be hiding itself in a hollow behind the everlasting massive rock wall, which rises endlessly below my slugging climbing boots.

I do not recall that I have read or heard any descriptions of these sandwiched slate features of passage in the Yellow Band during my mental preparations to venture into this unknown. This vast rock massif of layered, slippery slate-like flakes presents an unsafe footing and is becoming exceedingly dicier as snow intensifies. Nevertheless, I trust my feet and am confident with mixed climbing.

Now my seasons of practicing survival in rough, solitary winter conditions around Mont Blanc in Chamonix come to assistance. I trust my foot will remain where I stamp it in. Martin - dark-green, one-piece down suit - overtakes me on top of the rock massif, crossing the brink of the slate heap. He and Klev are the strongest climbers on our team; I am the strongest and fastest woman. My realities and verdicts are confirmed and put to the test after our month long acclimatizing procedures on the mountain. I am almost thrown off my feet by fierce gusts, I grasp and cling to the rock as I do not want to be blown of the mountain just as Alison Hargraves ended her climbing career, wafted of the flanks of K2 last summer.

"Hi Ngawang," the struggling Sherpa in front of me turns out to be OLD Ngawang, Lopsang's father. We call him Old Ngawang to distinguish him from all the other Ngawangs on the mountain. Sherpas are named after the day of the week on which they are born, so consequently identical names occur repeatedly, with so many Sherpas fortifying our expedition ventures. "Fantastic," we grin to each other. We're on the roll, having a ball. Some people thrive in cold, harsh, demanding environments and I am one such individual. I jog my memories of when I am sailing and the wind becomes rougher than most people feel comfortable in. As long as I know I can trust the boat not to break, I feel my sailing experience come into play and I become more and more delighted and invigorated through sailing for hours and hours, while less sea worthy individuals hang over the side, puking. Quite a few dates have ended after such a reality test. I perceive an equivalent kind of exhilarated delight, in Nawang's glittering eyes, reflecting my ecstatic state of mind. Steadily ascending from behind, Anatoli passes most of the climbers from Rob Hall's expedition and somewhere just above the Yellow Band he passes the leading climber on our team, Klev Schoening, who is still going strong. Anatoli notice, "Klev is ascending with a decent speed, almost like mine, and I have to press myself a little to keep ahead of the pace Klev is maintaining." When Anatoli arrives at the South Col around 2:00 P.M., he encounters an iced mayhem. In the freezing temperatures, amid a scatter of hundreds of depleted oxygen canisters abandoned by previous expeditions, the 50 mph wind is roaring across the exposed, corridor like plateau: our abode for the coming days and nights.

The Death Zone!

To prepare for the Everest attempt in the spring of 1996, all teams assembled at Base Camp, worked through nearly 6 weeks of acclimatizing and preparation and all groups aiming to summit on May 10 reached the highest camp, Camp 4 during the afternoon on May 9. We were around 50 people accumulated in this tiny community. Not a tight knit unity, but small self-contained and self-centered entities, exclusively preoccupied with ourselves and at best the other individuals in our particular group. On the entire duration of the expedition, we rarely intermingle with climbers from other expeditions. Non-expedition individuals often have a romanticized mental perception of the teamwork and life lasting bonding that ought to be a part of mountaineering. If you are truly fortunate, you are part of a sound functioning group, but that is a rarity, especially as individuals are more and more pressured when climbing day after day in more and more strenuous conditions. Even the guys amassed here, who are acquainted with each other from years of climbing together and surviving the same turf, mostly stick to their own expedition. The arduous process of gaining proper acclimatization, recuperating and remaining focused at the risky target ahead of us, maintains an invisible barriers between us and the others.

"One of the most dangerous encounters on Everest is these squalls that can easily tear you off the mountain, diminishing human beings to absolute insignificance. Storms this fierce, are one of my greatest enemies at high altitude", utters Anatoli gripping the edges of a tent with his gloved hands, assisting our Sherpas wrestling the flapping, flying material, fighting to tussle it to the ground. Anatoli has seen numerous expeditions halted, when a high-camp shelter became demolished by the uncontrollable forces of nature and the mountaineers forced to retreat from lack of protection against the elements up high. Struggling and utilizing their bodyweight to hold on to the rodeo tent, Klev arrives and crawls into our presumed shelter to pin it to the ground, while Anatoli and our Sherpas' manage to secure the tunnel designed tent. Our shelter is secured, for now. I bump into Anatoli in the cacophony, he is struggling unrelentingly to secure and protect our accommodation from the ripping forces of the gale force winds. Putting his mouth a few inches from my ears, Anatoli yells and points towards the entrance of the tent he is clutching, Martin and I worm our ways in and say hello to Klev, who is already settling in, marginally protected from the inferno outside.

"Lene and Martin look tired but are not complaining about any serious problems. Neal seems to be feeling the altitude." Anatoli recalls.

Gale force winds are skirmish to blow me away from my destination this afternoon. Notorious South Col. flip, flap- living inferno - while our Sherpas and Anatoli endeavor to pitch our tents. Empty oxygen bottles, shattered tent remnants, generously faded colorful unnatural items decorate this stark, rock-strewn uneven yet level ground. A monument to those, who have been here ahead of me, those who did not make it down and were therefore not able to assemble their equipment and bring their valuable belongings back with them. The debris at this altitude - The Death Zone - deciphers the terminated lives of all the driven individuals who lost their breath in the pursuit of their overtaxing dream. To me, the unsolicited items do not deface the barren uninhabitable landscape, but rather recounts a tale of men's- and women's destinies. In hundred years' time, it will provide material for researchers, like the kitchen middens of the Stone Age. I shoot pictures until the film ends, urgently aware not to remove my gloves and over mittens to change the roll as fingers have frozen for less.

My oxygen mask dangles from my neck. I need to fell the wind, sense the grandiosity of nature's force up here. I love it. Simply love it. Mother Goddess of the World, Chomolungma, Sagarmartha, you are truly the grandest mountain and I tread upon you with profound respect and awe. Your summit is all I desire! However, my brain realizes, thanks to my winter studies of high altitudes and the depletion of oxygen at elevation, that the air is so "thin" up here that I cannot breathe fast enough to get sufficient oxygen molecules in through my nose and mouth to sustain what my body needs. Even though our respiratory rates increase as we acclimatize it is just not sufficient. Here, in the Death Zone above 8,000 meters, my body, no matter how much I invest in acclimatization, I will not be able to withstand hypoxia for more than five days. So the crux is not to be caught in one of the repetitive storms here at the Col.

All I have, is a window of maximum five to 24 hours to get to the summit and safely back, never suppressing the fact that the longer I spend up here, the weaker I become no matter how much I rest. The same goes for my metabolism, no matter how many calories I consume, just playing with the thought that anyone brings food this high and if we did, I would not be able to consume any of it. A variety of factors contributes to the human body's weakness at high altitudes. Our bodies are not created to handle the incredibly frigid temperatures, the high winds, or the lack of oxygen, thus we are forced to come properly prepared mentally and physically. It goes without saying that ambient air temperature decreases with height, meaning that you will be much colder on the summit of an 8000-meter peak than you would when sitting on the beach in

Europe. Recent developments from specialized clothing manufacturers have alleviated some of the danger posed by the temperatures and winds, though oxygen concentration is a different joker altogether.

The true cause, for all types of altitude sickness, is the lack of atmospheric pressure. Pressure, defined as the weight exerted on the surface of the Earth by a column of air rising vertically to the very top of the atmosphere. Since mountains rise so much higher than land close to sealevel, the columns of air over them are much shorter and thus, there is much less weight (pressure) over that part of the surface. Because of this, the air molecules are dispersed, so there is actually less atmosphere up here - not just less oxygen - contributing to the significant risk of altitude sickness as well as sun scolding! At sea level, we bathe in air compressed by Earth's atmosphere, brimming with oxygen molecules.

At low altitude, most of us can walk easily without huffing and puffing and we can exercise with some huffing and puffing because we are used to it. However, at 8,848 meters above sea level, we need to work harder just to supply energy for essential functions, let alone exercise. The brain, arguably the most essential organ in the human body, is one of the greediest when it comes to oxygen consumption. The brain requires steady delivery of a large supply of oxygen. Blood flow to the brain increases, to meet oxygen demands. Of course, when people exercise at high altitude, they need even more oxygen to fuel efficient metabolic reactions.

The scarcity of oxygen at high elevations forces us to breathe harder, or slow down; and yet mountain climbers persist. Somehow, we manage to extract enough oxygen from the thin atmosphere to fuel our physical exertions and our greedy brains. Sea-level pressure, measured in millibars, usually tends to be around 1013mb, with some small variations based on weather phenomena. Vertical changes, however, produce huge changes in pressure. In fact, when standing on the summit of Mt. Everest, there is around 300-350 millibars, which also varies, based on the seasons (lower in winter). When you hear people say, "There is on 1/3 of the oxygen on the top of Everest compared with at sea-level", the truth is that that the pressure has decreased to only about 30% of what it is near the oceans. There is actually the same concentration of oxygen in the atmosphere regardless of elevation.

It is important to realize that the reduced pressure does not allow as much air into your lungs. Therefore your lungs cannot absorb as much oxygen as your body needs, which consequently causes medical problems, beginning with mild symptoms of acute mountain sickness escalating into the potentially fatal high altitude pulmonary edema (HAPE) and high altitude cerebral edema (HACE); the higher the altitude, the greater the risk. Research also indicates elevated risk of permanent brain damage in alpinists climbing to extreme altitudes. Numerous fatalities in high-altitude mountaineering have been caused by the effects of the Death Zone, either directly - loss of vital functions - or indirectly - wrong decisions made under stress- physical weakening leading to mishaps. An extended stay in the Zone without supplementary oxygen will result in deterioration of bodily functions, loss of consciousness and ultimately, death. In the "Death Zone," above 7,500m (24,600ft), acclimatization is virtually impossible.

There are a very few people with the genetic predisposition to be able to sustain life at these extreme elevations. Climbers like Anatoli Boukreev possess a better-than-average ability to absorb oxygen into their bloodstream. Modern medicine cannot do anything to boost this genetic aptitude. For those who "didn't choose their parents well", doctors can test this genetic ability to predict who may perform at altitude. Smart people should limit their exposure to altitudes to the minimum amount possible, as the human body is slowly going through the process of dying while up high. Almost everything we do - whether it is physical activity or a mental process - uses the same energy source: glucose. We use glucose as we walk, talk, breathe, and perform other physical tasks; climbing Everest craves up to ten times as much energy as dealing with our daily lives. We also use glucose when we perform effortful mental functions, such as making decisions, exerting self-control, suppressing emotional responses, and even solving math problems. Crucially, glucose - this fundamental source of both physical and mental energy - is a limited resource. We cannot eat enough calories at elevation to sustain our metabolic demands. Even if we had appetite or sufficient expedition resources, to haul ample food items up to Camp 4 with casualties involved, our bodies would not be able to extract sufficient nourishment out of the available diet. It craves a lot of energy to transform what we eat into crucial building blocks for our systems to function at its highest level, energy partially extracted from the sparse oxygen we breathe in. Because we are in an extreme environment our brains utilizes almost all available energy to preserve the crucial survival functions of the brain itself, as well as the energy necessary to keep the heart beating. When these vital tasks are sustained on an ongoing basis, there is absolutely no energy left for breaking down food into nourishment to sustain our hard working organisms. In addition, at high altitude, our heart beats faster, the stroke volume is slightly increased and non-essential bodily functions suppressed, resulting in a decline in food digestion efficiency as the body suppresses the digestive system in favor of increasing its cardiopulmonary reserves.

    At the South Col, we have entered the Death Zone and altitude sickness is a significant threat that can easily prove fatal. From Camp 3 at 7,300 meters and at Camp 4 and until we are back at Camp 2, it is difficult to sleep and most climbers' digestive systems have significantly slowed or completely stopped. At our current elevation, it is more efficient for the body to use stored energy sources - the protein in our muscles - than to digest food. Most climbers begin using supplemental oxygen leaving camp 3 to suppress the grueling effects of the environment we venture in to. We do loose appetite entirely up high, so I am not aware that any climber anticipates eating once we leave Camp 3. Instead, we let our bodies consume its own energy depots, fat and muscle. Only on 14 mountains worldwide, can one step beyond the 8,000-meter mark bringing you into realms where no amount of training or conditioning allow you to spend more than 5 to24 hours alive. In such conditions, odd things happen to human physical and mental states.

    A National Geographic climber described the unsettling hallucinogenic effects of running out of oxygen in the Death Zone. The insides of his tent seemed to rise above him, taking on cathedral-like dimensions, robbing him of all strength and clouding his judgment. Any stay in the Death Zone without supplementary oxygen is like being slowly choked all the while having to perform one of the hardest physical feats imaginable. We all resemble KZ prisoners after an 8000-meter peak expedition, because our bodies have consumed themselves to keep us alive. The South Col, the sharp-edged pass between Mount Everest and Lhotse is a relatively flat hollow between the highest and fourth highest mountain in the world. When we attempt to climb Everest from the southeast ridge in Nepal, our final camp - Camp 4 - is situated on the South Col.

The South Col is typically ravaged by high winds, leaving it free of significant snow accumulation. Today is no exception. The South Col is at 7,906 meters [25,938 feet]. The summit of Everest - the pinnacle of our pursuit - is 8,848 meters [29,029 feet] high. Realistically you should be able to climb 90 altitude meters [295 feet] per hour, so you should gain the difference between Camp 4 and the Summit in about 10 hours. Add a couple of rest stops and some time to enjoy the view on top, and you are looking at 12 hours up. Six hours for the descent makes it 18 hours round trip. Then there is the calculation of our oxygen consumption. At an average flow of two liters per minute, a bottle of oxygen will last six hours. You will carry two. With regulator and mask, they'll total maybe 15 pounds and your Sherpa support climbers will carry a third up in our oxygen depot below the summit, for your descend. That gives you 18 hours of total climbing time with supplemental oxygen. Clear weather and low winds are critical factors in deciding whether to initiate the summit attempt.

If weather does not cooperate within these few days, we will at best be forced to descend, many of us all the way down to Base Camp.

Mountaineers rarely get a second chance to return to the South Col within one season. Climbers typically only have a maximum of two or three days that they can endure at this altitude for making summit bids. A retreat will coast around one week of expedition time until we have restored sufficient energy to be ready to attempt another summit bid. One week of extra food, oxygen, risk of climbing down and up again and risk for the climbing Sherpas as well.

Most often, the true enemy being the insufficient amount of extra stamina and perseverance needed to sustain oneself in these hostile environments for yet an added week: a risk that we weigh against the risk of climbing higher. If we have to abandon our summit bid tonight due to the unstable weather, the expedition will in reality be over for most on our team. Heading back to Base Camp to recuperate is a must. Nowhere higher will our bodies be able to restore just marginal strength. But the total time we have spent at Base Camp and higher and the total amount of energy consumed to be where we are today, will not allow more than one or two of us on the mountain for another attempt in a week or so time. Our entire team will be so sapped that there is only on obvious choice, abandon Base Camp and wait until another year. Consequently - our summit bid is now or we will probably suffer defeat.

Every one of us who have made it this far, has a lot invested in climbing even higher; for Rob and Scott as expedition leaders even more so as they undoubtedly are influenced by their desire to come out successful to secure future business opportunities. As far as I am concerned Scott and Rob have not discussed their main objectives - but I assume they share a common vision – to get as many clients on the summit as possible and no casualties. Ambition must be weighed against the odds of turning around due to deterioration or not sufficiently improvement of the weather and whether it is wise to make the conscious choice of following our detailed expedition plan of leaving for the summit tonight at 11:00 P.M. High Stakes in a high-risk environment. Moreover, our brains just do not function at this altitude: a dichotomy because we have to make profoundly serious, well-thought out choices.

Death might be the outcome of the wrong decision and fame the result of the right bet, myriads of unknown factors that we cannot anticipate nor control. No matter what you do to try to preserve yourself you do die every second you remain above 8000 meters. The inkling is to get up and back down fast enough, such that you don't risk dying just from being up high. If you are not extremely careful and the weather with you, your time may run out: venturing into *"The Death Zone"* is mountaineering on borrowed time." We are in the abode of the jet streams and the weather is deteriorating. By the time I sort of settle into our spot at the South Col it is storming with gale force gusts. No surprise, it storms most days at this elevation. The wind accelerates in ferocity as it is funneled through the saddle between Everest and Lhotse. My base for the next days and nights... I stroll around slowly and slowly taking in the "world's highest junkyard," wanting nothing to be different from what it is. I stay close to our tent, not wandering far, partly because I'm exhausted and it's already 3:00 P.M. Our plan is a few hours rest and then final preparations for our summit bid at 11:00 P.M., if the wind loses some of its ferocious power before that time, that is. I know the camp area is "corpse free," but South Col is not. The climbers who remain up here, because they for one reason or the other are not able to move under their own volition, linger where they fall, adding another fragment to Mount Everest's history. For the time being, I cannot allow myself to consider or become confronted with that particular shadow side of my pursuit. *"To the summit and safe return."* I must control my mind and maintain my disciplined focus and not let my fears wander off and harbor the harrowing facts of how many lose their lives, pursuing their single minded dream of standing on top of the world.

  We Everest wannabe Summiteers know that the best time to climb to the summit is in the early morning. Accordingly, the New Zealand team plans to leave Camp 4 at 11.35 pm., followed by us - the US team-at 12 pm. Earlier this week, most of the leaders of the remaining expeditions seeking the summit, met, attempting to determine the order in which each team would start their final summit attempt. We are supposed to be the only two teams leaving for the summit from Camp 4, tonight on May 10. However, The Taiwanese expedition leader broke this apparent agreement and has assembled his group and seems determined to set out from Camp 4 between 12 am. and 1 am. with Sherpa guides. Well, Everest is free for all... I have reached higher than I have ever been before. No matter what, I have come this far and I feel a sensation of pride calming and nurturing me in the chilling blustery weather squalls. Where is Scott? Its 5:00 pm. and I am not aware of having observed either Scott or Sandy arriving at Camp 4. Oh Scott, where are you? Altitude and the resulting low levels of oxygen, can strongly affect the human brain and cognition.

The low oxygen levels at these altitudes can have detrimental impacts on our linguistic ability and the capacity to make decisions and alter plans, when circumstances change. Everest climbers with normal linguistic comprehension at lower altitudes might not understand slightly complex syntax such as "the girl was kissed by the boy" at altitudes over 6,500 meters. In fact, most of the climbers' speech at 6,500 meters resembled that of a person who has experienced a stroke. There are striking similarities between climbers at altitudes exceeding 6,500 meters and people with Alzheimer's in regard to their ability to adjust mentally to new situations.

Low oxygen levels in the brain impair the basal ganglia, which plays a major role in our capacity to adapt to changing circumstances like storms, malfunctioning equipment, and other unforeseen difficulties. Experienced mountaineers often switch into autopilot while climbing, and when something rare or unexpected occurs at high altitudes, they often find themselves mentally lost. It takes an extra mental push to process the altered situation and form a new good decision. The key is taking a moment to focus your thoughts. I must trust that I belong to the cluster of mountaineers, who cope at best up high, as I have to face serious decisions and extremely hard tasks from tonight and for the next 24 hours at least.

We plan to initiate our summit bid at 11:00 P.M tonight, reach the summit tomorrow May 10 early afternoon and then descend back down to the relative safety of our present Camp. Then descend towards Camp 3 for the first soup and food since we left 7,300 meters this morning at dawn. Will I be able to make life preserving choices, perform and execute to maintain life with a brain that at its best functions as a five years old's? Will I be able to start out on the ultimate self-quest tonight? Am I risk willing enough, competent enough, crazy enough or courageous enough? Will my brain manipulation and focus, service me or kill me? Before I dive into the flapping, Russian-made, tri-colored tunnel tent Anatoli has provided, I check our oxygen stock. A pile of orange pressurized canisters dumped between our two Mountain Madness expedition tents. We're stripped down to the absolute minimum in tents, stoves, food and personal kit, only what's crucial for summiting and surviving and absolutely nothing superfluous, no extravagance.

An entirely unknown sensation permeates my core. I have intellectually drilled myself for the fact, that at and beyond this elevation above sea level, there is no room for error, because rescue possibilities are next to none, once you've climbed into the Death Zone. Mobility under your own steam is a must. If you stumble from fatigue, twist an angle, lose you bearing and are caught out in the open after dark, there is high risk that you will not make it down alive: the very reasons why I have drilled self responsibility into my system.

Acknowledging that my best chances of making this adventure alive, is to be and remain able to take care of myself in every possible circumstance, keep moving under my own power, never harboring desires to give up and depend on anybody to do anything for me. I am alert. Creeping, seeping in to every cell of my organism is the proof of being in the death zone. I am literally embedded in a sentiment of slow deterioration, as if my survival instincts consciously make me aware and alert to the fact, that the Death Zone is not just a rhetoric construct. I am dying every second I remain here. My body detects the process and signals the deterioration to my consciousness. Odd, as well as unwelcome my body acknowledging its own destruction.....

The gale picks up even a notch more, fierce unrelenting natural forces, reducing humans to insignificance, fighting the fabric of our shelter, pressing it inwards as the wind perseveres blowing relentlessly. Klev as the Gentleman he has been consistently, since I first encountered him, has spent the entire afternoon melting snow for Martin and me. At higher altitudes, our bodies make adjustments, generates more red blood cells to carry oxygen through the bloodstream, pushing air into normally unused portions of the lungs and producing citrate synthase, a special enzyme that helps the oxygen found in hemoglobin make its way into body tissue.

The low humidity and low air pressure up here causes moisture from your skin and lungs to evaporate at a faster pace and your body's increased exertion requires even more liquid to keep it hydrated. Therefore, Klev's humble gesture of taking responsibility for replenishing our dehydrated depots is a true treat. We are waiting for the arrival of our fourth tent partner, Anatoli, who is helping our Sherpas' to erect our high camp.

Our temporary domicile bulges with the four of us and our summit gear. Diminutive ruck sacks ready for oxygen containers and nothing else. Weight equals chances of success from now on, so we bring nothing but the packages with Reload Gel, oxygen, mask and in the zipped chest pocket close at hand, the container with a Steroid syringe in case one of us collapses and needs a shot to be able to move down. I'm ploughed deep into my high camp specialized down sleeping bag, wearing as many layers of clothes as possible, except for my Everest One Sport outer shell. Wearing the outer boot would help me preserve body heat, but they are definitely too huge to fit into my sleeping quarter; so all our outer shells are shattered around the floor of the tent or utilized as pillows and gradually transforming themselves into blocks of ice.

Klev is in super condition and melts snow without a pause. In his calm dignified manner, he insists on continuing with this task, even though it is only fair that we take over. That's Klev, even at 26,000 feet! We are and our increased respiration and sweating from hard physical work dehydrates us very fast and for the next 24 Hours there won't be much opportunity for getting anything into our body or out for that matter. Solid food, apart from small foil packets of high-energy protein gel that tastes like …. - none of us seriously considers.

Ice forms from our respiratory condense on the inner side of our tent and sprinkles down, prickling us with every gust. The squalls correspondingly cause the tent opening to blow apart again and again and again. The tent entrance is shaped like a wind tunnel of nylon - you crawl through a narrow passageway of fabric on all fours - to keep out as much snowdrift as possible. The tunnel tent is meticulously constructed to avoid zippers that would truly make for the weakest link in the chain in this hostile environment.

The lack of zippers preserves us of the risk of frostbites, not having to remove our glove system to close the wind tunnel. Unfortunately, it's a hell of a task to draw the constantly escaping lilac tight in one glowed claw and hold on to the rodeo flapping long enough to tie the closing strings around the bundle.

The roaring gale keeps yanking the tent fabric from my paws, while I'm struggling to tie the aforementioned securely. Every time a climber seeks shelter with us or delivers a message and "Hot tea," are great and welcomed, but now I have to take up the fight with the escaping drapery once more. Speaking of messages, Pemba just arrived, reporting, "Lopsang is sick - he is coughing and vomiting, and most of our Sherpas' suffer headaches." As the wind continues to pick up through the dwindling afternoon, Anatoli is wondering how to proceed as the gale force winds obviously is threatening our summit bid. "I decide to speak with Rob Hall, whom I had seen supervising the construction of his own camp and when I approach him near one of his tents, we have to scream to be heard over the constant roar of wind. What are we going to do? I'm sure the weather is clearly not good enough for assaulting the summit." Anatoli's data is countered with Rob Hall's response, "My experience is that often it is calm after a squall like this and if it clears tonight, we will make our bid tomorrow. If the weather does not clear by midnight, my group will wait another twenty-four hours. If the weather is still think it highly unlikely the weather will stabilize." Anatoli's intuition continues to bother him and he does not expect us to climb at midnight. Ending his dialogue with Rob Hall and concerned that Scott has yet to arrive in camp, Anatoli begin plotting his way backtracking toward Camp 3. About 40 meters from our tents, through the snow blasts, Anatoli recognize Scott moving towards him with some more climbers in tow. Among them Anatoli recognizes Sandy Hill Pittman. Scott, yelling to be heard, asks Anatoli in what tents everyone should go. Anatoli articulates his concern to Scott "I don't think conditions are very good, and I think we should consider descending." Then he tells Scott. "I have discussed the weather with Rob, his intentions are to wait and see if the storm clears." It becomes clear to Anatoli that Scott agrees with Rob.

If the weather clears, we will climb.

I wish Scott wasn't taking the risk of being here. I wish he had remained at Base Camp. I wish he had listened during our winter get-togethers and had taken responsibility for being thoroughly recuperated and well rested for this break-through opportunity for his visions for the future. I wish I were able to shake him and make him pay attention to the care expressed by us, who love him. Fundamentally, I probably wish for Scott not to be so damn much Scott on this expedition. Scott' stressful lifestyle presumably put him under extreme pressure, to the point where he is exhausted, burnt out and increasingly unable to cope, from overworking himself. His extreme commitment has lead Scott to neglect his own needs. I perceive Scott's exhaustion as a normal reaction to pushing himself year after year, even though tiredness, physical and mental symptoms ought to stop him. Scott evidently displays emotional exhaustion, appearing drained and overloaded, tired and not having enough energy for what he attempts to accomplish. I progressively let go of my desire to preserve Scott from being Scott. He seems beyond reach and has been for a while. Scott appears to have increasingly distanced himself emotionally; from me at least, I have withdrawn into preserving myself a while ago.

Little insignificant incidents, drop by drop of less than desired action on his part, has caused my withdrawal from believing I can contribute anything, that will make him change his mode of operating for the time being, if ever. It saddens me, but I swiftly refocus on the more important task "To the summit and safe return." Probably around 5:30 pm. Anatoli joins me, Klev and Martin in our tent. Scott, Sandy, Charlotte and Tim are in the other. Wind blows relentlessly, excruciating noise, everyone hunkered down, pondering what decision the next few hours will unleash. "Stick to the winners." I have shared tents with winners since 7,300 meters.

Anatoli, Klev and Martin are trying to keep warm sharing this outer world time loop. I keep an eye on how my mates are behaving and performing now that we are all under influence of insufficient oxygen and under extreme psychological pressure. Can I trust myself and the less than yearlong programming of my subconscious *"To the summit and safe return?"* Now is definitely the time for my brain manipulation to kick in and take over the control of my survival genetic, because it's a universally accepted fact that you think with your ass at this height. You believe you're rational, certain you have your shit together and are making the most intelligent decisions, but the only thing you can be absolutely assured of is that you can't be sure you actually have your shit together, because your brain is oxygen deprived.

Having observed Scotts fluctuating health and lack of convincing strength and recuperation for the last half year, I wish that this time, Scott would "climb Everest via walkie-talkie.

When we were visiting Doctor Jim from the high-altitude clinic in Pheriche on our trek to Gorak Sheep, he shared what his team did when they were climbing Everest. They kept radio contact with their expedition leader, who stayed at base camp. Each time the climbing team had to make a demanding decision up high, they discussed it with the expedition leader, who, because he was at a lower altitude, presumably was more capable of thinking straight! But then again, we haven't had much luck so far maintaining radio contact on the mountain.

    The tiny yellow walkie-talkies David Breashears and the IMAX team utilize remind me of toys, but their reliability is beyond reproach. Our outdated sinister black antiquated radios can't be trusted, so above Camp 2 we've just accepted sporadic radio communication: suits me fine, as radios might add to a false sense of security. Who would pick me up if I phoned for help from the summit, anyway? No rescue exists up here; no helicopter can perform anything but crash at this altitude. So would human beings trying to come to my aid if I called 911? Climbing in the death zone is one of the most dangerous aspects of mountaineering. Lack of oxygen and treacherous terrain are not the only challenges on Everest; however ascents are rarely attempted outside a very short window between May and June when conditions are at their absolute best, with average temperatures of -27 degrees Celsius and 50 mph winds.

    Mount Everest is so high that the top actually penetrates into the stratosphere, where winds known as Jet Streams can drift up to 200 mph, driving temperatures down to minus 73 degrees Celsius. Any exposed skin at these altitudes is prone to frostbite. Frostbite is the freezing and crystallizing of fluids in the cellular spaces as a consequence of prolonged exposure to freezing temperatures. Frostbite may occur when skin and tissue is exposed to a temperature lower than 10°C. Frostbite is a reaction to extreme cold and starts when blood vessels in the skin contract to preserve core body temperature, in conditions where normal blood flow would lead to the body cooling dangerously fast. The resultant decrease in blood flow does not deliver sufficient heat to the tissue to prevent the formation of ice crystals. Hands, feet and exposed tissues, ears, nose, chicks and lips are most susceptible to frostbite. Climbers are by no means ignorant of these facts, which are reiterated in every book, film, in each article and for some cultures adds to the dangerous allure of the mountain.

Although abundant resources has been invested to create products that keep us warm in any situation, the Himalayas, still defy any attempt to be tamed by our efforts to make summiting the highest mountain in the world a safe walk in the park.

Everest is notorious for producing finger and toeless mountaineers. If you experience frostbite, you may not realize at first that anything is wrong, because the affected area will be numb. With prompt medical attention, most people recover fully. However, in severe frostbite, permanent damage is likely, depending on how long and how deeply the tissue is frozen. In severe cases, blood flow to the area may stop and blood vessels, muscles, nerves, tendons and bones may be permanently affected. If the frozen tissue dies, the area may need to be amputated. Because frostbite tends to occur in the same locality as hypothermia, most cases that are observed in High-altitude mountaineering, a variant of frostbite that combines tissue freezing with hypoxia and general body dehydration, has a worse prognosis.

The treatment of mild hypothermia involves warm drinks, warm clothing and staying active. In those with moderate hypothermia, heating blankets and warmed intravenous fluids are recommended. People with moderate or severe hypothermia should be moved gently. In severe hypothermia extracorporeal membrane oxygenation or cardiopulmonary bypass may be useful. In those without a pulse cardiopulmonary resuscitation is indicated along with the above measures. Rewarming is typically continued until a person's temperature is higher than 32 °C (90 °F). If there is no improvement at this point, revival may be terminated.

"Are we going to climb or are we not going to climb?" Our original strategy was that we would be where we are now - South Col, Camp 4- today and begin pushing for the summit at 23:00 pm tonight. Martin Adams expresses his frame of mind "The wind is blowing hard enough that you don't want to mess around with it." I check my plastic toothbrush case. Not that I have brought a toothbrush up with me. A toothbrush would just be unnecessary weight to haul up the mountain. The case is Dr. Ingrid's invention and just one more brick in her well-thought-out medical groundwork for our expedition. It contains a syringe filled with one injection of the steroid Dexamethasone for lifesaving steroid treatment for acute altitude sickness. One shot of "Dex" gives you a boost for six to twelve hours, enough oomph to be assisted in moving down the mountain, closer to safety. We have practiced and practiced symptom-recognition and talked about having the courage to inject someone in the butt, through clothes and what not. My kit for tonight's summit bid - if - consists of the toothbrush case with syringe, four Reload foil-packs, sun block, extra snow goggles, extra battery for my headlamp and extra mittens. I will also carry two oxygen cylinders in my pack and a ¾ liter water container in the inner pocket of my down suit where it shouldn't freeze.

All necessities to keep me alive for the next 24 hours and all I will have available no matter what those hours hold. By knowing our gear intimately and having systems and procedures in place, we know that we have done whatever we can to avoid unnecessary surprises and are prepared to look after ourselves in these extraordinary, challenging conditions. Our down suits are considered an indispensable piece of clothing in our hard ware wardrobe. When you are venturing to the cold extreme environment at altitude then a down suit, or a down jacket and down salopette combination, are absolutely essential.

Our summit suits are so specialized, that there isn't anywhere we can go and try on all of them, to test which one we like the best. Some are custom made for our individual purpose. When you bear in mind that you are wearing this gear to enable you to live, move and function in a pretty harsh environment, then the suits have got to live up to the highest standards. Sometimes you think what you have chosen is the best solution, but on the mountain you learn, that there is room for improvement. You want to be warm, and your gear has to be functional and usable whilst in windy, frozen, icy conditions and you need to be able to operate closures and zippers and access pockets without having to remove your gloves or mitts. Once you are on the move you don't really want to be taking your rucksack off and to that end plenty of pockets are the way ahead, so that drinks, food, spare gloves, sun block, camera etc. are all readily accessible. I had to make sure to try to negotiate every zipper, pocket and feature with my mitts on back home, because it's a bit late to discover drawbacks when you are on the mountain. You also need to remember to think about what you will be wearing under and over your suit - and then ponder how you are going to go to the toilet. There is a very subtle difference between the toileting options, a drop seat and an up and under zipper or pulling the thigh opening across.

When you bear in mind that you may well be wearing a climbing harness at the time, you will soon realize that the thigh opening choice is nowhere near as versatile as the other options. My down suit is a two-piece, with an extra wind suit to put on top in case of gale force winds. Mountain Equipment in England recommended this option instead of a one-piece suit, but I suffer when I have to tread off on behalf of nature, my suit seems to be a shit-flap short. So it's off with the down jacket and then down to mid thighs with the overalls - a tremendously exposed position - actually life threatening under certain conditions. Therefore, I time my toilet visits to happen in the plastic bottles in the fore appendix of our tent before leaving for the next challenging pitch of our climb. The wind cover is in my backpack with the sponsor flags, extra film and the valuable and heavy Nikon Camera. I will have to document myself on the summit to be trusted to have been there. An unwritten, strictly adhered to ethical rule amongst mountaineers to separate the wannabes from the real summiteers.

My pack is too heavy already and I haven't added the two oxygen canisters yet. My crampons and ice axe awaits me outside, securely fastened to the ropes pinning our tent to the frozen, snow-clad ground. Still the storm is roaring. Puffing and wheezing. I am wavering within myself. The old Lene, intelligent, sensible, serious and cautious by various standards wants the storm to continue so I can turn around now. It would be a wise decision to turn around because of the weather; we really have not experienced a full day of tranquil weather at this altitude yet. We are probably too early for the weather window.

My unconscious, programmed and drilled with "To the summit and safe return" mantra, massively argues to push for the summit, if the weather calms during the next hours. "Am I going to climb or am I not going to climb?" Conflict ridden, dilemma, not wanting the huge risks involved with accomplishing what I inertly desire - my most profound wish right here is to summit - yet survive. The death zone is beginning to creep into my resolve, facing the brutal facts that if I truly want to belong to the Big Boys - few girls network of 8,000 meter peak mountaineers- I need to construct more risk willingness than my intelligence and experience allows for. What to do? I now begin to fathom what it has taken for all who preceded me to actually climb Mount Everest. The stakes are so tremendous that no one in their right mind ought to climb further. Let alone seek the summit glory. How fortunate that I climb with Mountain Madness. Suddenly I grin, understanding the full impact of not needing to rationalize and intellectualize this adventurous quest. Klev, Martin and I exchange brief outbursts of our oxygen hampered thought processes - are we going to climb or not? Each of us considering our own risk willingness and break through commitment or not, depending on the weather.

In another tent at Camp 4, Rob Hall's team has parallel considerations and exchanges. Lou Kasischke, fifty-three, an attorney from Michigan, Andy Harris, Beck Weathers and Dough Hansen, all but the guide Andy Harris and obviously Rob Hall thought a summit bid around midnight would be a bad idea.

"It was a roaring storm and we were debating that we ought to wait it out. We were concerned that we really hadn't had a full day of good weather and we just thought it would be wise to wait a day... I mean, if it was still storming in twenty-four hours, we would have problems just getting off the mountain." Lou Kasischke recalls.

The few hours at Camp 4 before the summit attempt is one of the most important mental cruxes connected with climbing

Everest ; a final commitment or the contrary to push further or turn around, a brief time loop for concluding speculations, doubts, resolve, status and risk assessment. Mental preparation beyond what I have ever chosen previously. The Death Zone is breaking me down by the second. Is this what slow death feels like? I can climb higher if the weather permits my progress, or I can descend. I face a hard call. A choice I had hoped not to be antagonized by; a decision I am not sure I have the courage to deal with. My organism requires inactivity. I wonder if Scott and Rob will elect to proceed if the storm dies out. We have no weather forecast. I'm not aware if it is possible to get an accurate prognosis for the atmospheric conditions at our local position that is if we had the up-to-date equipment available, which we haven't. But I do what I also do when sailing and climbing in the Alp's, stick my head outside to find out what's going on. I hope we'll take off and simultaneously I don't want to because there is not enough of a stable weather pattern so far. Shifting through the oxygen canisters in our tent, sorting out the empty ones, Martin freights them through the rear entrance discarding them outside.

"Anatoli, wake up, I need the tool to loosen the nuts on some of the oxygen bottles, so the valves from the hoses to the oxygen masks can be screwed on." Imagine finding a full bottle in a critical situation and then not being able to suck the life restoring content because of a constipating nut. After controlling our oxygen supply and tanking fluids into my system by downing hot tea, I decide the best way to wait is to rest. Anatoli zips back down his bag and almost immediately fall asleep a second time: wise guy. Like SAS-soldiers. Sleep when you can and you will function better when you must. 6:00 pm- storm. 7:00 pm- storm. Hard to envision this inferno will transfer into a calm optimal climbing night or stay tranquil long enough for us to climb up and down as quickly as possible. Martin and I encounter a minor difficulty. Klev is threatening to leave the tent and sleep outside in the storm.

"When we were trying to sleep, Klev, who I think was suffering from AMS, starts yelling at us to move over, which is a little strange, because Lene, Toli and I are already squeezed into one-half of the tent while Klev is in the other half with our packs and oxygen." Martin and I exchange smiles and quizzical looks, because as Martin expresses, *"Klev is a great guy. We didn't take it personally. It wasn't his attitude, it is the altitude."* Emerging from unconsciousness, I must have dozed. Silence, I hear nothing except my oxygen mask covered breathing partners. A little gust of breeze plays with the tent textile and again silence. There is no fabric fluttering and the wind none existent. All I can hear is the characteristic familiar symphony of clattering mountaineering equipment. Now what? Will the aforementioned last? What time is it? 8:00pm.

Scott and Rob put their heads together in Rob's tent, sheltered from our inquisitive gazes - the rulers of this game meet to confer and decide. They are without hearing distance, so I cannot make out what their standpoints and arguments might be. Scott as well as Rob have invested tremendously, both aiming at having as many clients out of their team on the summit - being this close - just 900 altitude meter and at best 12 hours from the pinnacle of their visionary. I assume weather window speculations and the pressure on Scott and Rob to utilize this potential opportunity to push for the summit before too many on their climbers lose the necessary strength to actually climb for the summit by resting up high is intermingling. Both expedition leaders might also have calculated with just one summit push when storing oxygen.

The oxygen available for us at Camp 4 is minimal. Nine Zveda canisters reserved for sleeping on the night before our summit bid, as they are heavier than the 53 Poisks canisters allotted for our May 10 climb. We have six climbing Sherpas on our team and five of them planning to climb with oxygen. Our leader, Sirdar of the climbing Sherpas, Lopsang will climb without supplemental O2, which reduces the stress on our limited supply. At no time do I expect the Sherpas' to assist us while climbing. Their job is to support logistics and for some of them the opportunity to climb to the summit is a special favor and a reward that will secure their income for the years to follow. Any Sherpa would help a climber in trouble to the extent possible. But they are not salaried or have respect for saving white climbers, who do not prove themselves strong enough to be on the mountain. Sherpas seem to have their own unspoken ethical code of conduct when faced with life and death situations. They respect those who are strong, survivors and will not and should not be expected to risk their own lives trying to save those who jeopardize their own and the lives of others by venturing into terrain where only the strongest self-responsible and self leading individuals has what it takes to survive. They will never let you detect whether they consider you strong enough or the contrary. I assume they leave the judgment to their Mother Goddess of the Earth, Everest itself.

Lopsang will carry one oxygen canister for emergency purposes; the remaining five Sherpa each carry two canisters for their own use on the climb and are ferry an additional two canisters per person, for our consumption on the way down from the summit. In total our Sherpas' carry 22 bottles from Camp 4 up to our depot along the summit route. We each carry two bottles and Anatoli proceeds with one for emergencies: 17 bottles of oxygen. Totally our expedition carries 38 Poisk canister, which leaves 15 full Poisk canisters and whatever little is left of the Zvesdas we slept on till now. It is a slim margin of safety and certainly not enough for us to just wait 24 additional hours to see if the weather complies with our ambitions. It is now - in three hours to night - or not at all.

Scott probably also wants' the huge pressure of leading an expedition of this magnitude over and done with and with no casualties. Actually "Everest" is the first time in our acquaintance that he seems to truly take mature responsibility for the entire operation, surprisingly startling and to some extent disrupting. No climbing expedition that preceded our summit bid has reached the top probably because high winds have been raging up high since midday. Anatoli senses that no attempt should be made under the current weather conditions, but Scott and Rob do not include the more experienced Russian in their consultations nor do they confer with Rob Hall's guides or any of us. The stakes are high and the weather questionable. There is no evidence of an extended period of calmer weather. "Do I follow Scott and Rob's decision whatever it might be? It is my choice. Mine alone and I have to live with the consequences of my resolution, whatever it will be." Expedition leaders and us climbing, individuals dealing with high risk might be susceptible to overconfidence that can lead to an unwillingness to "cut one's losses. Without some degree of high self-confidence, no one would be able to climb Everest. When you're up here, you've spent years of training, months of preparation and weeks of climbing and at long last you're within grasp of the summit. In the back of your mind, you're telling yourself. "I will turn around, if we're late, otherwise I'm going to run out of oxygen." You see the summit and it draws you there. It's so magnetic that climbers tend to break or forget about their guidelines and go for the summit and, on a good day, you can get away with it. If you are not lucky, you'll die.

Scott and Rob's unanimous conclusion spreads like a steppe fire from tent to tent: "We'll start getting ready for the summit bid at 11:00 pm. if the weather remains calm, final departure time at 11:30 pm." That leaves us approximately one hour to doze before the unwieldy, uncomfortable drag of getting into our climbing harness and boots again. Can't help but admire Scott's decision. This kind of high stakes gambling must be what has gotten him to summits so many times. I would have chosen a wider margin of safety and waited below for more stable conditions just like the IMAX expedition choose by ascending yesterday. Practical for them though as well, as our expedition will be the first to climb to the summit and fix whatever ropes needs fixing. It is reducing risks of exposure when you climbing in the wake of other expeditions. Tonight the weather risk must seem acceptable for Scott and Rob. Each climber client now has an individual decision to make. I want to summit and have no more scruples. Apparently, nobody else has either, as I see no one take off towards Camp 3 during the moonlit clear bright hours approaching midnight May 9/10:
remaining loyal to our quest.

Loyalty is "the willing, practical and thoroughgoing devotion of a person to a vision". Loyalty is comprehensive in that it is not simply a casual interest but a wholehearted commitment to a cause. Social psychology provides a partial explanation for the phenomenon of misplaced loyalty to an imprudent or misguided cause; people usually stick to their vision even though reality has changed for the worse. Our plan is to leave at midnight, if the weather remains settled, offering no further disrupting complications. Moving on the recommended flow rate we can reasonable expect to be at the summit in 11 to 12 hours. Adding a minor pause somewhere on the route - it should take us 12-14 Hours to approach the summit around 12-13 o'clock May 10. Scrambling upwards for the next 12-14 Hours and arriving at the summit within the allotted timeframe will leave 1-2 Hours of oxygen in my bottles when I set foot on the highest point on this globe.

From the summit, assuming favorable weather conditions and no unexpected surprises, it will take me approximately one hour to descend to the South Summit. Here each of us will pick up the third canister of oxygen our Sherpas' have carried up for our descend, leaving me six hours of O2 to climb back down to our tent and oxygen depot at Camp 4. Darkness befalls approximately 6:30 pm. We are acquainted with the fact being caught out and spending the night exposed to the elements above 8000 meters, is almost certain death.

More climbers die on their way down than on their way up, so we must be back in Camp 4 before sunset. Scaling Everest from Camp 4 to the summit involves more than 18 Hours non-stop exerting our resources that are stretched to the utmost before the outset. In addition none of us have eaten or slept properly since before arriving in Camp 3 during the afternoon on May 8.

22

"The saddest people I've ever met in life are the ones who don't care deeply about anything at all. Passion and satisfaction go hand in hand, and without them, any happiness is only temporary, because there's nothing to make it last."

Nicholas Sparks

    The New Zealand team, lead by Rob Hall, consists of 15 members and is assisted by guides Mike Groom and Andy Harris. Andy is a professional mountain guide from New Zealand, certified by the International Federation of Mountain Guides Association: the highest credential a mountain guide can achieve. Andy has extensive experience with cold and harsh climates from Antarctica and the New Zealand mountain ranges. He is 32, soft spoken and physically imposing. He seems to be a fun-loving, strong guy and the sort of person who makes everybody around him feel that they are in safe hands. Andy was starting to really perform well as a high-altitude guide and he has the affection and respect of the other members of their team. He has no altitude experience though and is making his first Everest summit attempt tonight.

    From Camp 4, we will begin our summit push in less than two hours at around midnight, with hopes of reaching the summit (still another 1,000 meters above) within 10 to 12 hours. We should first reach "The Balcony" at 8,400 m (27,600 ft.), a small platform where we can rest and stare at the curve of the horizon, if we have the courage to take at peak in the early light rays of dawn. Continuing up the ridge, we are faced with a series of imposing rock steps, which usually forces climbers to the east into waist deep snow, a serious avalanche hazard. At 8,750 m (28,700 ft.), a small table-sized dome of ice and snow marks the South Summit. During our final 14-hour push to the summit, survival is to no small degree; a race against the clock. Ideally, if we begin our summit attempt at 12 am, we should reach the summit between 12 and 1 pm and head down soon after. In climbing teams, we typically establish turnaround times that represent chronological reminders for when we ought to abandon our fixated exertions to reach the summit and begin our descent towards more secure grounds. We know from previous Everest expeditions that they have aimed for turnaround times ranging from a conservative 12 noon to a risky 2 pm. It's 23.30 and pitch dark. Silence and only the familiar sound of my buddies' organizing their oxygen bottles, crampons and the first summiteers departing for the unknown, taking off into the starlit bright darkness, finally mobilizing ourselves for our long pursued summit bid. As usual, I am slow at getting myself mobilized and consequently late in leaving the tent. It took me 1½ Hour to pull myself together to get out of the comforting warm cocoon of my bulgy sleeping bag and into my down suit and Everest One Sport boots. It's taxing on all levels to perform the simplest tasks. It seems to take forever, like moving in slow motion.

I watch my contemporaries on Rob Hall's team, forming a glittering string of glowing pearls, leading up the glaciated terrain into the dark void. As planned they are ½ an hour ahead of us. Realizing my team is about to leave camp, my oxygen deprived brain grasp the urgency, as I am now on my own, but for one person crawling out of our second high camp tent. It must be Scott. I hurry towards him; grinning noticing his summit down suit is dark blue and shows clear signs of wear. I want to be able to recognize him by his colors when we are on the move.

"Hi Scott, are we running on two oxygen bottles from now on?"

I have forgiven him on his intrusion upon my wish to summit without using supplemental oxygen last week. Since I first accepted Scott's invitation of climbing Everest with him, I've wanted to summit without using supplemental oxygen. Scott has continuously supported my pristine ambition of pursuing Everest in the simplest and most genuine manner. Last week Scott cooped me and gave me an ultimatum, "You either utilize oxygen on the summit bid or you do not climb at all". I hated him for his pronouncement. I sensed his confrontation was not based on my capacity as tested and exposed on the mountain, but much more an expression of his despairing need to get this expedition over and done with. His disloyalty towards our common planning of me summiting without O2 truly pissed me off. I withdrew into my tent, for the first time in this entire process for a split second contemplated abandoning the whole spectacle. It was only until a mental picture dawned in front of me of a huge delicious lollipop in one hand, exchanged by a smaller in the other.

Whining and inwardly protesting and contesting his authority, I unsurprisingly decided to take on the offer of the smaller lollipop and at no point since have I looked back or regretted not being endorsed to attempt my summit bid without O2. My flamboyant laughing exchange with Scott reinforces my acceptance and vaporizes long buried grudges. "Yeap! Scott grins back and we exchange our "Good Lucks". I hug him tight and long, before I sort of astronaut slog in direction of the diminishing row of headlamps. I must stick with my team and not fall behind.

What happens next enters the folklore of the copious myths spinning around the regions and creatures trespassing unto the highest mountain on earth. Every person provides a dissimilar narrative. Sagas shaped by oxygen deprived entities and the transforming process of psychic adaptation and time passed. Now I truly am venturing into the unknown: my first happenstance with Mother Nature and myself above 8,000 meters. Initially I pass over an almost level patch of rock slate and ice, characterized by scattered oxygen bottles and shredded remnants of discarded tents. After 5-10 minutes the human debris begins to diminish. Cast offs from former Everest seekers seem to mark the favorite spot for us climbers to establish a thin community of feeling sheltered at South Col. I detect nothing but crystal hard blue ice for my crampons to negotiate in the midnight darkness. Steep, up heaved blue ice slates. Crevasses ubiquitously and frozen traps hard to spot in the obscure gloom. Excitedly I am catching up with the rear headlamps of the looters leading upwards and I feel safer for now, embedded within the sheer numbers of my team. Klev, Neal, Sandy, Tim, Charlotte, Martin and where is Anatoli? My guiding token. Located - there he is, lingering in the proximity of our cluster, a steep ice face leading us upwards. One fall here and you are.... No, keep your wandering thoughts in check; do not give in to fear. Concentrate on one step at a time, focus on whoever is in front and I permit myself to be drawn into the false sensation of feeling secure, cocooned by the safety in numbers.

When are we encountering the fixed ropes? I have grown accustomed to clipping unto these "safety lines" dangling in the riskiest sections of Everest and here, where the climbing is truly precarious, we have none. Ron Hall's and our strongest Sherpas' have it as their main objective to constantly be ahead of us by at least a day, fixing ropes for paying clients and whoever else is here to summit, to clip unto. We fix ahead of our surging crowds to avoid the "Bottlenecks" that might cause unwanted delays, if we wait in line on the most arduous sections. This causes the whole caravan to slow down and stop, risking lives by not adhering to the "Speed equals safety in the mountains", even more accentuated here on the highest mountain in the world. Our survival is intimately bonded with our ability to ascend and descend fast enough, while we still have oxygen available in our canisters.

We are running on borrowed time: irreversible parameters that control our very existence. How thoroughly silly of me! On other mountains, I would never have allowed myself to grow psychologically dependent of fixed ropes. However, here I have conditioned myself out of the added emotional strain of being the lead climber, breaking trail and leading the route. Anyway I am satisfied with the fundamental set-up here on Everest. After all - I am a Novice and it is the first time I attempt to scale this huge thing and it sure does take some getting used to.

At long last, a snow spear with orange line attached. I breathe; exhale, relieved and clip on to this navel cord, guiding my every step upwards and upwards and upwards. Even sucking on O_2 to counter agonizing dawdling movement is excruciating.

Upwards, high, high and guess what, climbing to the top of the world involves a ton of upward steps. How could that be a surprise? My orange attachment only takes me 50-75 meters and then I am on my own again, unattached to any crutch to feel secure. Confronted with what I ingenuously yarned for: motoring in the "Death Zone" on my own volition and choice. Holy Moly! How am I to descend this section in the distant future of late afternoon with so many hours yet ahead of me and how exhausted might I be? Focus; do not think ahead. Focus on one step at a time. I pass Yasuku where our team is catching up with the front sluggers, consisting of Rob Hall's team members and we circumvent them, still adhering to each other in our group. I spot Anatoli, slightly behind us - green down suit – with no oxygen mask. Lopsang is distinctly recognizable in his white Sherpa outfit on top of his down gear. What's that in his pack? A Flagpole? Interrupted by coughing spells Lopsang manages to convey that he and Scott have planned a terrific stunt for when they reach the summit on Everest. I can't tease out of him what it's all about.

Lopsang is vomiting again, but nobody reacts, not even me. How long have we been on the move, climbing and dragging our carcasses upwards? One hour? Two? Our team schleps themselves over a wall requiring mixed climbing, at snail's pace. Wish I also had the sticky glue that secures the snail from tumbling to its death on its vertical adventures. I detect fear- fear of falling- anxious about how on earth I am imagining descending this death trap. At times, I crawl toddler style, on all fours, just to have as much friction through contact with the steep rocky foundation as possible. I will admit, I am not growing fond of free climbing at this altitude but I choose to carry onwards through doing and moving as necessary as I come more to my senses.

Acknowledging that trying to climb to the top of the world is in truth extremely real and excruciatingly hazardous, which is exactly what compelled me to want to attempt to scale Mount Everest; overtaxing, demanding beyond imagination is exactly what this ordeal ought to be. If today turns out to be a mere "walk in the park," Mother Goddess will profoundly disappoint me. She must not and until this second, she does not.

The supreme about mountaineering and climbing is that you cannot diminish what it takes, can't bereave it of its value and can't get away with "That it's probably not that steep, not that risky and not that fatal in reality. Those who climb just give an inflated imagery, in their pursuit of standing apart, delusional by grandiosity." Mountains are real. They are dangerous and exceedingly demanding. They reveal who and what you truly are and what you can and cannot do. They disclose to you, who others are and how they conduct themselves. They confront you with the fundamental randomness of existences and the inequalities you are powerlessly victimized by. By not acknowledging the actual price of wanting Everest, by diminishing what it takes, we reject our envy, neglect contemplating what we truly desire from life, distancing ourselves from our lack of balls as well as network to pursue the adventures we might deep down dream about for ourselves.

Mountaineering is true to its projection, not inflated sales talk. An arena that consumes everything you have in you and more, if you want to participate in this existential game. It exposes you while teaching you about your limitation, learning to accept what it craves to grow, expand your potential through risk taking and investing heavily in becoming better at what you are doing by doing more of it. It helps you to become a better version of yourself. Shortcuts are not available. Accepting hard won experience is the route to bigger adventures, just like in any other venue of existence. Mount Everest is for real. Nothing changes especially for you, no matter what you are accustomed to in horizontal life. No special treatment. Up here, we are all exposed to equal terms. Everest plays us by the same rules whether we are women, men, Russian or Danish. Mount Everest simply doesn't care. It is up to you and random luck; simple and brutal. Take it or leave it.

    I am willing myself upward. The 848 meters to the summit will crave at least an additional 12 Hours arduous physical investment. No cause for false hope just yet and for that matter the numerous hours ahead. At about 5.3o am., three members of our team reach the beginning of a long narrow ridge running between 27,200 and 28,000 ft. known as the Southeast Ridge Balcony and avalanche prone without a doubt. We come to a halt, doubt induced, taking an unplanned yet much desired break and fixed safety ropes are not secured beyond this point. All three expeditions, The New Zealand, US and Taiwanese team intermingle, as we pacified by the daunting task ahead, waiting for somebody other than ourselves to work out, who has the courage as well as rope at hand to secure the line that will improve the safekeeping of the next steep traverse of our climb. And in addition, lead us to our first oxygen depot.

    Our inactiveness creates the first of several bottlenecks that occurs in the course of our climb. Suddenly out of the lifting early morning dusk, we detect Lopsang on the cliff on the other side of the snowfield where he is placing an orange beamer, a directorial buoy in the white and one lightening oxygen canister, waiting in the snow to guide us. I set out on my long traverse towards the orange focus, fighting against the snow, sinking into my hips at places.

The traverse forces me to stop and await my breath, several breathing stops to cross. Fuck! I must negotiate this snow hell again while descending. F U C K! One misplaced foothold, snow slide and it's "Good Bye." Pull yourself together... Up on the ridge the first rays of sunlight, gleams through the diminishing darkness and I envision a lot of tiny colorful specks scattered around on a rocky outcrop in the middle of an ocean of snow. Is it birds? Can't be at this altitude, nothing lives up here. Hallucinations? Human beings? The sun begins to gain momentum, cloudless, clear blue sky: a panoramic view, literally over Nepal and the adjoining mountains below me. Anxious to take in the fabulous scenery, not daring to gaze around and especially down - really. It is simply to overwhelmingly big and too far down. I am in the "Death Zone", the fuller impact hammering into my awareness. Withdraw into the mental safe haven of "Tunnel vision", not to become paralyzed by the magnitude of what I am placing myself in the mercy of. Lamed through the Grandiosity, the madness and the surreal fact "I am here! F U C K! I am in fact climbing towards the top of the world! It is so grand and scary!" I thoroughly and completely comprehend how people die up here. Here is more to die - than to live off.

The tiniest bit of snow or deteriorations in weather conditions will make this death trap snap with immediate effect. No margin for error. Here there is no safety margin; none whatsoever. After hours of hard, physical effort, I have fallen into a familiar trance. I'm moving instinctively - not thinking, not feeling, not reflecting - just moving and occasionally checking the bubble in the hose to see if the oxygen is flowing as it ought to. Carabiner onto the fixed rope and Jumar is on the next length of rope. Which rope looks the least aged? I almost don't care. Upward. How will I get down these steep, yellow sheets of rock safely? Onward. A snow ridge, could that be the summit up ahead? I can see some rock formations and try to force my brain to remember what the summit looked like in all the photographs I've studied.

What did it look like on the video Scott made in 1994? Can't use the images anyway, for the amount of snow constantly changes the appearance and contours of the mountain. Slowly upward, gasping for breath. My poor lungs are panting like crazy. I hope they can cope with the overload. My breathing has adapted to the environment: rapid and not very deep. I pause and then move onward and upwards. Our team sticks together. We move at an almost identical pace. Then we stop, some down suits are gathered in a small hollow and five to ten bulky crouching persons are sheltered a little from the rising winds and with a view of the Western Cwm a mile and a quarter below. I will myself to sit down, hammering my crampons solidly into the snow, not to slide out of the hollow and a long tumbling way down. I can decipher the South Summit; it certainly helps recognizing specific features in the landscape and get to an upright position.

There is the Hillary Step! It's probably 11 or maybe noon. It seems I have lost track of time. It's is cold and I am tired. Tim helps me check the oxygen content of my bottle. It's damn hard work to take off the backpack up here. You have to untangle yourself from the hose connecting the bottle to the mask, control the gauge and then run through the whole procedure in reverse. I appreciate the help from Tim. "Almost empty", he reports. Must think now, from here to the summit and back again, how many hours? Three to five? Probably at high flow rate and the hardest climbing is still ahead of us. I've got to find a full bottle of oxygen among those lying scattered around us here. Off course, it must be one of those belonging to us. It's unthinkable to take one from Rob's cache.

Nobody has been on the summit ridge this season; therefore, there are no fixed ropes, only the shreds that have survived past years summit attempts. The remaining expeditions at Base Camp supported our two teams' summit bid. Whoever climbs first, will make it easier for all those coming up after us this season, if we fix new ropes, just as we are using the fixed lines left by our predecessors'. I stare athwart the cornices, haphazardly shielding the solid ridge somewhere underneath, towards Tibet and observe fixed ropes from previous years expeditions, dangling in open space, spanning an almost vertical drop of two to three kilometers, like high voltage telephone wires, 30-50 feet below me. The faded, shredded lines emerge from the snow wall in one place and disappear again through another whole into obscurity. I wonder if I could manage to grab hold of one if I slipped and fell…..

Everything and everybody seems to have come to a stop, the entire locomotion dwindling into inertia. Voices are being raised - a little desperately - debates back and forth - attempting to figure out whose job it is to take the lead and fix lines on the next pitch of steep traverse and consequently, who will be the rope fixer on Hillary Step? Neal exclaims that it ought to have been taken care of already, but obviously, no one did. Who has rope? Who has stakes? Nobody. More feverish gesticulation. Anatoli sets out, followed by Neal and somebody in a blue down suit from Rob's team, who suddenly shoots ahead with a rope on his arm. Who is that? He doesn't seem okay. I huddle in a crouching position, freezing in the rising wind. Charlotte, Tim and I agree to stick together. Charlotte is honest, "I simply don't like this situation."

I watch Anatoli with deep respect. The Russian man climbs deliberately up the Hillary Step, a fly at nearly 28,900 feet above sea level, his years of mountaineering experience expressed in his assurance. No frustration, no anxiety, no words, no desire for admiration and praise. Anatoli does what needs to be done. And does it well! I hold my breath until he has scaled the stretch safely, but know he won't slip. He is too good.

There are no sufficient feet of rope to secure us and no usable old ropes as they are covered by the winter snowfall and impossible to pull out. The first stretch on the ridge is an extremely exposed traverse - spooky - like walking a tightrope in a strong wind. Knowing there is no rescue if you stumble, if the crampons catch your trouser leg, if the ice axe's grip isn't good enough. I start out, I have to turn back to return to the imaginary security of the hollow which feels so protected in comparison with the exposure on the traverse, I just detest traverses. I must think. Is the summit worth this kind of risk? If I slip and slide, I'm dead. I can turn around here and venture down towards camp 4 as others have.

The wind has picked up and I can see the snow drifting across the summit ridge. Here there is absolutely no safety beyond my own capabilities. How unscrupulous do I want the summit? I contemplate what it will feel and be like when I return home, what will I feel every single time I envision the Summit Ridge and Hillary Step in my mind, being forced to face and acknowledge my defeat. Ones more packed down by my inner fear I think of my assurance and promises to my sponsors, who have contributed to the financial puzzle of my present venture. I ponder on what alluring possibilities and options I will miss out on, if I turn back now, as I have previously abandoned my ambitions on lower peaks countless times.

   I am bursting with this burning desire to get to the top of the highest mountain in the world; I am so close. I want to be the first Danish woman to reach the summit of Mount Everest. I know I have the experience to scale and negotiate the next pitch, to realize that it's only old fears that paralyze me, to recognize that I harbor the resources and mindset to break through old limiting patterns and socialized dysfunctions. I want to summit at whatever cost, so I get up and once more initiate the traverse on my way to the top of the world.

   I'm climbing like a novice; stiff, ungraceful, unsteady, and staggering and therefore, a real hazard to myself. Lopsang observes me. He has never seen me in this state before. My sweet friend takes my hand, which helps, even though I know it's more dangerous for us to move like this, than if he hadn't. After barely a few steps, I am an adult again. The paralysis disappears and my body moves fluently anew. In goes my ice axe with the shaft pointing down. I hold on to the blade and have better support than without it. Lousy axe for climbing, what was Scott thinking of when he recommended this particular lightweight aluminum model? Has he forgotten what it's like up here? Aluminum featherweight is great if you only have to consider weight, which is crucial off course, but it is so light that I cannot arrest myself with it. I would have felt much better with a long-handled classical axe. Well, next time I have more experience and will trust my own know-how instead of taking advice from someone else. I move up across the snow ridge. Every time I pull the axe out of the snow cover below my crampons,

I make a tiny peephole through which I can see down into Tibet - here is next to nothing to balance on, but we keep doing it. It's like walking on a cloud really. I trust myself again and begin to enjoy the madness of being so close to the top on a dangerous stretch of climbing towards the pinnacle of the world. I can make it. I have what Everest takes.

While climbing, I am fully immersed in a feeling of energizing focus and comprehensively involved as well as fused with delightful enjoyment. I am thoroughly absorbed in and by what I carry out: supreme focused motivation.

Climbing is a single-minded absorption and perhaps represents the ultimate experience in harnessing ones emotions in the provision of performing and transgressing everything you know about yourself and your former capabilities. Emotions are contained, disciplined and positively channeled, physically you become energized and 100% aligned through this challenging task. I experience the activity as intrinsically rewarding: the sublime merging of action and awareness. I am in the universe of FLOW, with an intense and attentive concentration on the present moment. I lose reflective self-consciousness: a sense of personal control. Even though my distortion of temporal experience is obvious as my subjective experience of time is altered, I am permeated by the conviction that I have the potential to succeed. I am so engrossed in this experience, that all other needs become negligible. I feel spontaneous joy, I have profound focus on nothing but moving, not even on my reflections or myself.

23

"To the summit and safe return"
Lene Gammelgaard

I am on the top of the world. By climbing Everest I live my wildest dreams, not because of what it will prove or get me, but because it is all I want. I am transcended by an immense calming all-encompassing and identity altering sensation of massive, profound inner peace. Something within: deep-seated self-reflections, self-doubts and judgments, conflicting focuses and complexities of a multifaceted personality characterized by internal struggles fall into place.

SERENITY!

I am who I am because I am.

20 minutes of complete and all-encompassing bliss stressed by an ever louder non-negligible reminder from my survival instincts. This might be the top of the world but that's the very reason, why you have to get yourself up from your butt position

and get into gear before time invested in enjoying the exhilarating fact, steals away the last of your already exhausted resources. I hurry to catch up with the others, who have pointed the tips of their crampons downwards. No way am I to be alone up here. I am thoroughly grateful that our group is truly watching out for each other today. I will not drop behind. I need to stick with the others. What! it looks as if Klev is helping somebody across at the South Summit, or are they taking a break? Down, down, keep your balance - most of my fellow climbers who perish on Everest do so on the descent. "To the summit and safe return," my subconscious mantra is supposed to kick in now and take over. The ultimate strategy of my self-programming is to keep me alert and alive all the way back down to Base Camp; nobody wants to hire a dead climber. I might create history if I perish now, but I sure desire to bask in the aftermath of having been able to summit. Set your crampon precisely, place the ice axe and take just one step. Reposition yourself, don't hurry, and don't get sloppy with details. Clip into that bit of weather-beaten rope and get down the Hillary Step.

I made it.

I fucking made it!

I have just climbed the highest mountain on earth. Now I just have to survive the hours to the South Col and to our tent at Camp 4, then to Camp 3…..Descend, down, down past the traverse where I had to stop and reconsider on my ascend. Now I hardly recognize it - doesn't seem as steep from this angle. Next - our oxygen cache. How is my oxygen situation? The monitor shows almost empty, just as planned.

Lene Gammelgaard First Scandinavian Woman to summit Everest May 10 1996

I am running low on O2 and must remember to change to a full bottle to get me through the next 6 Hours...How many of us are up here? Are there enough cylinders for all of us? How many full or not completely empty canisters? Shifting through bottles, disarray, I check several bottles in our pile, empty, almost full, full - here's no system any longer.

Detailed planned and meticulous order has dissolved into chaos, I am wasting valuable minutes, losing track of time. I exchange my oxygen bottle. The content of this new partly full oxygen canister will hardly be sufficient for me to reach the South Col, but the further down I manage to climb, the safer I will be. Therefore, down is mandatory. I clip onto the ancient deteriorating fixed ropes from those who were here years in advance of me.
Better than no ropes at all. Rounding the curve of the rocky cave, and POW! Shit! Full gale-force winds and knee-deep fresh snow. Shit! This is serious.

The cloud cover I observed from the summit must have been a snowstorm building up further down and we are heading right into it. We are heading down into a full-scale storm on the highest mountain in the world. The only path towards safety is through. Snow falling reduces my visibility by each slippery step and it's almost impossible to distinguish the terrain under my feet. I know from winter randonne' skiing that it can be impossible to detect what is up and down when a complete white out engulfs you. Everest is notorious for countless accounts of mountaineers descending in snowstorms with close to no visibility - not being able to see what is below and disappearing of the side - falling to their deaths far below. Extremely difficult to distinguish solid footing from the ever present free falls to either side of the ridge we attempt to negotiate with impaired vision and insecure footing, as we cannot be certain weather we place our boots in snow or air.

Tim rises to the occasion - being who and what he is - his decisiveness indications of what stuff he's made of. One of the unsung heroes', never displaying his true humble strength, but when it's spoken for like now he is calm and deliberate, proving himself capable of responding superbly, whenever the situation and circumstances get truly critical. Charlotte is a lucky woman. I wear large expedition gloves, huge bulgy paws, thwarting my descent; I'm on the fixed rope and hurry down after Charlotte and Sandy. Tim is right behind me. What? Sandy splashes in front of me and just collapses in the snowdrift. More dread, I cannot detect if we are descending into the storm or the storm is moving up to consume us. Clouds and snow rolls around us, engulfing the route, as we knew it, visibility and movability shrinking by the second. Sandy doesn't want to move and just sits there like a giant yellow panda. "If you don't pull yourself together right now, you will die!" Charlotte unzips her down suit, finding the emergency kit Dr. Ingrid gracefully and knowingly distributed to each of us and gives Sandy the shot of Dex just as prescribed and rehearsed, in Sandy's feather clad buttock, right through her clothes and the whole caboodle. It helps a bit, Sandy stirs. We confer, yelling to overtrump the roaring wind because by now it is clear that we are descending down into bad weather: the snow intensifies, the wind speeds up, new snow covering the terrain and route finding becomes increasingly harder.

    We double check Sandy's oxygen canisters and discover she has had the flow rate yanked up on 5 instead of the 3 which is necessary to adhere to, so as not to run out of oxygen before we are back at South Col. As a consequence Sandy's oxygen bottle is completely empty. Does this woman not realize that Everest is for real? That this is not an American movie, where someone comes and rescues her, when things turn really nasty?

I am stronger than Sandy and I exchange my full canister for Sandy's practically empty bottle. I hurry on. I want down and it is late. I clip my karabiner onto the rope leading down across yellow sheets of rock.

Where there was naked stone five hours ago, there is now a covering of seemingly bottomless snow, like slippery, sucking, brown soap. This snow is scary, like quicksand under my feet. Though I can no longer see very far, I know that there is a drop-off to our left and that hope the fixed ropes can stand the weight of our bodies because we have all clipped in. Neal has taken hold of Sandy, willing her to descend and she doesn't seem to be all together - or is she? At least she is moving with the rest of us. To let her sit where she collapsed will be equivalent of leaving her to the slow scrutinizing process of freezing to death. We do what has to be done, stick together and proceeds down into the incessantly severing whiteout.

Strange impossible snow, I never experienced conditions this weird. I quickly discover it's not possible to glissade upright in this snow, so I do as children do, nearing my core of gravity to the ground not to lose control and stumble, I sit down on my ass and slide down Mount Everest.

Whenever my speed threatens to get out of hand, I lean against the fixed rope with my whole body and try to brake a little with the karabiner. If the fixed rope snaps, I'm done for. No chance my lightweight aluminum summit axe will be able to arrest in this loose snow, no hard surface underneath for the tip to grip unto... We stagger, fall, crawl, swim, slide our way down the mountain. Our worst nightmare is materializing around us - foul weather! Shear survival now. I keep losing track of time, descending in the haze of whirling snow crystals, it seems like it's taking forever to get down. Neal is fighting to save Sandy and is having trouble navigating her as well as himself. Charlotte, Tim and I are in fine shape - considering... in the course of a few hours, we get down to the spot where we took a break coming up in the opposite direction almost 12 hours ago, at sunrise in superb conditions.

    I gaze towards my climbing buddies, breaking off the ice that keeps forming around my mouth as it condenses from my exhale, instantly freezing when it leaves the warmth of my body and gets in contact with the dropping temperature up here. Neal is steadfastly with Sandy. Tim and Charlotte are sticking together, looking out for each other and doing fine. I am descending faster than the rest of my team, even climbing without oxygen as Sandy has gotten my last bottle and not feeling hampered by not having oxygen available. I slide down the deepening snow layer and detect a human contour; somebody is sitting on the route in front of me, Klev. I hurry in an attempt to join him. I encounter my hero of the highs as Klev is taking a short break. Good for me, otherwise I would not have been able to catch up with him. He is preparing to descend the rocky flank leading directly down towards camp 4. In fair weather, it would take no more than one and a half to two hours to get back to relative, temporary safety and protected from the hostile elements: our tents at South Col. Who knows how long in these conditions. We set in motion directly down the snow flank, where there's high risk of avalanches - accident prone angle of the terrain - even more so now with the snow falling and piling up. My organism is running on fumes, almost finished, exhausted, no food or drink since when? Yesterday afternoon? It feels like an eternity. Weary, exhausting, grueling, lethargic, so slow, slow motion, I start to struggle to keep moving.

Shit! I'm out of oxygen.

"Stop, Lene. Oxygen! Breathe deeply and keep breathing. Take some more!" Klev takes one glance in the direction of my exposed mouth and immediately insist we share his oxygen mask, like deep sea divers, running short of sufficient equipment. Evidently, the sudden loss of my supplemental oxygen made me hyperventilate. Klev can see how blue my face is. Myself, I didn't notice anything. I didn't feel any different.

We work our way down Everest and Klev insists despite my protests on sharing his remaining oxygen with me and for some time he climbs down and I continue sliding on my ass. My down suit tears and the tiny white down creates its own snowfall. It doesn't matter now, a down suit can be replaced and I fell safest sliding down this way. It reduces the risk of stumbling to my death through sluggish footwork. Darkness sets around us and our visibility dwindles by the minute, going from truly bad to even worse as nightfall combines itself with increasing snow and howling winds. Sliding on my bottom, I at least reduce the risk of tripping over my own feet.

There's a fixed rope, so at least we are in a place on this humongous mountain, where living entities have been before us. Comforting, who's that in front of us emerging through the storm? Yasuku Namba, peculiar how one recognizes fellow human beings up here: body language and down suits, little inklings of clues as to whom we encounter ingrained in the most rudimentary parts of our brains, probably the ancient part of our brains that might function better than the civilized veneer under these brutal survival circumstances. It gives hope to see someone else. I am glad Yasuku is on her way down as well.

After following in her wake for a spell, Klev and I work our way around

Yasuku on the fixed rope and pass her. We were faster than most climbers on Rob Hall's team coming up and as it proves now, we are also faster coming down. Being a fellow woman, it's good to see that Yasuku is getting off the mountain in fair enough time, just so slow, that we decide to descend ahead of her, knowing that several from her team are still coming off the mountain. Me running against time, with no oxygen to keep me warm or lasting for long, I need to stay very focused. We are now on the icy bulgy slope leading down towards South Col and we do not dare to lose time and precious life sustaining resources. There is steep, glazed hard blue ice crevasses, distinguish ability shifting with the velocity of the storm. If we move too far off the fixed rope to our right, we risk falling 1, 5 kilometer down into Nepal, too far to the left; we would plunge 2.3 kilometer down the Kangshung Face into Tibet. Visibility is deteriorating, snow swirling, black spots dancing before my eyes; the roar of the storm distorts any sense of direction and the lack of oxygen affects my effectiveness.

Klev and I descend the last run of fixed ropes from 8,350 meters as Martin stumbles across Jon Krakauer further down our slippery route.

Neal, Tim, Charlotte and Sandy are above us about to descend from
8,350 meters. Neal who does not have visual contact with us finds Yasuku, "We encounter someone, hanging face down on the rope." Yasuku Namba is almost motionless, moving excruciating slow; we try to make her move with us." Neal assumes Yasuku is me, as we both climbed clad in red down suits. Neal starts yelling at the slumped figure, trying to get "me" up and moving, still believing it's me who is semi unconscious. Yasuku is not mowing, so Neal jiggles off her

oxygen mask, freeing her face from ice, trying to get a response, realizing it was not me, but Yasuku Namba from Rob Hall's expedition.

"She was not moving whatsoever," Beidleman says, "most likely out of oxygen. I tried to show her how to move down the line faster. After few minutes, I realized she either didn't understand English or was incapable of doing what I was asking her to do. I grasped her harness and started sliding, standing or rolling, depending on the terrain, down with her behind me. Several times her crampons went through my down suit and into my back. She seemed to be capable of understanding what was going on, but was incapable of physically helping the process much. We eventually got down to the bottom of the fixed rope after several times of falling into crevasses. I believe Tim helped me more than a few times in picking her up, throwing her, pushing her and pulling her over those crevasses."

Yasuku Namba had been climbing with Mike Groom higher up until they encountered Beck Weathers who was still waiting on the Balcony, where Rob Hall half a day ago, had told Beck to wait for his descent, because Beck got trouble seeing as he climbed up this morning. Who tells a person to sit still above 8,000 meters? It's equivalent to signing a death sentence. Why did Beck not move instead of trusting his life to a person, who was oblivious of the ground rules of surviving in the mountains?

Rob Hall as well as Beck must already have been suffering severely form the altitude at this early point of the summit bid, to form such hazardous strategies. Beck Weathers was still waiting for help, practically frozen to the cliff, where Rob had asked him to wait upon his arrival. New Zealand team member Beck Weathers was directed by Rob Hall not to descend before Hall returned from climbing to the summit. Fatefully ridiculous lack of accurate knowledge of the predicaments doomed to follow such a prolonged immobilization. Beck Weathers had at least two opportunities to descend with other climbers from his own expedition, but refused to go downhill because of his pact with the guide. He agreed to descend 12 hours later without Rob Hall, but only after assistant guide Groom, got permission from Rob Hall via radio. Jon Krakauer passed his teammate Beck, on his descent, apparently insensitive to the fact that Beck needed help and fast, after sitting immobile for approximately 10-12 Hours..

I guess it's probably close to 6:00 P.M, so we simply have to be off this hostile outlandish altitude. Neal, at 8,200 meters and within approximately 200 lateral meters of Camp 4 recalled when things went to hell. "At the bottom of the fixed line the storm had intensified. Periodically you could see a light at Camp 4. I got one last fix on the direction and that was it. That was the last I saw of Camp 4."

Darkness becomes almost impenetrable. My headlamp ran out of battery climbing upwards in the dark last night, I have a spare battery in my backpack, but neither Klev nor I consider it worthwhile to struggle with changing the battery right now. It might not function due to the dropping temperatures anyway. Just the process of removing my waterproof over mitten and the insulating mitten and risk frozen fingers even though I have protective gloves underneath the other layers, is just insurmountable hazards right now. The advantage of the headlamp is that you can see better within the field of the light beam; the disadvantage is that your eyes adjust to the light and you can no longer see the outlines of the landscape around you. For me it is a matter of weighing how best to find my way with or without a light. The beam seems to reflect off the snow, turning the whiteout into a snow wall. So for now, I manage better without.

"Klev, I think we should keep to the right at the couloirs, don't you see something there that could be the lights from camp?"

"Yeah, let's head for that."

We struggle downward. The whiteout gale-force gusts make it almost impossible to get our bearings. Every outline of the rock scape has been blotted out; fatigue and lack of oxygen does not help either. The roar of the storm prevents us from hearing any yells from Camp 4 and Klev and I are reluctant to tax our decreasing resources by crying out ourselves, fundamentally knowing that it would only be an act of panic and useless waste of resources we need to survive. We harbor no desire to become added to the numbers of mountain climbers who lose their orientation here and walk over the edge of the precipice on the Tibetan or the Nepalese side. Cool calm pervades us both. Survival   !

"What is that over there to the left?" Klev and I can feel the ground under our crampons becoming less steep. A sign we've probably reached the outskirts of the South Col and are down from the steepest descent. We're trying desperately to detect or recognize something, anything that will give us a hint of our camp's location. Why didn't anyone think of fixing ropes all the way down the steepest section? Rope ought to have been secured all the way to our camp. It's easy to be wise after the fact and all speculations of what ought to have been done isn't going to help us now anyway. We stop and struggle with the elements to talk about the most plausible strategy of finding our way back to camp, so that we don't end up as permanent yet famous post mortem inhabitants of the South Col.

"Quite a bit of light over there. But I think the camp is to our right."

"I totally agree."

Yet, still we decide to investigate some lights beams flickering close by, to our left and begin to scuffle through the incessant rising storm. It's enormously exhausting and focus demanding just to find foothold and will my boots to move one step forward in this lunar landscape.

The lights are our teammates: Tim, Charlotte, Neal and Sandy. Also two Sherpas' and two down suits, one of which I think is Yasuku Namba, the other is silent and we later we detect is Beck Weathers. Standing still will kill us so Klev and I decide to put our trust in the two Sherpas', who assumingly are most familiar with Everest; after all we are only guests in their universe. We defer to the Sherpa's experience as they have been here before. Therefore we choose to follow them through the darkness.

Searching for familiar terrain, they poke their ice axes down into the layer of virgin snow and examine what lies underneath it, rock, ice or nothing. How long do we all trail the Sherpas', a quarter of an hour? Half an hour? Longer, before we realize they are lost? It becomes evident that they don't seem to have the slightest idea where they are and they begin to stroll around in a bewildered manner, obviously without any apparent plan. It's very dark now, stormy, a blizzard really. If the Sherpas' can't find their way, it means the worst is happening. We are lost, lost in the Death Zone.

My methodical substantial life preserving brain programming is triggered. Isn't this what I have prepared myself for since I crossed the Atlantic when I was 18? Foreseeing with horror the worst imaginable scenario? Studying survivor's tales and amassing grueling insights, storing mental homework, accumulation of skills, seeking one rough experience in the mountains on top of my already survived encounters with nature, when it's showing its prongs and establishing the proper relation to the illusion that we can control everything in our modern context.

"Okay, what now? We need to stick together and agree on an action plan so we don't waste energy." I am permeated with a phrase I carry with me - my older brother trained as a fighter pilot in the army- and through his 196 stories, I learnt useful facts for climbing high: one being the sentence that now serves to keep me cool, as it is drilled into the brains of the pilots it's supposed to keep cool. The chant sounds like a joke, but it helps me stay calm in circumstances like this: "I am not lost; I just don't know where I am right now." My brother's experiences with oxygen deprivation have also drilled me towards acknowledging, that in these altitudes we believe we are acting like mature sound grown-ups, but reality is, that at best we function at the level of a five year old and that's on a grand day. Our capacity to perceive reality correctly is dramatically reduced without us knowing.

Klev and I agree, we hardly need words to discern what the other thinks, and we do what we consider most expedient. I leave it to Klev to communicate with Neal. Gender bias seems to be obstructing Neal's ability to pay heed to my contributions, so why bother trying? Calmness is the only mechanism that works in catastrophic circumstances.

We stagger around in the blizzard, the forces of wind so fierce we are thrown off balance. We begin to search the South Col, sticking together, holding on to whoever is nearby, not letting anyone wander off on his or her own, stick together and we will all have better chances of surviving. Yasuko is extremely scrawny, clearly on the verge of losing consciousness, but there is nothing any of us can do for her now, other than try, to the best of our ability, to get her to follow the rest of us. Neal has already done a great deed of bringing her this far down the mountain, as it seems no one from her own expedition managed to help her. One foot in front of the other, snailing our way into the gale with snowdrift so dense we cannot see. I can't perceive where I place my crampons, can't hear what someone is trying to yell, totally at the mercy of the forces of nature. We are engulfed at 8,000 meters at the highest mountain on earth. I can't detect any contours, it's hard to keep upright and I can't see anything or do anything. A little upward, a little downward, just dragging my crampons close to the terrain, escaping the danger of stepping into nothingness by sliding, not walking. It takes all I've got left in me just to stay remotely upright, let alone move my feet, hunching against the direction of the wind. Ice, rock, snow piling around every invisible outline, difficult and demanding terrain to move in, from one attempt to find camp to the next discourages hopes of rescue. We allow no one to sit down, to fall behind and give in to exhaustion and despair. We know immobility equals death here. Blizzard, hope of rescue, the unreality of this living nightmare, my deepest harbored fears come to life, making us exclaim again and again and again....

"There is light. I can hear voices." But again and again and again disappointment and disillusionment....The two Sherpa's we entrusted to lead us back to camp in our momentary belief in other than ourselves have disappeared stepping into the white wall of impenetrable crystals, stinging whatever skin is exposed. There is a giant monstrosity of snow threatening to engulf us. Where are they? The terrain under my feet is all wide of the mark: too much rock, too steep and wrong angle. Last night, when I started out, I was moving on blue ice, hard blue ice, now there's too little ice under my crampon spikes and too few oxygen canisters for our present position to be even in the vicinity of our camp area. Seemingly several of us simultaneously realizes we are heading towards the abyss of Kangshung Face and all we can see is snow, stinging and swirling before our eyes, in our eyes and the roar of the storm excluding exchange of words, deafening and disorienting. Based on experience we decide on emergency plan number two. We have rambled all over the place, staggering around and around, using crucial survival energy reserves in our vain search for our camp and relative safety from the pounding storm, that is threatening to blow us off our feet and so off the diagonal flat we try to decipher, to save ourselves and as many of our party as possible. Obviously, we haven't succeeded; on the contrary our disoriented attempts have led us into the unknown with danger lurking at literally every step. We are truly lost the next survival option and the best for the time being is not to waste further energy. Our best chance to stay alive is to find a hollow, a boulder, something, just anything that can provide us with the slightest shelter against the raging snowstorm, huddle together and watch for a break in the weather later tonight. Or worst case scenario, keep each other warm enough and awake so we stand a chance of surviving our night out on Everest, at least some of us....

I lie next to Klev - no - half on top of him. Klev has his one arm tugged securing around me. Neal and Tim are on our right. Up against my body, Sandy lies moaning, "I know I am going to die. My face and my hands are freezing off." Charlotte lies next to Sandy, lifeless. Charlotte had given up, letting go of her will to survive. A while ago, she expressed her despair, "Just let me be,

I just want to die in peace". Our yelling, hitting and bantering to keep everyone aware, disturbs her, drifting into the bliss of unconsciousness. A little further away in the darkness is the Yasuku bundle, toppled over and her companion, Beck Weathers, who have not expressed a sound or anything, since we hooked up what seems a whole night ago. A zombie, barely alive when we encountered him and now even further gone, motionless and unconscious, just lying there, dead still....

"Keep moving your hands and feet say something, shout, and keep the person next to you awake!" Neal, Klev and I take turns shouting, moving and hitting those who do not comply. Klev shakes me. I shake him and kick Sandy every few minutes. "Are you awake? You must not let yourself fall asleep. Hold out!" Sandy groans, "I just want to die."

Tim is nothing but amazing and fantastic. This soft-spoken humble sired guy does all the right things in the right way and takes care of everybody in the group. He is calm and deliberately in total control in spite of our terrifying circumstances. Neal tries to guide, but I sense what I interpret as fear underneath his words.

Full force gale, null visibility and fast-dropping temperatures as the night keep getting denser. It's even darker now as most of the headlamp batteries have given out. No one has any oxygen left in their tanks but we keep the masks on in spite of the ice that forms faster than we can remove it from the fluid in our breathing out. Yasuku's face resembles a block of ice and I can't see the other climber through the impenetrable blackness; maybe he already expired?

"Charlotte, are you awake." Tim shouts and shakes her mercilessly. Charlotte is lifeless. Snowdrift starts to pile up on top of Klev and me, we must shake it off not to end up just another contour in this moon like landscape. I get halfway up and brush most of the snow cover off. Snow crystals begin to penetrate my down suit, collecting in the seams and melting as it gets close to the core of my body soaking through my last armor, quietly, inevitably and lethal. Do I have enough stamina to remove my backpack? I debate with myself. The buckle broke on the summit, so the hip belt is tied around my waist, no way can I untangle that now with my huge mittens and under gloves on. I'd have to take off my expedition mittens and work the stiff knot loose with my bare hands. A climber never takes her gloves of, it's so easy to suffer frost bite in the deep freezer like, subzero temperatures, especially with high winds but it might be worth the risk, for at the bottom of my pack, I have my wind suit. That would keep out the gale force snow penetration, at least for a while…. but I'd also have to get my climbing harness off….and the two click on crampons…. I don't have strength for so much activity and the risk of losing a glove or… too huge…. I lie down again….

"Sandy, wake up. You are not going to die."

"My hands," the yellow suit next to my body whimpers,

"They're freezing off."

How tragic. Has Sandy reached the summit she aspired to manage for so long, just to die or end up maimed?

I fear for Yasuku and her bundle over there with absolutely no sign of life.

I am so cold, the marrow of my bones resembles chunks of ice and I cannot feel my fingers anymore. I listen to Sandy's moaning through the howling gale and blinding snowstorm, she seems to be hallucinating, babbling about a musician playing the violin and wanting to remove her clothes as she is so hot. "It hurts so much just let my die," she keeps repeating her pledge that neither Klev, Tim nor I want to comply with. Sandy's body still has a lot of strength left for survival, but she seems to have given up mentally and is slipping into unconscious pre death coma. We keep banging at her, yelling to keep her conscious and connected to life. Klev shelters me with his huge frame, trying to protect me as much as possible from the grueling storm gusts. I am unafraid. I am not lost; I just do not know where I am right now. Permeated by a white, strong feeling that this is not where I am going to die. I just instinctively know "I am not going to die. I am not going to die." Not a conscious will statement, but a calm, serene feeling making me do what has to be done - to prevent dying. How long have we been lying here?

I know I'm not going to die tonight. I just know it... I am not frightened. I comprehend the predicament we are in devoid of fear or panic. My turn has not come yet.... I am not going to breathe my last breath just yet......

I can still move my toes inside my huge lilac Everest One Sport Expedition Boots. I guess they are all right so far not frozen solid at least: bend- stretch, bend - stretch bend - on and on and on, relentlessly willing myself to preserve what can be preserved. My fingers are cold, so darn cold... I move them, one by one, beating them against each other, whenever I can to raise the energy needed. Bend, stretch... Damned gloves: not good enough for Everest. The outer mitten cover is stiff as a board, long frozen to ice. But it protects me against the gale. Try to stick the mittens under my armpits to protect my hands against the chill factors of this kind of storm. Too much snow collects making me still colder ... Bend, stretch...bend, stretch....

"Klev, are you awake?" Of course he is.

Tim works tirelessly. He and Neal try to get Charlotte and Sandy to sit upright, any tiny fragment of movement, the smallest sign of will to live rather than apathetic surrender. Yasuku stopped responding a while previously. She is blessed in a way, obscure to the excruciating intensity of experiencing your body freeze solid from the extremities towards the core.

Is the person bug led over next to her, deceased?

   I kick Sandy. Better to listen to her snivel; moaning and squeaking equals life.

"Sandy, check if Charlotte is conscious or kick her till she awakens." Bend, stretch, bend, stretch….

Lying across Klev, shaking uncontrollable from the life stealing cold, my teeth chatter in my mouth, I have never been this cold; the shaking is not of this world.

Bend, stretch, bend, stretch….make fists with my hands inside my mittens, move my toes… bend, stretch, bend stretch….

   How long have we been lying here… one hour, two hours? I don't know, but through our wordless communication Klev and I start rising to our feet, collecting what is very likely the last strength we have stored, reserved for ultimate survival. Instinctively, we know, without having to discuss that our only chance and consequently, the group's only chance to get us out of this predicament, is to perform the impossible right now; get up and find camp. Our last hope of surviving this nightmare…

Neal is of the same conclusion and just then, the weather Gods of Mother Goddess of the Earth look upon us with mercy. The gale and snowstorm pauses a split second, just long enough for a mountain massif to emerge out of the broil at our right. "I think I recognized a star." Neal regains a sense of direction from his knowledge of the fix points in the sky.

We, a trio, Klev, Neal and I stagger forward. Klev is trying to drag somebody. Yasuku? Charlotte? Yasuku....He can't lift her, he is not able to slip her either, nobody can carry anyone up here. Oh, my heroic friend has to let go. There is nothing this strong decent man can do to follow suit on his inclinations to do the decent thing. Klev must shake the person off his arm; otherwise he will die from trying. It takes everything we have left, just to keep hunching kind of upright enough to shoulder the storm and more than that, we have to move our feet. Sheer will: will to survive.

I am confronted with having to make those close calls, deciding to live or die from rescuing another fellow climber. I am a woman and therefore not strong enough to carry anybody, through my gender am freed from the burden of ever being confronted with - why didn't you? Nobody including myself ever embraces those expectations to one of my gender, but for a huge, strong man not to be able to save another.... That's a different psychological battle field all together. I am aware, alive and so cold. Without communication, we are fueled by the gruesome fact, that if we do not erect sufficient strength in ourselves to make a final live saving attempt to locate our high Camp, we will likely succumb in the Death Zone on Everest as so many have before us. Moreover, the others in our huddle will stand no chance of survival, if we do not get on our feet and start staggering around again, we must, plain and simple invent yet some more will to restore ourselves to relative safety, through finding Camp 4.

"I know where we are, and I know where camp is," Klev's voice is permeated with a sense of focus and the certainty in his movements make me believe he actually does. I follow; Neal is on my other side. He seems quite effected by the efforts he has donned to get Yasuku and Sandy off the mountain and the lack of oxygen. He's confused, yet struggles to remain in control. I just have to remain on my feet and not stumble. All my mental energy devoted to my next step and my next step, not stumble and disappear. Walk! Now I spot Everest to the right and Lhotse to my left.

"Klev, light! Ahead to the left....I'm quite certain."

"Klev, there is light from the Camp, we must turn left. It's there!" Combining our last resources and capacities, Klev, Neal and I struggle to remain on our feet in the gale-force whiteout. Focusing intensely whenever there is a slight opening in the snow drifts that blog out any contours and possibility for making a bearing, trying to get a glimpse of rock, oxygen canisters or any tiny fragment that will help our quest for survival. Then the tiny speck, just a glimpse, a trembling flicker of light through the white, roaring hopelessness: Anatoli's headlamp. "Sometime, about 6:00 pm., I understood I needed to go up again as none from our team had arrived back to camp. The weather was deteriorating above me, but at the South Col it was still okay, stronger and increasing wind, but okay."

Anatoli headed back up - to where the fixed ropes began at 8,200 meters. No more than ten to fifteen minutes walking distance from our two tents, the cloud cover that had been hovering above him engulfed the South Col. Simultaneously; a lateral gust of ice crystals propelled by wind of at least forty to fifty miles per hour began to bombard Anatoli. The sky changed suddenly from grayish to whiteout.

"I kept looking behind me to see if I could keep a bearing of Camp 4, I could see some people flashing lights - trying to guide the climbers who were still out, so I felt okay to continue my search. I moved unto some steep ice, understanding intuitively this was the right way to the fixed ropes, but the deteriorating visibility made them impossible to see. I was using my ice axe, being careful, understanding that if I moved too far off my course, I could slip and fall down the Lhotse Face."

An upward step would cause Anatoli to lose sight of the lights flashed at Camp 4. One step down would restore his connection with camp. Anatoli's life was tethered to a beam of light. To go any higher, to search any longer was foolish. Dead he wouldn't be able to help anyone.

"About thirty meters from the tents, my power was almost gone. I took off my pack, sat on it and put my head into my hands, trying to think, trying to rest. I was trying to understand the situation of the climbers. What is their situation, their condition? I am considering this. The wind is driving snow in to my back, but I am almost too powerless to move. How long I was here, I don't remember. It is here that I start to lose track of time, because I am so tired, so exhausted. Someone I do not know approached me out of the darkness and snow and he spoke with me as if I was his friend, but I did not recognize him. I thought maybe he was from the Taiwanese Expedition or from Rob Hall's team, but I was not certain, he asks, "Do you need help?" "No. It is okay." And so he told me he had to return to blinking the lights and I assured him I could make it back to my tent. After some time, I don't know how much, I found my tent, took off my pack and crampons, knocked the snow and ice off my boots and without any power crawled into the tent. It was empty. Nobody had come. Nobody."

A stone's throw away Lou Kasischke from Rob Hall's expedition, who had decided to turn around instead of summiting, was also alone. Andy Harris, Beck Weathers and Dough Hansen had not returned.

"I got back to camp about 4:30 or 5:00 pm," Kasischke recalls, "and I just collapse from exhaustion in my sleeping. I don't think I had a molecule of energy left in me. Later I awoke or regained consciousness and it was terrifying, the wind woke me up. It was just pushing me around inside my tent. It was actually getting under the tent floor, picking me right up in my sleeping bag and slamming me back down, whirling me around. I regained consciousness and I couldn't see! It was probably the worst moment of my life. I'm figuring it's eight, nine o'clock... I'm snow blind ... alone... my tent mates - nobody's there...This went on for hours. I couldn't figure out why I was alone. I was able to control my anxiety enough to know that I had to stick to my sleeping bag, if I try to do anything I was probably going to die. I yelled for help, but figured out nobody could hear anything. I mean, it was just like a hundred freight trains running on top of you and I was screaming, but you know, a person five feet away couldn't hear anything."

Martin Adams, after his glissade down behind Jon Krakauer, had picked up the last run of fixed ropes and had reached the end at 8,200 meters sometime after Anatoli had given up his first attempt to come to our aid. "I started out across the South Col and I'm moving pretty well and then I step into a narrow crevasse. I pull myself out of that and then the lights went out, it had turned dark. Then I went just a short distance and fell into another crevasse, this one was worse. My right leg and arm went in, and they were dangling down. I thought this might be it, I was afraid to move. I surveyed my situation and could see a solid patch of blue ice off to my right and above eyelevel and I swung my ice axe and got a securing with the pick. Somehow I was able to leverage myself out and I just picked myself up and continued on down."

As Martin pulls himself out of the second crevasse, his face encrusted with snow and ice; his lips had turned morgue blue. "Right after I start down again, I saw the light of a headlamp and I walk up on somebody just sitting there about one hundred yards away from Camp 4. I'm wondering, who is this guy?"

Martin had run into Jon Krakauer, but neither of them in their debilitated conditions recognized the other in the darkness. "Where are the tents?" In response of his question "the guy" - Krakauer - points off to his right.
"Yeah, that's what I thought. What are you doing here?"

Martin thought he had run into somebody from one of our expeditions, who had wandered out from Camp 4 and was particularly confused when "the guy" according to Adam's recollection says, "Watch out. It's steeper here than it looks. Be careful. Go back to the tents and get rope and some ice screws."

"I'm thinking at that point," Martin says, "I've almost died coming down the mountain, this guy has been in camp all day and has the brass to tell me to go down, get some rope and come back up to solve his problem! You gotta' be kidding!" Martin had been descending without oxygen, motoring on instinct and experience, scrambling for survival. Martin surveyed the slope of ice he'd been warned against, but didn't see it as particularly dangerous. "You needed to pay attention", but it wasn't a big deal. You could see the bottom where it flattened out. There was no hazardous exposure."

Martin took a few steps down the slope, tripped and slid unto the ice until he landed in the South Col. "It was maybe a hundred feet and I got up, turned around and waved at the guy and headed, what I thought was in the direction of our tents, which by then had disappeared from view."

24

"I have not failed. I've just found 10.000 ways that won't work."

Thomas A. Edison

Hope.... Stagger along one step at a time.... To stay alive..... survival instinct is all there is ..... the will to live.....Spotting a shape, there's a tent, two odd shapes emerging through the whirling snowdrift. I need to pee. I pee in my down suit. Nothing I can do about that. I am exhausted. Anatoli, it is his headlamp: the light through the whiteout. Neal disappears into the tent he intended to share with Scott, Sandy, Charlotte and Tim. Klev tumbles into ours, falling to the ground like the trunk of a tree. The giant fallen at last. I look into Anatoli's eyes through the storm. Anatoli gazes silently at me distinguishing that the situation is serious, he bends down and takes off my crampons.

"Anatoli, the others are out there. They are dying."
"Where?"
"Not far. Walk straight ahead. That way."
I point towards the white wall we just escaped from, the direction where Sandy, Charlotte, Tim, Yasuku and Beck Weathers are dependent on someone else to come to their rescue. Tim could have gone with Klev, Neal and I and by now saved himself from the perils of huddling out in the storm, but no way would he leave Charlotte to die on her own. Tim actively decided to remain with Charlotte, investing his life in wanting

her to stick to life. I crawl into our tent, acknowledging this is the exact time when people die from mere exhaustion up here. Martin is here, dead to the world with an oxygen mask attached onto his nose and mouth. He made it! Klev has done absolutely everything he could and now he is out. He lost consciousness the second he fell on his sleeping bag. I am so cold, shaking, involuntarily whimpering like a beaten dog. My body reacts, programmed to tremble to prevent me from freezing to death, shaking and bolting to restore some body heat into my system, hypoxia prevention, if it succeeds. My brain takes care of….Oxygen! Where's is an oxygen bottle with something still in it? I take Klev's empty bottle, unscrew the tube and mount it on a full canister I've located in the chaos the tent has exploded into. I manage somehow, in spite of my heebie-jeebies to attach it to the face of my hero. I can't do more for Klev just now, he's asleep. Liquids! Water! No snow, only a block of ice in the aluminum pot we normally use to transform snow into life preserving fluid. I cannot get the gas burner lit. I just cannot get it lit. Shaking and moaning…. Oxygen for myself…. I have to do what I can to help sustain my exhausted body. I prepare a space for Anatoli to sleep when he returns. Where is Scott? Probably already in the other tent with Neal. By now Scott must be off the mountain, not having spent unaccounted for hours, being lost in this God forsaken place, like I just have. The storm drives right through the tent fabric, leaving a fine dust of snow in the air inside. I crawl into my sleeping bag, lie there shaking, shivering with cold fits, the marrow in my bones must be frozen solid. My fingers begin to ache. Are they thawing? It's extremely hazardous if a thick clot of frozen blood breaks loose in the unfreezing process and blocks my heart. It's a very risky process being reheated and there is nothing I can do though. Am I crying? I moan unwillingly. My body speaks its own language, telling a tale of being on the verge to the abyss of death. Somehow I muster enough togetherness to find dry mittens to protect my blackening hands.

"Where are they?" Anatoli yanks the entrance tunnel open, letting in yet more cold and snow. "Where are they?" Anatoli is back from his first search and rescue venture and indignantly demands an answer from me. I never experienced his anger until this night.

"You have to head straight across the rocky ground, not upward across the ice, straight across the rock, no longer than half an hour."

Then he's gone. Anatoli rushing into the night. Apparently, he couldn't find Charlotte, Tim, Sandy, Yasuku and the other down suit in his first attempt, but I gave him the best direction I have. I know exactly where they are, but I can't join Anatoli to make sure he finds them. I'm powerless. I sincerely hope Anatoli does not get lost in this unforgiving storm as well. I must get the tent opening closed after Anatoli's abrupt departure. I must, to preserve all of us from the never relenting snowdrift. The wind keeps roaring and threatening to tear the tent from the ground with the three of us in it. I wrestle and keep trying without using my aching fingers. I cannot! I must keep the snow out! I struggle, battle and fight the bloody whopping tent fabric and finally succeed in tugging the designated cords around the bulging and breathing opening channel. I lie down, shaking with convulsions and hear myself, howling. Howling…. I cannot stop my thrilling howl. The sound of a human animal, beyond the finer of civilization, layers peeled off, exposing the sheer instinct to survive, no matter what. And the howling… the howling we bond with wild untamed animals in wilderness, humans reduced to an involuntarily howling creature… Howling for hours…

howling... What time is it? 2:00 am? 3:00 am? Pemba, the only one of our Sherpas' who is still functioning, the only human still operative it seems, apart from Anatoli, enters our tent with enough tea to cover the bottom of one of the big cooking pots. I am deeply grateful and touched at the gesture, what an incredible amount of work it must have been for him to melt and boil water for this cup of tea.

"No more gas," he says. No gas, no fluid, no reheating, no rehydration, no surviving...

Am I waking up Klev? The cup of tea Pemba so preciously poured for me splashes over my sleeping bag. My shaking fits make it impossible to keep the cup still. It wishes and sways as if I were on a ship in a hurricane on the Atlantic, all caused by my body's programming to keep me alive in spite of too low body core temperatures. It's working on overtime.

I have to get a few sips inside of me, instead of bathing in it. How long has it been since I drank anything? I detect human scrambling a few meters from where I fight my body shakes to no avail. Anatoli is bringing Charlotte back, he found my teammates. And is on his way back!

The almost hurricane-like gale continues. I doze, shake and whimper. The artificial oxygen surely makes a difference and I have turned the crane on high flow rate. Now what? Lopsang suddenly crawls halfway through the tent opening, sort of entangled in the fabric tube. Even in this ghostlike atmosphere, there is no doubt it is him. His white Sherpa ceremonious suit that he wears when he and Scoot celebrate their common summit successes distinguishes him, as does his golden earring and shiny black ponytail. Scott's glorious protégée and a great guy too. It must be three or four in the morning.

"Where is Scott, Lopsang? And how are you?"

"I'm fine. Scott decided to bivouac up at the ridge Camp 1. The weather is too harsh to come down."

Then Lopsang is gone again. "Camp 1"is the name the Sherpas' have given our first summit morning stop, on the South East Ridge. What can Scott bivouac in up there? Nevertheless, Scott has survived foul weather in snow wholes previously, so he knows what it takes to survive when things turn sour. Peculiar decision though and why is Lopsang down here on his own? I know Scott and Lopsang arranged to meet on the summit for their boyish celebration tradition, which they have perfected over the years of climbing together. I know they met on the summit yesterday afternoon. Did they not descend together? In this kind of weather and in the light of what I have just been through, bivouacking is not an incomprehensible decision though. If you cannot keep moving, which is the best strategy, switch into hunkering down, stay as warm as possible and wait for fair conditions. Lopsang seems quite calm and collected. I just hope Scott will be as fortunate as we - Klev, Neal and I - and find his way back here soon. Slumber. Awaken. Anatoli is back. Daybreak approaching, judging by the increasing light. I watch Anatoli begin to swell in slow motion. He is kaput, totally drained. Finished! Not an atom of energy or anything resembling Anatoli's customary modus operandi left in this genius of the mountains. Anatoli has completely exhausted whatever abnormal forte that made it possible for him to save the lives of three people, who without a doubt would have succumbed to the monstrosity of spending the night in the South Col. How is it possible for this extraordinary being to be capable of doing what no one else up here can? What ingrained ethic leads Anatoli to risk his own life in his pursuit of saving the lives of his fellow beings? Why does he do what no one else is willing or proficient of? I sincerely wish there were more Anatoli's this night. More Anatoli's in the world as such. The world would be a better place for more of his kind.

Exchanging glances, we don't need to say anything. I know he managed to get Charlotte, Sandy and Tim "safely home", half-dragging, half-carrying the two women Tim stayed behind with, not to abandon them to a solitary destiny. I think "the Russian Man" ventured back for Yasuku and the other unconscious bundle, Beck Weathers, lying snow-blind, frostbitten and in a hypothermal coma a few hundred feet from camp.

Two human beings from Rob Hall's team, left to die on their own, no one proving capable of doing anything for them. The following day, Stuart Hutchinson, one of the clients on Adventure Consultants, organized a search party to find both Namba and Weathers. Hutchinson found both in such horrible shape, unlikely to live long enough to be carried down to Base Camp and he decided to leave the two alone to save limited resources for the other climbers.

While Beck Weathers endured, after being left for dead twice, Namba never moved again. She expired alone, breathing her last breath from exhaustion and exposure to the harsh conditions of the mountain.

Somehow, Beck Weathers was miraculously capable of staggering back to life the following day. He suffered severe frost injuries. Since Everest Beck Weathers has undergone eight major surgeries. His right arm was amputated, he lost the fingers of his left hand and his nose was removed and later remodeled.

Anatoli's nose is a raw swelling lump of blackening meat, not even in the vicinity of resembling the normal human attribute. His hands are swelling to enormous proportions as I watch him struggle to get into his sleeping bag. Anatoli's hands are almost as huge and deform as mine were with the summit expedition mittens on, but his are bare. I zip Anatoli's bag as far up as possible with my frost-damaged fingers. Kiss this gentle, humble giant of a man on the forehead. Anatoli is finished and he is very quiet, vanished deep inside himself.

"Anatoli, Scott is still up there. We have to send some Sherpas up to search for him", the tone of my voice revealing and expressing my utmost concern. Lopsang crawls into our tent, with him the chilling tokens of drifting snow and high winds.

"Lopsang, you have to arouse a couple of Sherpas to climb up and assist Scott down." I persist.

"Anatoli, the last thing Scott said to me before ushering me off was: "Get Anatoli, he is strong, he can get me down." Lopsang tries to rouse Anatoli but Anatoli is kaput. Lopsang is finished and no Sherpa is capable, willing or obliged to climb up Everest again today. From a cynical objective point of view, it is simply too hazardous. Anyone venturing into this hurricane-like blizzard faces a severe risk of getting herself or himself killed. I myself would probably collapse like several of my fellow mountaineers, vegetating in their tents up here, if I tried any major kind of exertion.

"We have to get somebody up to Scott." Scott is so close and yet beyond salvation for the time being. Why the Hell did Scott decide to spend the night up there? Why did he not climb down with Lopsang? If he can only preserve sufficient body heat to avoid severe injuries! Scott is not cut out to live as an amputee for the rest of his life, but how should he be able to remain warm? Apparently, he is on his own. At least we were together and could help each other stay awake and keep moral as high as possible during the grueling hours of being lost. Lopsang appears unruffled as always, so nothing serious can have transpired? Factually, there is nothing we can do, no rescue mission will be possible, until somebody has gotten some repose and the snowstorm has lessened. I struggle to lace up the opening of the tent, again. The winds seem to attack us with unrelenting roars, making my task excessively laborious. Nevertheless, I must keep the gale and frozenness at bay, I must tie the strings around the wind tunnel to keep us inside the cocoon as safe from the hazardous elements as possible. I know we are purely surviving on a thin margin and must not leave anything to chance, that are within my control. Lacing up the tunnel is bloody well within my control, although the force with which the tent fabric is repeatedly yanked out of my aching hands, wants to convince me of the opposite.

25

"When you have lost hope, you have lost everything. And when you think all is lost, when all is dire and bleak, there is always hope."

Pittacus Lore

Rob Hall, one of the golden boys of climbing. Big, handsome, charming is trapped high on the mountain and slowly dying, he is using his cell phone to get through to his wife back in New Zealand. She knew her husband's voice and she could tell he was in trouble, but almost a hemisphere away, could do no more than encourage him. Everest is at all times a high-risk environment and since the first attempts of scaling the mountain, multiple motivators, for pursuing the summit, have driven people. Most of us need sponsors or clients to be able to afford our quest, adding risks of second agendas. Rob Hall had set a turnaround time at around noon on May 10. Why did he continue to climb many hours after that? And why did he assist Doug Hanson upwards, a client who to me already the previous morning showed observable signs of being too slow, incoherent and clearly discernible, not able to climb across the yellow band unaided by Rob? Dough had a long resume in the European Alps and Asia. Significantly, he was a member of Rob's 1995 Everest Expedition that turned round at the South Summit, 85 meters from the top. Every day since the 1995 turn around Dough expressed that he thought about Everest. Doug seemed rather obsessed, but summiting Everest this year appeared to be all consuming. In 1996, Dough was back for another attempt, fully backed by Rob Hall, who had also reduced his costs for participating on this expedition. Doug was fully committed to dissolving his profound disappointment from the previous year and accomplishing the final 85 meters to stand on top of the world. Whatever the reason, once it became apparent that Doug Hanson was deteriorating fast in the afternoon blizzard on May 10, Rob Hall decided that he would linger with his client. Even when Guy Cotter, a colleague pleaded with Rob on the radio to abandon a hopeless case, Rob insisted on remaining with the stricken Dough, fact being that at nearly 29,000 feet neither of them could survive long. Rob Hall remained near the summit with his dying client Doug Hansen as the oncoming unremitting storm made one and all vulnerable to passing away, as oxygen supplies ran out. Doug Hanson died that night. The following evening, on 11 May, too weak and frostbitten to move, Rob spoke for the last time on the radio to his wife Jan Arnold in New Zealand. She was seven months pregnant with their first child. The poignancy of that farewell was almost unbearable, but there is some consolation in knowing that Jan Arnold had climbed Everest herself with Hall in 1993. She had shared his dreams and she understood the risks and she knew that Rob was in a situation where "Every man for himself" is the norm.

    Was Rob Hall affected by losing his friend Gary Ball on Dhaulagiri? In some distorted way trying to make up for not being able to save his best friend? Was Rob falling victim to the effects of altitude and confusing Dough with Gary? Or was Rob controlled by other motives? When we are in danger, it is natural to feel afraid. Our fear triggers countless split-second changes in the body to prepare to defend against the endangerment or to avoid it.

This "fight-or-flight" response is a healthy reaction intended to protect us from harm. Psychologically traumatic experiences often involve physical trauma that threatens one's survival and sense of security. A wide variety of events can cause trauma, but there are common aspects. There is frequently a violation of the person's familiar ideas about the world and of their human rights, placing the person in a state of extreme confusion and insecurity. When a human being is exposed to an overload of destruction and death, some react with post-traumatic stress disorder (PTSD). In PTSD the inherent sound survival and preserving flight or fight reaction becomes over stimulated and our adequate reactions are changed or damaged. PTSD develops after a terrifying ordeal that involved physical harm or the threat of physical harm. The person who develops PTSD may have been the one who was harmed, or the individual may have witnessed an injurious event that affected someone else. Psychological trauma is a type of damage to the psyche that occurs because of a severely distressing occurrence. Trauma, psychological "injury" is often the result of an overwhelming amount of stress that exceeds one's ability to cope or integrate the emotions involved with the tragedy. The brain suffers from sensory overload. A traumatic occurrence involves the sense of being overwhelmed. People who have PTSD may feel stressed or frightened when they are no longer endangered. The nervous system seems to be in constant alert mode and unable to distinguish between minor input and traumatizing circumstances.

The reaction to a sensory overload can be delayed by weeks, years, or even decades as the person struggles to cope with the immediate circumstances, eventually leading to serious, long-term negative consequences. If you are traumatized you may experience flashbacks in which you intensely relive the trauma, as if it were really happening again. You may feel all the same emotions and sensory influences repeatedly. You do not lose consciousness during a flashback, but you may have difficulty distinguishing here-and-now reality when a flashback consumes you. You may see, hear, smell, taste or feel things related to the past traumatic ordeals that are not actually there in your current reality. This does not mean that you are "losing your mind". Such remembrances are an entirely normal part of the response to trauma as you struggle to rework and integrate the experience.

If you had other traumatic experience years before this one, you may even find that sudden flashbacks about that previous experience are mixed up with flashbacks about your more recent traumatic experience. We react individually when caught in taxing circumstances. One individual might be altered for life while another is hardly emotionally affected at all. Why did Rob not save himself, his wife was 7 months pregnant? Was Rob Hall already suffering so much from the lack of oxygen, that his professionalism and experience was elapsed in the single-minded quest to get as many participants as possible to the summit? Every soldier, rescue worker etc. are drilled with the common sense as to rescue what can be rescued with the means available. If there are not sufficient resources and manpower to save all in peril, you must save yourself instead of two people dying. It truly serves no purpose whatsoever that two people die instead of one. But Rob's entire conduct on summit day points in the direction that he was actually not responsible.

Already the day before, I was puzzled, having to wait in line on the avalanche prone Lhotse Face, as Rob assists Dough up over the Yellow Band. Dough displayed clear signs of not being able to move coherently and fast enough not to cause harm to himself or others. Various eye witness accounts seems to support the fact that Dough himself wanted to descend above Camp 4 on May 10th but that Rob Hall convinced or insisted Dough could make it to the summit. In addition, how could Rob tell Beck Weathers to remain and wait for him for hours on end, so Rob could come and fetch him on the descent? Some years before attempting Everest, Beck Weathers had his eyes operated to be able to see without glasses. Apparently, this laser operation influences the eyes adaptability to contract in freezing temperatures, so practically Beck suffered increasing disturbances of vision the higher he mounted.

"I did not mention my impaired vision to anyone, as i felt slightly bothered by the problem rather than downright handicapped. Neither did I panic, when my alteration of eyesight dawned 8,300 meters altitude. I was practically blind but anticipated the solution would come with the break of daylight. Assuming that the bright light reflected so massively by the glittering snow cover that it can burn the inside of your mouth. If you remove your goggles, the rays can fry you corona in less than 10 minutes. I expected my coronaries would automatically contract once the sun hit the mountain and then I would be capable of seeing again. I was thoroughly convinced I had it figured out correctly. It just had to work this way. I was nevertheless too blind to continue climbing in the dusk of dawn, so I left my trot in the colonne and let others pass by me and swiftly dwindled from climbing as number four out of a row of approximately 30 something climbers to becoming the absolute last. I actually quite enjoyed standing still; just observing the others scramble by. I just stood there, chatted and exchanged handshakes with everybody until the sun began projecting its lucid rays upon the upper slopes. My vision improved just as I had anticipated and I was able to hammer the tips of my crampons into the ice and traverse across the ridge." "Unfortunately, I caused deterioration in my condition as I wiped off my face with my stiff frozen glove. An ice crystal tore a rip in my right corona, so now my sight on the right eye became completely blurred and I lost all sense of depth - not very smart -taking into consideration where I was. My left eye gave me an okay, yet rather grained view upon my surroundings. I did realize though that I would be unable to climb any higher than my current position - a mere 500 meters from the summit - unless my eyesight improved dramatically. I still convinced myself that I would be recovering full vision as I rather optimistically told Rob. "Just go ahead and slide up that hill. I will follow as swift as my eyes allow me to."

It was half past seven in the morning.

"Beck", Rob replied with his characteristic kiwi-accent. "I do not support that idea. You have 30 minutes. If you are able to climb in half an hour then do so. If not, I will not permit you to climb."

"Okay." I hesitated. "I accept." It was not a complying and constructive reply. I had come too far to give up the Summit being this close. But I acknowledged the prudence in Rob's reply.

"You know what? If I cannot see within the 30 minutes window you have given me, I will descend to Camp 4 as soon as I am able to." Hall turned down that proposal as well.

"I dislike that suggestion just as much as your first input" Robb exclaimed. "If I descend from the summit and do not find you here, how am I to know whether you have descended safely or gotten yourself lost up here? You have to promise me and I am serious about this, you MUST stay here till I return." So I committed myself to a very stupid deal.

"Rob. I promise, I will not move from this very spot."

"The thought that Rob might never return to get me down never dawned on me. I waited all morning. It was a magnificently gorgeous day. High blue sky, crystal clear with no clouds what so ever. Perfectly wind still. The enormous cathedral of mountains reached as far as my good eye was able to grasp. The curve of the earth was easily discernible in the horizon. Around noon three climbers from my team scrambled down towards me: Stuart Hutchison, Lou Kasischke and John Taske. They communicated that a bottleneck was forming on the upper ridge caused by too many and too slow climbers attempting to scale the Hillary Step. They had all realized that it would not be possible to wait it out and still reach the summit before our allotted turn -around time at 14.00, 2 pm.

I had been close to motionless since around 8 o'clock this morning and just gotten colder and colder. "Come on down with us." "Well, I have truly backed myself into a corner here. I promised Rob I would stay put until he returns from the summit. We are not carrying a walkie-talkie, so I could let him know I headed down together with you guys. I don't think it's a good idea. Rob will just be left with the impression that I am not trustworthy. So I don't think I can join you."

Stuart, Lou and John continued down: three wise men. "Off course, I should have joined them. But I was unaware of the immediate danger I exposed myself to. The weather was dazzling. Even though I deep down were acknowledging that I would not make the summit today, I still loathed admitting that I had given up. As soon as I moved one step downhill with the others that would mean that I would be forced to admit, that I had failed in my quest." So Beck Weathers, a grown man, doctor of 45 years of age, did nothing.

For Rob to tell Beck to wait above 8,000 meters and for Beck to surrender all mature common sense to the judgment of another adult, no matter how experienced that leader might appear and self-promote, is almost the equivalent of signing your death warrant above 8,000 meters. Twelve days after Rob's last conversation with his pregnant wife during the night where we all gave up on Rob, his body was found under a light blanket of snow, below the summit of Everest.

26

*"It **doesn't** matter if you try and try and try again and fail.*
*It **does** matter if you try and fail and fail to try again."*

"Scott is above us, not very far", I am listening to Lopsang breaking down. Denial lifting, exposing him to the entire brutality of what he has been through, listening to the tiny nuances that wills my hope not to declare Scott forgone just yet. Scott you must stay alive, keep fighting dear beloved Scott, you cannot die. I almost howl in inconsolable agony. I want to push the finality of that circumstance out of existence, denying the undeniable, and the irrevocable with all my mental power. I cannot let myself give up hope, not you Scott, even though I have prepared myself for his death since I first meet him. I have come to love him, experiencing his survival year after year; he made me have faith in that he was not going to die in the mountains. Although I have followed him and felt my loyalty dwindle, as Scott unlike his usual self, acted out his frustrations as a consequence of organizing this expedition, aiming to make it big- time

Late in the day of May 10, as bad weather closed in, Scott approached the summit after 3:30 pm. "Just below the summit of Everest, I anchored my ice axe and fixed a 15-meter rope at a dangerous spot so that all remaining team members could get down safely. I then waited for Scott to arrive." Scott Fischer finally got to the top of Everest and reached Lopsang, who was waiting for him. "He finally arrived very late and we started down. Just as we reached my ice axe, Rob Hall and Doug Hansen were coming up my rope. After they passed, I sent Scott down and waited next to my ice axe in wind and extreme cold for them to summit and return so that they could get safely down. Once they were off my rope, I left and quickly caught Scott. From the South Summit, I physically dragged Scott down through the storm until he could move no further. There I waited with Scott, determined to save him or die. Finally, he threatened me, to cajole me into saving myself, saying he would jump off if I did not go down. I was, in fact, the last person to leave Scott Fischer and Makalu Gau that night."

Scott Fischer finally succeeded in urging Lopsang to leave him behind and descend alone. Just above the Balcony (27,559 feet), Scott in his peril, encouraged Lopsang to depart downwards without him and send back Anatoli Boukreev, to help. Suffering from hypoxia and probably cerebral edema, Scott buckled, sat down on the snow covered rocky ground, never to get up again.

The temptation to give up when exhausted, dehydrated and frozen to the core of your being is common and nobody is exempt. Ignominy isn't something many of us can handle gracefully. In addition, even though we know it's a common human condition, we're somehow always surprised when it happens to us. Finally Lopsang had to leave Scott behind, huddling in a shallow depression on Everest, lying next to the Taiwanese expedition leader Makalu Gau, who too was unable to move under his own steam and had apparently been abandoned by all his team members. I never heard details about what brought Makalu Gau in this disastrous predicament. Lopsang had to leave the two fellow climbers to save his own life. He did the right thing under the circumstances. There must be something we can do to get to Scott; to help him.

I will Scott to live, be part of the future we planned that fueled our vision for Everest. I need Scott to be alive, unfrozen. I need my jolly, frail companion to continue to experience the adventures life has to offer. I need Scott to dream big and make the dreams viable by following through with his life mantra. "Let's make it happen - and have fun!"

I am filled with serenity of having survived and proven myself strong enough for what I overwhelmingly desired, but doubted I would be capable of accomplishing. Thanks to Scott, the greatest adventure of my life so far, has become a part of who I have now become.

I am eternally grateful, but now I want to assemble a rescue team that can push through the hostile forces of Mother Nature and come to Scott's aid. I know from the involuntary shakes of my body and my blackening, frozen fingertips that I will die myself, if I consider going up Everest again to locate where Scott is. I am too weak and I would never in a lifetime, be able to drag him downwards anyway. Nothing I can do.

I cannot believe my strong beloved friend is dying. I want to climb up and will Scott back to consciousness. Scott cannot be giving up. It takes quite a long time to freeze to death, maybe Scott is just severely frostbitten and we can still save him, although I doubt Scott will be able to adapt gracefully to a life without hands and feet. Surviving these circumstances will cost him some of his awesome body, that's a given.

I wait. I do not cry, I breathe oxygen and focus on remaining alive, knowing that we will have to move off this colossal mountain very soon so as to preserve ourselves. We must descend to base camp today. Weather permitting our retreat or not, we must. If we remain here in the death zone, some of us will not make it through another night alive.

We wait, no body outers our concerns. Anatoli is bloated, a human balloon, totally wasted, with nothing left in him to move as much as a single step. Anatoli waits with the patience of experience, knowing his limitations due to years and years of surviving at high altitude.

He saved the lives of three people, ferrying them in during last night, from the claws of the storm and exceeded even his humongous will power and strength and now suffers the consequences. When your body loses fluid through its blood vessels, it tries to counteract the effect by holding water and sodium in your kidneys. As a result, more fluid builds up in your body and more trickles out of your blood vessels. This fluid can get into your body tissue and causes the edema I observe happening in Anatoli, as he collapsed some hours ago. I was howling from the intense agony of rewarming after hypothermia, as I stared at him swelling like a Michelin man, his face, legs and feet, bloated to abnormal dimensions. This harrowing condition isn't always an indicator of altitude sickness, but is a physiologic reaction at altitude. This type of outer earthly swelling worsens with ascent, but it usually resolves itself when you descend. As for myself, I am powerless. Howling and shivering.....

Perseverance is the tough grind you deliver after you are worn-out by delivering the grueling effort you already exhausted your innermost resources undertaking. Without outstanding individual's perseverance, we may never identify human icons. The icons: the singled out humans, who seem to have a larger than life impact on humankind globally. What if these people had given up? What if Anatoli gives up? One of the most common causes of failure is the habit of quitting, when we are overtaken by temporary defeat. It doesn't matter if you try and try and try again, and fail. It does matter if you try and fail and fail to try again. I know Anatoli yarns to rush to help Scott, do whatever he can, to get his iconic friend down into safety. But he is too experienced to even try for now. He needs to rest and recuperate as much as it is humanely possible here at Camp 4, before he can survive attempting to save more lives.

"Wake up! Wake up, Lene, we need to get his upper body down." Pemba sticks through the tunnel opening into our tent. "Get everybody ready for ten o'clock."

It is still storming. Gusts threatening to flatten our tiny tent we emotionally equal with being safe, to the rocky, corpse-strewn ground. I just feel like lying still. Need to rest, just twenty-four hours more. Just leave me alone and let me go back to sleep. However, my brain distinguishes resting will not restore me, or help me recuperate and regain strength at this exposed altitude. My desire for rest will only further weaken me. I am cold, so cold and still shivering compulsorily. I must check the oxygen gauge - the canister is empty! I'm whimpering like an exhausted child. I try to suppress my shivering and whining, but my body's extreme reactions seem beyond my mental control. I shake, whimper, shake... I acknowledge we have to get down to survive, time has run out for us, but haven't got the faintest idea how I am going to mobilize the required focus and force to even consider getting up, organizing and initiate moving.

"What about Scott? Has he come down during the night?"

I have been deeply engulfed in a blissful, comatose nothingness and have been able to keep reality at bay while unconscious at least for some hours escaping the express train roars of South Col.
"Maybe Scott is on his way down, descending now that it's light?" We must send up a team with oxygen for him, so we can support him. How far up the mountain is he?"
"Martin, Klev - wake up! We have to descend. We must get down the mountain. We're taking off at ten o'clock!"
I wonder if we can climb through this storm at all. Thoughts of other mountaineers who have succumbed from exhaustion under similar conditions, caught at high altitudes in tempestuous weather conditions, rush through my head. We have to get down.

It's 8:00 am. I kneel in my sleeping bag, trying to melt some water for us. The cooking pot is frozen solid, the lighter won't work and my fingers seem to have taken on a stale life of their own volition, they just will not obey me. I scream - overwhelmed by an intense burst of excessive pain - my lower legs are cramping. I scramble around the tent floor, struggling to find an oxygen bottle with just a little tiny bit of invigorating O 2 left in it, focused like an addict, the bottles all appear to be empty. We have exhausted all our meticulously premeditated supplies. All details, planned to keep us safe and sound under calculable conditions. This particular morning we are far beyond that matrix. Having sucked all oxygen for the summit bid and subsequent descend plus the emergency canisters, there is no more O 2 available. Klev wakes up, but cannot open his eyes. Snow blind, he must have taken off his goggles at some point yesterday, maybe to clear the ice that kept freezing over our oxygen masks and threatened to suffocate us inside the equipment supposed to keep us alive. Although he is in pain and robbed of his eyesight, he and Martin start massaging my aching legs.

"Lene, do you have Ingrid's eye ointment nearby? Would you make a patch for my eye?

Time is dragging by. It is still storming and my hands are useless, aching, blackening claws where my fingertips were 24 hours ago. How dependent one is of those insignificant centimeters.

How are we going to descend? I wonder. We must. I finally excavate an oxygen bottle with some blobbing still inside, as I shake it for testers and put on my mask again, sucking greedily on the invisible fluid. My involuntary whimpering dwindles. Next is a protective patch for Klev's eye. How am I going to gain access to my inside pocket - unzipping? Close to my body in the breast pocket, is where the ointment is, in the emergency toothbrush case. Even with the strings I tied to all my zippers in preparation for climbing, my fingers cannot really get a grip to open the pocket. My attempts seem to take forever, as every other task does up here, but finally I manage: ointment, toilet paper and sports tape for minor strains. Under different circumstances, we would most definitely be howling with laughter at the building blocks for Klev's eye patch. However right now, as my bawling has stopped with the intake of oxygen, the howling is entirely up to the wind. Anatoli is quiet just lying there. Lopsang appears again through our tunnel opening. He is as white as the snowdrift following his entre still wearing his ceremonial white Sherpa outfit on top of his down suit. He's changed, less calm, less composed, than when he first arrived during last night.

"We must get somebody up to get Scott. He is ill, very ill. He cannot come down by himself. I had to leave him with Makalu Gau not to die myself. Scott kept insisting: Go down and get Anatoli. Tell him to come and carry me down. Anatoli is strong. He can do it."

Sadly Anatoli cannot comply with Scott's innermost wishes for the time being. He is not capable of anything just yet. This night's rescues have taken everything out of him.

"Lopsang, get a hold of some of the other Sherpas'. We have to get somebody up to salvage Scott."

How many individuals are we up here? How many are scattered around in the various high-tech tents? At some point during last night, I tried to find someone willing and capable of helping those left further up the mountain, but no one seemed to hear my pleading. No one, out of maybe 20, no one..... Anatoli is totally out for now, but I know he will stay at the South Col until he has regained enough strength to climb up to Scott. I just know.... That's the way this grand guy is.

"Klev, Martin we have to get down!"

None of us wants to move. Nevertheless, we must. If we can, infinitely exhausting to worm out of the comforts of my sleeping bag and to get my down suit on. My companions wisely still wear theirs, but I was forced to take mine off, not to acquire frost injuries where the pie had flattened the thick down shelter. Is it dry now? It doesn't matter. My body clearly displays it's used up, so I have to protect it as much as possible. So on with the down suit. What seems like an eternity passes by. We are so drained. No news about Scott. Where are you big guy? Are you holding up? I unwillingly acknowledge that by now, Scott will have suffered lasting damage due to frostbites and lack of oxygen, but I fathom him striding into the camp area with his gregarious white teeth grin, Scott being Scott, as always.

"How far up are Scott and Makalu lying, Lopsang?" "Up there - maybe an hour, maybe two hours from here." Lopsang points towards the route. You idiot, Scott, you are so close to camp and then not coming down. Mountain climbers have survived nights out in the open here before but not without losing fingers and toes. You're such an idiot Scott. This is so unlike you, my charming big man. Come on, get your act together and haul your muscular ass down here, to the rest of us. Come on.....I am wasted, depleted. There is nothing I can do, other than get down alive and try to speak firmly enough to mobilize the strongest, most competent Sherpas' to climb back up and search for Scott. But basically, I have no right to ask anybody to risk their life for mountaineers who proves too weak for the conditions of Mother Goddess of the Earth. Sherpas', I learn, have their own experience-based ethics above 8,000 meters, which I neither will, wish to, nor can interfere with. They want to survive - just as much as any of us, who are here for entire selfish, recreational reasons. Most Sherpas' risk their lives, preparing the route and camps to make our attempts less strenuous and taxing. They are here, because it's the best paid job in the entire region, maybe even the highest paid job possibility in Nepal as such. Sherpas' are not employees we can order to do whatever we need and want them to, they are independent spirits, strong yet humble and very much in tune with the rules of nature' forces. I respect them. I respect their choices. Lopsang will do the right thing. On May 10 to 11, no

Sherpa died, none had to be rescued, and none were injured in the storm. Out of the tent, I am crawling through the wind tunnel on all fours, probably for the last time. Klev will need help to find his way down Everest, not being able to see with his snow blinded, hurting eyes.

"Come on, we have to get down."

Pemba grasps my arm and declares something I don't quite catch, his words blown away into the storm. Something in the vicinity of "All the Sherpas' love you; therefore I want to assist you down." I scarcely know him, this young mature man, who has appointed himself my guardian angel today. Pemba starts walking, pulls at my mitten protected hand and I have no choice but to follow him through the storm. Martin is trailing close behind.

From Camp 4 to Camp 3, this young Sherpa supports me. He shifts my karabiner from one fixed rope to the next. My fingers are still useless, so he clips me in and takes me off each rope quickly and efficiently. I follow him downwards, tailing him at a pace I could not have set in my battered condition without the close protection of this angel of mine. What was it he whispered up there? Did I interpret correctly? The further down the mountain we get, the more the storm weakens. How outlandish it is suddenly to be able to hear Martin saying something behind me. We have been existing in a bubble of chaos and incessant noise for so long, it's liberating just to get out of the roaring 8000 meters. I wonder how Klev is doing. The sun is shining…..Pemba is good, very competent. He only makes the utmost necessary movements. First he secures himself and then he safeguards me. I'm not allowed to use my hands. He is steady, everything he does serves a purpose; nothing is superfluous. I wear the oxygen mask to do the little I can to prevent my body from collapsing. Outside of Rob Hall's Camp 3 at 7,300 meters, people come out to meet us, tears welling up in their eyes.

"Welcome down. How fantastic it is to see you alive."

People are on their way up to offer any help and assistance they can contribute up there into the inferno we just escaped. I tumble into our yellow Camp 3 tent. Martin throws himself in after me. We cannot detect Klev. Sandy and the others are further up on the route. Pemba waits patiently for some time, but as I seem fine and not in any rush to get off my butt, he's off and on his way down. I try to rest, recuperate somewhat, but start to whimper again. Funny, I cannot help it. No words exchanged. Nothing to say. Martin and I would like to stay and rest, but at the altitude of 7,300 meters, there is no recreation to be found, only slow but certain death. We have to get down, we take off together. Martin as habitually, is faster than I am and we part. I am particularly and meticulously careful to secure myself to the fixed ropes all the time. "To the summit and safe return." I acknowledge it's at this point that fatigue can lead to a careless and possibly fatal mistake. Slowly, slowly I move down across the avalanche prone Lhotse Face, hoping that no rocks propelling from above, will cause my descend to be less than successful, pausing more often than I have ever done before.

"Lene, how good to see you, is there anything we can do for you?" David Breashears and Ed Viesturs greet me severely on their way up.

How strong and normal they appear……

"Do you have anything to drink? I am so thirty. Dehydrated. I can't remember when I last had any fluid."

David squeezes my hand. "We thought you were all dead. Last night twenty -one were reported missing."

So, that's why people are so happy to see us emerging from the front yard of hell.

"How is Sandy?"

"She is on her way down. She must be on route to Camp 3, she probably has frostbites, but she is alive." Rather fortunate to be so, pondering all the near calls she was rescued from, to be one of those able to leave the frozen graveyard but with traumatic memories.

I drink and drink, cautiously in small sips, not to get sick.

"Rob Hall is lying below the South Summit with a dead client. His feet are frozen so when he tries to get up and walk, he keeps stumbling and falling.
But he has radio contact most of the time. Many fears Scott is dead. Sherpas' are on their way from Camp 2 with more help." David shares. We part. Ed and David are on their way up to help. They have an oxygen cache at the South Col and are in excellent shape, so they will be a welcome encounter.

"On the night of May 10, 1996, I had a profound feeling of dread and disbelief," says David Breashears from the IMAX expedition. "These feelings were rooted in the death of the Taiwanese climber Chen Yu-Nan on the Lhotse Face, the day before, Chen had been injured, tumbling down the Lhotse Face from Camp 3, taking a leak in the early morning and had later expired suddenly amidst the group of Sherpas' who were trying to evacuate him down the mountain to safety. It had been up to

Ed Viesturs and myself to bring Chen's lifeless body down to the bottom of the Lhotse Face and then into Camp 2, where we were met by other climbers. It had disturbed me considerably to grapple with Chen's dead body as we lowered him with a rope over a steep ice cliff. The next day, now May 10, we knew many of the climbers had reached the summit of Everest much later than is normal and outside the window of safety".

Accounts of when we individually reached the summit of Everest on May 10 conflict. However, between 1:12 and 1:25pm., eight members of the New Zealand and our team reached the summit. Several more members of each team arrived at the summit between 2:00 and 2:15 pm. and several more arrived at about 3 pm. At about 3:30 pm., members of both teams continued to the summit. "Most alarming was when we learned that Rob Hall and Doug Hansen had been on the summit unusually late at 4:30 in the afternoon. Soon after discovering that, we were informed by way of radio calls from Rob Hall that Doug had collapsed above the Hillary Step. An extremely problematic situation only worsened as the storm swept up the mountain and all through the night, we listened to the fearsome wind battering and punishing the mountain high above us. We were aware that many climbers had not returned to camp and it was unthinkable to conceive they were outside, exposed to that vicious storm away from the shelter of their tents. A Sherpa woke me early in the morning requesting that I come to Rob Hall's communication tent. From the look in his eyes, I knew things were not good." Rob Hall, still conscious, was patched through by satellite phone to his wife in New Zealand. He had survived for more than 32 hours at close to 28,700 ft. but was frostbitten, without supplemental oxygen and unable to move. Ed Viesturs and David Breashears, joined the rescue efforts. Working with the stronger surviving expedition members, they helped weaker members, including Beck Weathers and Gau, down to a lower camp. They were both lifted out of the South Col in a rescue stunt that had never been attempted above 18,000 feet, Nepalese Army Pilot; Lt. Col. Madan K.C. arrived in a helicopter and hovered above a makeshift landing strip marked by pink Kool Aid. Because a helicopter's ability to fly is unpredictable at higher altitudes, no one knew if it could lift off with the weight of even one extra passenger; Gau was lifted first and about 45 minutes later, Madan K.C. returned to take Beck Weathers to safety. Attempts to rescue Rob Hall were aborted due to weather at 6:40 pm. on May 11.

Don't think. I'll believe Scott is dead when I hear it directly from someone who's seen him dead. I still silently hope he will come bumping back to base camp with his usual irresistible, sheepish, genuine roguish grin. Both Lopsang and Anatoli are still up there, not too far from Scott. They have not given up. Down below I can see a line of antlike black dots milling towards the Lhotse Face along the trail in the Western Cwm. Looking forward to being down there myself, aching for someone to carry my diminished pack and craving for more to drink. Negotiating the steep, rugged bergschrund, ice climbing. My body does not want to labor this hard anymore. Whoops! One of my outer mittens flies off. Huge mistake, disclosing how distracted I am due to the ordeal I am about to climb back from. Doesn't matter now, I'm not planning to scramble back up; it's at the bottom of a deep crevasse. I don't feel the need to slide down there to get it back. Better the mitten than me ends its endeavor buried in a grave of excruciating chill and darkness.

We are finally at Camp 2. Someone takes my pack and I take of my crampons, harness and everything else I don't need for safety. Another merciful soul hands me a mug of steaming hot tea, black with loads of sugar. Just the way I prefer it in the realms of the highest peaks on earth. Nowhere else do I drink black tea, thick with sugar. I stride through camp. "Congratulations" resonances around me. Heads emerge from tent openings. "Well done" from a subdued voice. An atmosphere of gloom and pent-up emotions hangs in the air among the brilliantly colored tents. I am lead inside Mal Duffs tent. He looks forlorn. I believe he and Rob are best friends. I fell instantly welcome and taken care of. Henry Todd stands outside with big bear hug and comforting laughs. "Ah, those fingers are nothing. Mine have looked like that lots of times. In six months they will be completely healed."

"Are you ok, Henry?"

"Yes, I am quite fine. Michael and the others are at the South Col, but I've told everybody to come down, except for the two strongest ones, who'll stay there and help out."

Photos are taken, and then I am finally home again, in our own advanced camp at 6,100 meters, Gyalzen, Ramen noodle soup and into my sleeping bag and drink, drink, drink. But where is Scott? Anatoli? Lopsang? The rest of my team is slowly on their way down greeted by helpful Sherpas'.

But what about Scott?

27

"The things you do for yourself are gone when you are gone, but the things you do for others remain as your legacy."
Kalu Ndukwe Kalu

May 12, 1996

The majority of our team is assembled again. Klev, Martin, Charlotte, Tim, Sandy and me. Somebody must have strolled through camp during the night and beaten us up, one after the other, with at least a baseball bat, judging by the way that we appear. Swollen eyes, boxer's nose, black cheeks and lips, flesh peeling off. Crying and laughing alternating as reality sets in, in the doses, our mental protective mechanisms are able and willing to cope with brutal facts. We are still not down at relative safety in Base Camp. First we have to get through the labyrinth of crevasses making up the Western Cwm. then through the notorious Icefall one last time. Suppressed tension of months' exposure to high risk is replaced by conscious apprehension of the myriad of things that can still go terribly wrong. Disciplining of will discerning focus on the actual risks, crumbles, as the end seems within reach. Reportedly, Lopsang is on his way down, and I'm anxious to greet him. There he is appearing over the rugged moraine edge. We are waiting. The Sherpas' are waiting. I go to meet him.

"Scott is dead." Lopsang sobs and collapses in my arms, his defense mechanisms giving in to reality. Experienced, mature beyond his western comparisons yet still a youngster in his twenties. "My father climbed up to get him down. My expedition leader is dead. Scott is lying up there in the snow Lene, frozen. Lene, he was ill already at the summit. He came up to me saying he was tired, so tired. Scott took a picture of me. I had to put a rope on Scott on the way down. He tripped, fell and would not move. I could not get Scott to move. On the snow flank, he tried to glissade down towards Tibet. I had to lower myself with a rope to get down to him and get him up again. I have never seen Scott like that before, Lene. He just gave up. He said he was going to jump right down into Base Camp. I dragged him and begged him to keep moving, but on the ridge, he just did not want to trudge any longer. I could not get him to do it.

Lopsang Sherpa   Everest Base Camp 1996

Scott took off his oxygen mask - he would not wear it even though there was more oxygen - and he just kept saying, "Lopsang, I am so ill, so ill. You have to get hold of a helicopter." I did not know what to do and he said I should go down and get Anatoli. "He is strong, Lopsang, he can carry me down. Tell Anatoli to come and get me." I lost him, Lene, I could not save him. Scott gave me his camera with all the photos."

After the storm subsided, on May 11, two Sherpas' one being Lopsang's father Ngawang Sya Kya climbed from Camp 4. They located Scott and Makalu Gau, the Taiwanese expedition leader, where Lopsang had dug a platform for them the night before. On May 10, 1996, after a decade's preparation, Makalu Gau leader of the Taiwanese National Expedition finally realized his dream of reaching the top of Mt. Everest. However, a few hours into what should have been the proudest time of his life; Makalu Gau was caught in the unexpected snowstorm.

Unable to save himself and trapped overnight at an altitude of 8,300 meters and a temperature of -60 C. The storm was still brutal and the rescue team knew they only had capacity to save one of the stranded climbers. Scott was barely breathing and had almost no response at all to the oxygen and hot drinks offered, whereas Gau was fully conscious in spite of his severe damages due to the subzero blizzard. The Sherpas placed an oxygen mask over Scott's face and rescued Gau, who they carried down to Camp 4. The Sherpa's took care of the strongest, with better prospects of surviving. They had to leave Scott behind. Left Scott to die... Makalu Gau, who jokingly refers to himself as having "blood type M (for mountain)," has had a lifelong passion for mountaineering. "I've knocked off the most difficult peaks, all in order to push my own limitations and overcome my own narrow perspective and cowardice," says

Makalu Gau. Even the Sherpas had given up on Gau, yet he miraculously survived.

Suffering severe frostbite, after his rescue Gau had to have his fingers, nose, toes and part of his feet amputated. Despite the awful price he had to pay for summiting Everest, he continues to face the future with positivity. After undergoing surgery, including reconstructive surgery 15 times, Gau was discharged from the hospital to face his new reality. He began his different life having to relearn to wash his face and brush his teeth and after he had learned to walk again, he eventually returned to the world of climbing, visiting places like Tibet and Xinjiang to continue to record climbs of China's famous 100 peaks. Since his recovery in 1998, Gau's madness for mountaineering has seen him tackle 25 more of those hundred.

It would turn out to be the last full night of Scott's life and for most of it, he must have been severely hallucinatory, affected by Cerebral Edema and Hypoxia, freezing from his extremities to the core of his body, neither unconscious nor awake, until he lost semi consciousness entirely. It would probably not have been able to thaw and defrost Scott without inflicting a heart attack, as his body warmed up.

How long does it take to freeze to death? What does it fell to be left alone in a raging storm, without the remotest chance of restoring yourself back to the capacity to move under your own power? What might Scott have contemplated? What is it like to be entirely dependent on someone stronger than you to; first be able to locate you in a humongous remote vastness, secondly be able and decide to struggle through deathly weather and still harboring enough strength for surviving themselves, as well as the strength to ferry a dead weight, literally down?

I sincerely hope Scott hallucinated and felt the warmth of dying of hypothermia, instead of lying awake, sensing the dreadfulness of being caught out high on Everest, bit by bit losing his precious body, tissue turning into solid ice. The very situation Scott so often almost begged me to protect him from, willing me to save him from himself. Pleading with me to keep provoking the part in him that wanted something different from life, something he had not yet managed to adapt into.

Anatoli climbed up to Scott and found him dead. He did what he could, under the circumstances, to cover Scott's body and took a few small talismans of Scott's to bring back to Scott's wife and two children. Scott used to carry a small Indian inspired cloth bag around his neck when attempting the high regions, containing hair clippings from his precious children. I can still hear the deep, encompassing love Scott felt for those kids, detecting his profound emotions while saying their names and sharing little tales of the memories Scott cherished from when he spent time with them. "Andy and Kathy Rose…" I know that Scott was profoundly attached to his children, realizing that they were the most important in the world, yet failing to make the conscious life altering choices that would have made it probable he could live and follow them growing up. Scott lived to turn 40.

"Sorry, I came too late Scott." Anatoli concludes his speech to his deceased mountaineering companion tears streaming down his marred face at our memorial ceremony at Base Camp.

Through tears and surrounded by the familiar smell of incense from the altar, I let go for the first time.

"Thank you for making this possible Scott. I will continue to live life the way we believed life should be lived "Let's make it happen and have fun! I will miss you Scott." I so much desire to have been able to ease his discomfort, but it was out of everyone's hands. Scott slipped into the cold realms of his beloved and hazardous playground, dying in the very environment, where he had pleaded with me not to let him die.

"I do not want to die in the mountains, Lene please don't let me die."

In death, Scott still remains close to the spot where he was left for death and did eventually pass away.

Our three teams suffered eight deaths, including the three guides: Rob Hall, Scott Fischer and assistant guide Andy Harris as well as climbers Dough Hanson and Yasuku Namba, plus the Taiwanese climber who had died earlier in the expedition. On our team only our leader Scott did not make it down.

In the immediate aftermath of our climb, I desperately need time alone to deal with what has transpired. I need time here at Base Camp, time to reflect, ponder and grieve. Authentically trying to come to terms with the fact that my ultimate athletic challenge and grand adventure in company of some of the most impressive personalities I have ever shared life with, individuals I have unconsciously searched for as a globetrotter, has partly transmuted into a devastating tragedy. I felt extremely vulnerable and emotionally frozen as well as resting content in the serenity of having come to peace with my inner conflicting selves having survived "To the summit and safe return."

When did I give up trying to influence Scott? Why did I give up attempting to sway him?

I remain as long as possible, to be among the mountain climbers who share my story, taking proper leave of Mother Goddess of the Earth, who keeps my great friend, to let myself heal just a little from having escaped the storm of climbing high: life altering. Reality can never be the same again. I need to stay here long enough to say a proper good bye to Scott, in my own way, before I start the journey back to civilization and the hectic times I expect once I'm back in Denmark. Scott and Rob's death stirring and mobilizing massive media attention: the publicity they both invested in.

Anatoli, the strong Russian man, unfortunately I cannot claim him as my Russian Man, as much as I would love to, is physically and mentally "out of order". Anatoli will climb Lhotse, fulfilling the plan he and Scott agreed upon back when meeting in Katmandu in February. I cannot bear to lose the two most important men in my life on one expedition. Loosing Scott will surely keep me grieving for quite some foreseeable future. Having yet to learn the full extent of what it will mean not to have Scoot as an inspiring beacon to grow through. Who am I supposed to empty beer bottles an' masse with now, so we can play Scott's favorite game of walking on them afterwards?

The mountain climber in me knows Anatoli has to climb high; he has what he has to do to become complete again. That is just the way it is.

Doctor Ingrid does not understand. She is truly in scrambles over the many lost lives. If she continues to return to the big mountains, she will gradually come to understand. I understand that she does not understand.

I have started digesting vitamin pills again. "Can I have the ration Scott used to devour?" Anatoli probes. I gladly carry out the popping ritual, even though it is difficult to get the tablets out of the foil packages and plastic bottles with these grossly bandaged hands. Doctor Ingrid becomes quite skilled at making bandages that don't get torn to shreds during the twenty-four hours between bandage changes. Velcro is on everything these days: a sleeping bag, tent openings and clothing, how does a person with gauze boxing gloves for hands keep from looking like a serpentine stream er?

Little was I to know what I had truly lost and that I would soon loose several more adventurous friends.

28

"Many of the great achievements of the world were accomplished by tired and discouraged men who kept on working."

Unknown

May 13, 1996

Everest - the highest mountain on earth kept one of ours and Anatoli is the last of us, to have seen Scott. I have an urge to ask Anatoli a need to share, as we all seek togetherness in the blueness of our mess tent. The Huge Starbucks Banner, reminds me of Scott's inventiveness, when it came to hook sponsors for our gourmet expedition.

Sitting close to Anatoli, my instincts, intuition and common sense take over: "Drink your tea, Anatoli." Every time he looks away, a teammate fills his cup anew. Anatoli is a proud, self-contained man and difficult for anyone "to take care off". However, even the strongest are also human.

"Anatoli, where is your down parka?"

"I do not need it."

Sure he does. "Steve, will you fetch Anatoli's down jacket?" my fingers are bandaged like boxing gloves to protect my frost damaged fingers against further injuries and hazard of infections, so I need help myself for the most trivial tasks. However, I can still command. When Steven puts his own jacket around Anatoli's shoulders, Anatoli wakes up a little, stride to his flower-strewn tent and puts on his big blue down jacket. In the meantime more tea is poured. Then this remarkable Russian man puts an end to all my hidden hopes with his grueling account of how he found Scott's lifeless corpse. Anatoli is a changed man. Worn out and clearly weighed down by Scott's death. I so want to comfort him, nurture some light back into his eyes. I wonder if he feels guilt about not having been able to fulfill his friend's last wish. "Anatoli is strong, he can carry me down.....", at least Scott with his pledge restored Anatoli back to his originally intended position on our expedition. The strong Russian Climber, who can outperform any other mountaineer on Everest, if shit hits the fan. Instead of attempting to reduce Anatoli to a socialite entertaining lap dog. "Anatoli is strong, he can carry my down...." an impossible burden to carry.

We were nine climbers on our summit bid. We all turned our vision of standing on top of the world into reality. We all made it to the top. One died on the way down: our expedition leader and my life companion Scott Fischer. Scott would have been satisfied with his team. How I wish Scott was among us now and alive to harvest the fruits of his fortuitous investments. Instead, he succumbed to the risks of Climbing High, dying alone in the mountains. The type of death he explicitly feared. However, he himself chose to climb. Nobody forced Scott to pursue Everest and the fame it entails. Five days after our summit bid and the loss of Scott, we were nine human beings sitting in a circle amongst our tents in Everest Base Camp. The Mountain Madness Team, recording our memories and individualized experiences and notions of what actually transpired up above. Some more than others express a profound need to try to piece together our fragmented accounts, in an attempt to gain a bigger picture or to fill in personal blackouts and memory gaps: an effort at truth telling and self reflection, verbally comprehending the uncontrollably.

When we find ourselves in life threatening circumstances, causing extreme pressure, comparable to the night of May 10, 1996; where we were profoundly sleep-deprived, oxygen-starved and dehydrated while staggering around in the dark in the blizzard, you find out if you're a person who gives help, asks for help, or just gives up and lies down to die. I am passionately intent to unravel what it is, that makes some people sit down and give up, sometimes within shouting distance of safety. Are you one of the climbers who master the realization that, not only will you not be able to help anyone else in trouble, but if you mess up, in any way or luck runs out, no one will likely be able to help you either? In extreme state of affairs we are stripped of our ability to be anything but our true selves and this confrontation with who and what we are is one of the undercurrents in why some people reorganize their memories or try to blame others after surviving trauma. Day by day, our recollections alter. Probably we all rework past reality to a storyboard we can live with, re-scripting facts. Scientific testing has repeatedly proven that the human being is unable to recollect incidences 100% truthful. As time passes, the more we transform facts and reality according to subjective matrixes.

29

"Courage is not having the strength to go on, it is going on when you don't have the strength."

Theodore Roosevelt

"There is one boarding pass too many," Ngima shouts through the intensifying rudder spectacle oozing from the orange Everest Air Helicopter.

I am about to embark on my first serious step of my journey home, the airborne stretch to Katmandu and the world press.

Klev, Neal, Pete, Martin and our climbing Sherpas' wait in the morning fog while the helicopter prepares for takeoff.

Charlotte departed from Base Camp with helicopter some days ago. When we finally got down through the Icefall and she took off her boots, her toes were bloody lumps. Injuries so severe she was ordered to utilize the emergency exit – airborne - that are reserved exclusively for seriously injured personnel: sparse, expensive and dangerous. For the less severe casualties- injured individuals unable to stagger out on their own or supported by others - Yaks are reserved.

Sandy called her soon to become ex-husbands secretary back in the US and ordered a helicopter for her luxury departure. So she was airlifted from Pheriche a few days ago apparently in a hurry to leave and return to more civilized grounds in Katmandu. Ingrid and Tim joined her ride for free.

"I bet it's for Anatoli. He will probably show up at the very last moment." Anatoli, where are you? You promised me you were going to fly out with us today. Rumors reached us that Anatoli summited Lhotse and that my fellow Dane, Michael Jørgensen, who summited Everest with Anatoli in 1995, turned back just below the summit because of deteriorating weather. They are both alive and that's all that matters. The helicopter, delayed due to fog, is about to take off, as I detect a woolen hat appearing at the end of the runway. Anatoli! Serene lines mark his face, a familiar glow ignited, lightening sparks invigorating his blue gaze, clearly reflects to me. He is in order again. He has initiated his own healing process - summiting the fourth highest mountain in the world – his catharsis after our ordeal on Everest, where the burden he has to cope with is presumably considerably heavier than mine is. To honor his promise - Anatoli ran all night - bringing his guitar.

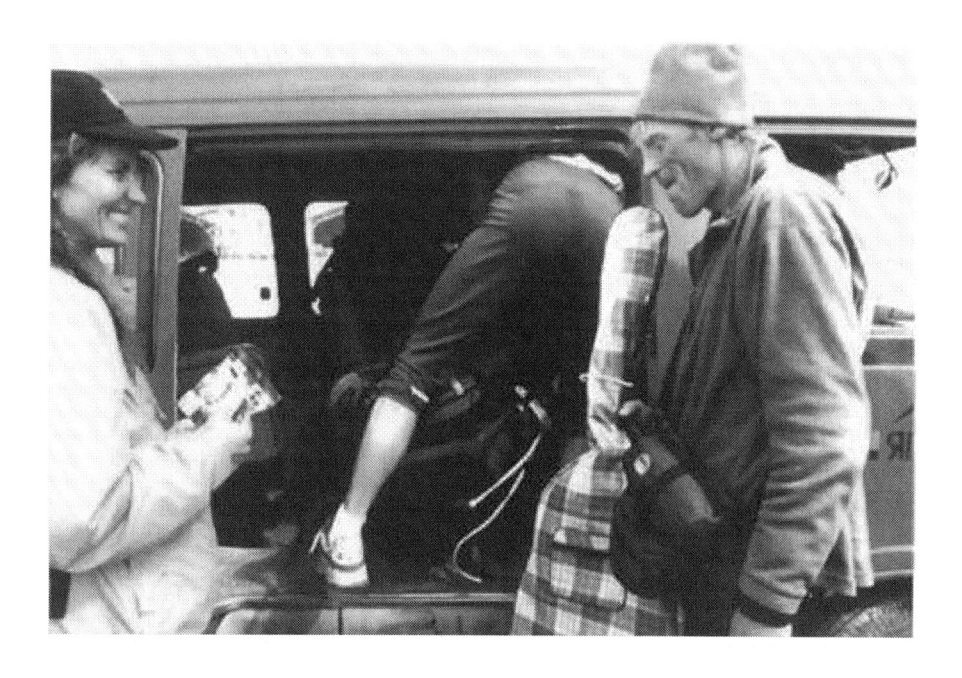

Lene Gammelgaard and Anatoli Boukreev after our helicopter airlift from Namche Bazar

Simply unbelievable!

30

"Develop success from failures. Discouragement and failure are two of the surest stepping stones to success."
Dale Carnegie

I knew before I lived the years to come, that I am going to live the rest of my life without Scott. I did not know what an immense impact his death would initiate. Our chance encounter in Solo Khumbu 5 years ago had been the beginning of who I have become now - Scott's death - the end of me. The amount that I loved him without needing to possess him was beyond quantifiable. My appreciation and passion for the life Scott has given me is all encompassing and unembellished. Scott in the truest sense gave me myself through inviting me to share the grandiosity of Everest.

Climbing high made me and killed him. Scott died alone. He, who truly did not seek solitude for himself, succumbed to the consequences of climbing high. How I wish there was something I could do to unravel reality, willing him back to life all in one piece: big handsome Scott sound and sane. Although I gradually distanced myself from, him as he turned his attention and entire focus to "Bagging the Big E" displaying signs of burnout reactions that was less than conducive, I am grateful. On the summit of Everest I felt something clicking fundamentally into place, serenity growing in me, something real and strong.

A change that has never altered since and has carried me through the rough life experiences that followed, without Scott, I would not have been who and what I am today.

Scientists have reconstructed the climatological circumstances associated with the fatal outbreak of high-impact weather on Mount Everest that occurred, when we were climbing down from the summit in May 1996. These studies indicate that during my descent, two jet streams were present in the proximity of Mount Everest. Meanwhile, in the lower troposphere, there was merging of water vapor transport from both the Arabian Sea and the Bay of Bengal into the region south of Mount Everest. Research propose that the storms in combination with the anomalous availability of moisture in the region, triggered convective activity. The resulting high-impact weather trapped over 20 of us on Mount Everest's exposed upper slopes leading to the deaths of eight. In addition, the extraordinary dropping barometric pressure and the presence of ozone-rich stratospheric air that occurred near the summit of Mount Everest during our climb could have budged a coping climber from a state of brittle tolerance to physiological distress. In 1996 we did not have sophisticated equipment that could have predicted and warned us about the extreme, unusual weather patterns.

After 1996 seismological instruments have been positioned on Everest, transmitting detailed information to satellites for climbers to download meticulous weather forecasts. There has been a lot of writing, debate, research, criticism as well as dramatized reconstruction and distortion of facts. Turn-around times for example. I am not aware that we in our group had an explicit turnaround time on summit day. Maybe I have overheard a statement. Maybe I were so affected by lack of oxygen at Camp 4 that I did not pay attention. Maybe I was somewhere else when a claimed turnaround time was fixed. Maybe our turnaround time was never a raised issue. If you have ever climbed mountains during the winter season, be it the Alps, Himalayas or Rocky Mountains, you know you have to get your ass off the mountain as swiftly as possible. It is not something we need to discuss and address, as if it was a special feature connected only with climbing Everest, explicit turn-around time or not.

All mountaineers with experience just have ourselves to either thank or blame for having adhered or the contrary to the knowledge we ought to have from years of dealing with ourselves in the Winter Mountains. Would I have turned around if anyone had told me to or ordered me to? What would that person have done, if I had not complied? No one has resources to impose any consequences whatsoever at altitude. At best, someone wanting to control my whereabouts could have become mad enough to push me off the mountain. So the debate and blame based on transgressing a specific agreed or ordered turn-around time, burns down to people's inability to live with imperfect reality. Therefore rewriting real life events into a more simplified and controllable scenario. That goes for us who were there as well as everyone writing and utilizing Everest for their own purpose. Many climbers' recollections of who did what, why and when, changed during the aftermath of Everest.

Lopsang's actions during that summit climb, as that of others, came under some degree of scrutiny in the aftermath of May 10 1996. Prior to the summit assault on 10 May, he had carried an especially large load of equipment, including 30 pounds of technological gear Sandy and consequently Scott needed for her reporting for NBC via email dispatches sent via satellite telephone and computer all the way up the mountain. In addition, at times Lopsang had closely assisted Sandy Pittman using a "short rope" technique. He later explained that he himself made such decisions, so as to provide assistance to any team member "who was having trouble" "Scott Fischer did not order me, nor did Sandy Pittman offer a "hefty" cash bonus to short-rope her to make it to the top. On ten other expeditions, I have short-roped any team member who has trouble. This year it was Sandy. I wanted to ensure that all group members had a good chance of making it to the summit. This was my goal, our team's goal. I worked very hard on this expedition and all members of my group would agree. I do not understand how Jon Krakauer, involved in a different expedition, could write statements that judge my work habits or intentions."

Lopsang acknowledged that on the day of this fateful summit push, he suffered from vomiting and fatigue. He explained, "I have been over 8,000 meters many times, each time I vomit. It is just something I do. It means nothing. Jon Krakauer makes critical references to my vomiting in his writing, implying that I was weak and unable to do my job; that it affected my performance. This was wrong. I have been over 8,000 meters many times, and each time I vomit. It is just something that happens to me and has nothing to do with altitude sickness. I have done it on all expeditions. It just happens. I did it at Camp 1, 2, etc.

On the way to the summit, Neal Beidleman saw me vomit and also misunderstood this. He took the load of ropes out of my pack and took off in the lead with Anatoli. I assumed they would fix lines for the group. My job then became that of seeing to the rest of the team, making sure they got to the summit. I in no way "lost sight of what I was supposed to be doing up there..." It would have been very bad for all three guides to go ahead and summit without the others. Again, I was doing my job. I thought that Neal and Anatoli were doing theirs. Also, if I was sick and weak, then why would I wait so long on the summit for Scott, Rob Hall and Doug Hansen? If I was sick and weak, how could I spend hours dragging Scott back down from the South Summit? My choice to summit Everest without oxygen was questioned by Krakauer. I have summited Everest three times without oxygen before this year's expedition.

On summit day of Rob Hall's 1995 Everest expedition, I broke trail through deep snow and then fixed ropes from the south summit to the top. There I waited for one hour for other team members, who unlike me were using oxygen. No one else came. You may wish to know that I netted $2,000 for this expedition, not to mention that fact that to save Sandy Pittman, I gave her my personal oxygen bottle on the way up, at 8,820 meters. I also carried an 80-pound load from Camp 3 to Camp 4 the day prior to the summit bid, which included 30 pounds of other member's personal gear.
There was no personal financial incentive for this.

Money is not important for me. I always give my best, I am my father's only child and I have many uncles and family. We help each other and live very well in Kathmandu. In reference to the complaint about the fixing of the lines, let it be understood that on all expeditions, whoever goes first from Camp 4 is supposed to fix ropes. Rob Hall's group left 45 minutes ahead of us. In my group there were two guides who were paid considerably more money than me - Anatoli Boukreev and Neal Beidleman. That these strong professional guides would waste precious time sitting on the South Summit waiting for "Sherpas" or me to come up and fix lines for them is ridiculous."

On May 10, 33 climbers went up Everest from the south side of the mountain. Only two of those climbers were not using oxygen: Anatoli Boukreev and my friend and our climbing Sirdar (manager), Lopsang Jangbu Sherpa. Anatoli and Lopsang were the only individuals who were capable of extending their physical efforts in an attempt to save other people's lives on Everest during May 10 and 11. Lopsang Jangbu Sherpa struggled for more than five hours to bring Scott Fischer down from 8,400 meters, where Scott had collapsed. Anatoli was the only person who ventured out into the storm that night from 1 am to 5 am when there was a lateral knockback of snow and little visibility. He made two forays out into 60 to 70-mile-an-hour winds in sub-zero temperatures. I write this to point out that everyone else on the entire mountain had either collapsed or were psychologically or physically unable to endure what Anatoli and Lopsang were able to accomplish.

Although technology allowed Rob Hall to talk to his wife in New Zealand by satellite phone, there was nothing that could be done to save the eight climbers, including both Rob Hall and Scott Fischer, who could not make it back to camp. I was there, I myself tried to assemble rescue teams with no response from any one present at Camp 4. Lopsang was well regarded in the mountaineering community and had in spite of his young age summited Everest four times. I got to know Lopsang on the trip to Pakistan, where Scott brought three of his favorite Sherpa friends to adventure, assist and explore the world outside Nepal. Lopsang was killed in an avalanche in September 1996, on an expedition to climb Everest again for what would have been a fifth ascent. He was swept off the Lhotse Face, almost from the spot, where I observed Dough Hansen display considerable difficulties scaling the Yellow Band in 1996 and where he and Rob caused a "bottle neck" pack up of climbers heading for Camp 4, due to their sluggish and lethargic proceeding. I was pain strikingly aware of how avalanche prone the stretch where I waited was. How exposed to heightened risk I became, because someone in front of me occupied the fixed rope for way to long, due to trouble with the altitude. At that exact stretch Lopsang lost his life within one year of having left his great friend and mentor Scott, higher up on Everest. I lost yet another of my gregarious life-infusing companions. Lopsang died, leaving his infant baby daughter to grow up fatherless and the mother of the child to fend for their survival as best as she could, without the financial infusion from the well earning young father. Denial and shock: the human psyches tendency to shape a history where we come out on top, whether it's true or not, plays a huge role in Everest Tragedy constructs.

I am a strong advocate for self-responsibility. What can 1996 teach us about leaders and the phenomena of wanting to be led? Are they a liability when their egos seem to lose grip of reality and their own limitations, as their reputation, status and experience expands? Are leaders the greatest risk? People tend to seem to want someone, an Icon, a heroic gestalt to lead them They harbor a false sense of comfort and security by avoiding self-responsibility. However, are leaders, who keep control of their team often the cause that ventures do not succeed? Our team consisted of highly self-reliant, antiauthoritarian individuals, never wanting or even considering being coxed by Scott. Moreover, Scott did not harbor any desire or inkling to construct a hierarchic anachronistic leadership structure either.

We survived. I am utterly convinced that you cannot guide Everest: in the sense that a guide ought to be the leader and strongest, who have the experience and capacity to handhold you safely into and back from an environment, where you are not yet capable of surviving under your own steam. Is that not why we hire guides? Follow leaders? To take us where we in reality do not dare to venture ourselves? Unconsciously or often demanding as well as expecting our icons to be the heroic superhuman we need to live the picture of ourselves that we prefer. Would we venture into the same situations, adventures etc. without the false security of someone stronger and wiser than us to take responsibility, when we abstain from wanting that burden? Even though it literally is our lives, we place in the doubtful care of just another human being? Guided expeditions are here to stay. History just proves that, year after year. The commercial industry is just growing and growing. Organizing permits, oxygen, logistics etc. might be safe to leave to a guided expedition. But when it truly comes to climbing, you must be certain that you have what it takes to save yourself if Everest shows her true magnitude. And she will, every year... In 2015, 500 people were waiting to attempt Everest when an earthquake struck.

Surviving Everest is shedding off every remaining layer of naivety. Most climbers taxed beyond their resources, countless become so excessively focused on the summit, that they step over dead or dying people to fulfill their desire. When catastrophe hits, everyone except the very few, transgresses all civilized socialization and are reduced to survival entities, including when it comes to leaving the weaker behind to preserve our own lives. Rightly so, that is the proven pattern of survival throughout history in various demanding environments.

We yearn for heroes, guides who are light year smarter than we are. But our risk adverse admiration is a life threatening escapism. Any deficiency in being capable and wanting to take full responsibility for yourself might be deadly. Existence above 8,000 meter is an entirely different universe and rules stripped of any resemblance with what we play by at water level. During the process of climbing high-sleeping low up and down our route, I had never been able to keep up with Anatoli. Speed is safety in the mountains. Anatoli was in another league altogether. I shared the occasional picnic with him at Camp 1 and we shared tents from Camp 3 and up.

"Stick to the winners," I put the slogan into action, that I learned working with drug addicts, before venturing to Everest. If you want to excel, do not drag the weak with you, stick to the winners - were their well wish upon my departure. I could rest next to Anatoli, but never climb in his presence. He was just so fast. Therefore, I did not harbor any expectation, that the process would be any different on summit day. Anatoli being the strongest on the entire mountain would make the passage for everyone following in his wake easier, by breaking trail and fixing the most exposed passages with the rope we would all clip our jumars onto. Rope fixed to the mountain with aluminum ice screws or snow spears. Rope routes, that the IMAX expedition and other teams for the reminder of the season would profit from. So many individuals truly depended to a certain degree of our expedition to be the first to break trail for the summit this spring. Therefore, on summit day I never wondered where Anatoli was and whether he was fulfilling his responsibilities as a guide.

I knew he had been in the forefront fixing ropes on the route for us. I never expected him or Scott to be at my side. He did what he always did in the high mountains, *"To the summit and safe return"* as expedient as possible. Speed is equivalent with safety. I would have loved Anatoli's company, but I had to wait to camp to exchange life with this extraordinary Russian. "To the summit and safe return" Anatoli was the fixer. Fixing rope on the exposed stretches no other wanted or dared to fix for the progress of the hordes that followed. Client climbers who did not want to undertake this added risk themselves. Fixing rope, especially on the intimidating traverses on the Summit Ridge was one task that I as an Everest novice gladly, ungracefully and gratefully abstained from proving my readiness of being up high, by taking upon me. I waited for the Guides and climbing Sherpas' to fix the most dangerous sections.

So did everyone else. That's what I anticipated from Anatoli's guiding role. A responsibility he could shoulder due to his massive experience and competence. "To the summit and safe return combined with speed is safety in the mountains," ought to be the ingrained steering program in everyone who sets foot on Everest. He did what he always did as a highly experienced mountaineer. Broke trail, fixed the sections that needed fixing, summited in the process and climbed back to Camp 4. "Business as usual" and not leaving me or those I climbed with any second thoughts in this regard. Based on experience, I never expected Scott, Anatoli or least of all Neal to help or rescue me. Never as much as for a split second. I knew I was on my own. Not harboring a naïve preconception that our guides were there to save my ass. I didn't much care about where they were on summit day, except my concern that Scott was so far behind and seemed weak. At the same time I had had to let go, in the process of being on Everest, acknowledging that Scott was beyond my reach, beyond any of his friends and loved ones desires to influence and preserve him. Scott resembled a drug addict you waste your life to save, ultimately having to let go of that person and your desires for possible outcomes, "What if?" Scott was beyond anybody's control and paid with his life, for not having been able to truly pay attention to himself as well as those of us, who saw his predicament and wanted him to change mode of operation. We couldn't, he didn't and then he died. Losing all opportunity of ever making the change of life, he momentarily contemplated: too late.

Now that Scott and Anatoli are both dead, I mobilize an inner drive, a purity ignited by who I fundamentally am, fueled by the sharing of life with two dissimilar ostentatious personalities. Anatoli and Scott are living in me. The admirable parts of them, their example, made me grow and change as a human being. Scott's inviting me onto the Everest Expedition made my subconscious aspire to unfold hidden resources deeply imbedded within, untapped potential that needed to be exposed, for me to thrive and come to terms with life as it is, with me as I am. Sustaining my self-mobilization, as well as validation of the fact that whenever life gets rough again - I am alive - they are dead. I have the exuberant opportunity of dealing with the ups and downs of life. Their struggles came to a halt. I do not wish for troubles to be over with once and for all through losing life.

31

"Technology can't replace experience"

I have questions that did not occur to me while preparing to summit Everest. Could we or anyone else have foreseen the extreme weather pattern that lay ahead of us? There were after all no shortage of computers and technology assembled at Base Camp. Scientific analysis conducted years after our summit approach reveals severely unusual weather end environmental conditions around May 10 1996 unpresented even by Everest standards. Why did I/we not carry a GPS that could easily have led us back to Camp 4 during the storm before nightfall? We were down in good time, but got lost, which led to at least two people dying. A GPS would have brought me back to our tent no later than 17:30-18:00 o'clock May 10. I never go sailing without my handheld Garmin, but didn't bring it to Everest. It might be a good lifesaver next time. While I was googling for information about why we did not use GPS back in 1996, I found this amusing note on Explorer's Net on how to tackle the route to the summit of Everest.

The Washburn map of Everest is for sale on the streets of Kathmandu. Bring also a small compass. Use it to take a bearing from Camp 4 to the wall when going for the summit. There are no ropes on this section and people have been lost on their way down when clouds or night set in. Much of the tragedy in 1996 could have been avoided if people had found their way back to C4. Sometimes, strobe light is used by expeditions on C4 for direction in foul weather on descent. Another option is the use of a small, handheld GPS unit. Do use some of the options and fix ropes wherever possible. The equipment needs to withstand temperatures of minus 70 degrees Celsius.

GPS stands for Global Positioning System. It can provide people with their exact position on Earth; tell them how to get to another location, how fast they are moving, where they have been, how far they have gone, what time it is and more. The system consists of a constellation of 24 satellites that orbit about 12,000 miles (19.312 km) above Earth's surface and travel approximately 7,000 miles (11.265 km) per hour. To use GPS, you must have a GPS receiver. The receiver gets information from the GPS satellites that circle the Earth twice a day and transmit signals. The receiver compares the signals from several satellites to find the difference between the time the satellite sent the signal and the time the signal is received. That information allows the GPS receiver to calculate how far away the satellite is and determine the location of the GPS user. If the GPS receiver locks onto the signal of three satellites, it can calculate latitude and longitude and track movement. With signals from four or more satellites, the receiver can also calculate altitude. Now, a GPS tracker is monitoring at the pinnacle of Mount Everest. This tracker was positioned by an American team in 1999. According to Ballinger, who has summited Mount Everest six times, as well as many of the other 8,000-meter peaks throughout the world, technology has allowed climbers to go further faster and more safely, while telling their stories in real time. For example, Ballinger brings

Wi-Fi to base camp for his teams, hauling in full Wi-Fi satellite terminals and routers to let his teams' access unlimited data plans with full Internet access. Nepalese telecom company Ncell installed 3G services at the base camp of Mount Everest in 2010 and last summer Huawei and China Mobile CHL installed 4G service there. Last year, Dubai-based mobile satellite communications provider Thuraya introduced satellite sleeves that turn cell phones into satellite phones that now provide smart phone capabilities for other peaks that lack wireless service. "This lets us access expedition weather reports, including high-altitude wind and weather maps with hourly breakdowns," said Ballinger. "They're incredibly accurate, so we can choose the best hours to be on the summit."

Thanks to laptops and improved communications on the mountains, many sponsors expect daily expedition updates. The downside is that communications technology can also divert climbers from the climb. Promoting yourself becomes a distraction. Rather than enjoying the moment and focusing on the task of climbing, mountaineers are busy updating their blogs. That said, access to information on the mountain's conditions doesn't lessen the skills needed, but it does make expeditions safer. "We've analyzed the successes and failures, looking at where, when and how accidents happened during the past 10 to 20 years, to determine the riskiest times to be in certain sections of the mountain. For example, The Khumbu Icefall, just above base camp, moves three to six feet per day.

Chunks of ice the size of houses tumble." After analyzing two years of time-lapsed images, Ballinger changed his expeditions' routes through the icefall; analyzing accident data caused him to change the time of day his teams climb it. "We assumed the icefall was safest to climb during the day, but the most ice movement is in the afternoon. Now we leave base camp around 1:00 A.M. to clear the icefall by mid-morning." Before mounting an expedition, Ballinger also downloads all the maps he may need onto an iPad, which performs well in cold, wet conditions. "Everest has fixed lines, so you don't need maps, but I use the iPad on other mountains to help find routes in whiteouts," he said. "Professional climbers also use its tracking feature as proof of summits," Ballinger said. Despite all the tools now available to elite climbers, technology is no replacement for knowledge and technical skills. Weather reports may determine a window of opportunity for a climb, "but you should still check the clouds and your own barometer.

If things change, you should be willing to turn around and go down." Modern professional climbers use a combination of high- and low-tech methods for climbs. "The technology almost makes climbing more dangerous. If the technology fails, many climbers today may lack the necessary survival skills, including route finding. For example, climbers who rely on GPS to mark difficult routes are out of luck during their return if the device is damaged or its batteries die. In contrast, those who mark their ascent routes with "willow wands," which extend well above the snow, can find those routes during their descents."

Nowadays climbing Everest is perceived as mainstream as well as business. With the territory come decisions, objectives as well as tactical decisions, including who can pay for the slot. Does the client climber have sufficient experience and money? Do sufficient funds outweigh proper considerations as to the risk involved? The down side of this development is increased crowds on the routes, new regulations, hampering the freedom that we used to escape to in the mountains and the implication that high altitude adventure trips are just like any other charter holiday. The up side is that the crowds that flock to Everest Base Camp are proof that living conditions have shifted for the better, for more people around the globe. Technology and access to cheap transport opens the world for others than the elite, shaping the opportunities for more human beings and allowing them to follow dreams and inspire more in their quest. It might downgrade "our" status that blind, one-legged, young and old people are in fact able to climb and survive climbing the highest mountain in the world. However, the expanded attentiveness most profoundly alters the way we perceive human limitations and that is for the greater good of humankind.

32

"Mountaineering is a model of the ordinary life of all human beings placed in an extreme environment. We strip away all the polite layers that make it easy to ignore the truth. We work hard, we deny ourselves comfort, and face the uncertain future with our skills. What comes of this effort is that we know ourselves better. That is what we offer the public. Everyone in his or her life must ask the questions "Who am I?" "What am I doing here?" If we were honest and fair, this is what we can report from our adventure that is important."

Anatoli Boukreev

"Early in the trip, I thought Scott's laid back system "Just a group of friends out having fun" was fucked. It ended up being better than our regulated system and that shows you how little I know. I remember thinking Anatoli is this great strong guy, but he's terrible with people. He's never around and he's always up front with his Sherpa.

I thought the Mountain Madness expedition members were looking for trouble, because none of the guides were around, climbing with the team. Some of us on the Adventure Consultants team were smug that our group was sort of the safest, that it was more conservatively guided. And we worried about Scott's group and his laissez-faire, let people do what they want. In the end, all Scott's clients survived. Anatoli is who he is. He's going to be always up front. And, as it happened, this time he was down, he just happened to be down (at Camp 4) and strong enough to save people when the time came."

Who is the member of the Adventure Consultants' team who offered this testimony within days of the Everest tragedy and before the media began to seriously hunger for someone to blame? Jon Krakauer. Based on brutal real life experiences I truly desire to promote critical thinking. Critical thinking and less bias towards our own limited controllable worldview might serve us all. To gain useful insights from the fatalities on Everest - a meaningful vantage point- is to separate the expeditions into the three microcosms that we truly were. We had very little to do with each other on Everest and at base camp. Moreover, the leaders and the individuals on the three teams were rather different in their psychological makeup and age. Illuminating crucial factors when it comes to dissecting the reasons apart from pure luck or the contrary, that some survived where others did not.

During the storm of 1996, some of us narrowly escaped, others succumbed close to where I was huddling to wait for a way out. Several climbers descended to the South Col during late afternoon on May 10, involuntarily leaving behind slower moving individuals who died. During traumatic events, we as a race are biologically compelled to find immediate ways to survive. In the chaos, arousal and propulsion to self protect, actions may be taken, that we later regret. When we are in life threatening danger, survival becomes a neuro-biological as well as an emotional imperative. Our body responds neuro-chemically to propel us to protective action, counter-aggression, stillness or flight. If we think about how we would cope in challenging scenarios, most of us have personal and cultural expectations of how we will conduct ourselves in life-threatening circumstances. Not giving up, striving to overcome the hazards, to help and protect others are common conceptions. However, acting according to these values in practice might be severely limited or impossible.

At the time of the trauma, there is an immediate sense that we should respond according to one's ordinary standards, in certain constructive ways, by halting the track of the trauma or malevolent reality, or by helping other people in a beneficial way. Neither of these wishful scenarios may be possible during extreme distress. At the very most, the response that is conceivable is less than our ideal belief.

Often, people who have experienced traumatic occurrence are particularly troubled by the fact that they were unable to exert control over what was happening. When you experience death around you for the first time, some predictable reactive patterns seem to be common. One peculiar reaction in novices is what has become known as survivor's guilt. Guilt is an emotional experience that arises when a person realizes or believes - accurately or not - that he or she has compromised his or her own standards of conduct or has violated a moral standard and bears significant responsibility for that violation. Feeling guilty is closely related to the awareness of remorse. Following traumatic events, an individual may experience "real" guilt for acts of omission, which resulted in the physical or emotional endangerment, harm or death of others. "Imagined" guilt, the crippling concept of survivor's guilt occurs when a person unconsciously believes that they have done wrong by surviving a catastrophe where others did not. Once the immediate threat to one's life is over, the "whys" surface, as the survivor begins to question why he or she was spared? "What could I have done to prevent the tragedy?" "Why did I get spared?" "Why did I deserve to live while others died?" Survivor guilt is empathy or selflessness twisted back upon itself. Guilt can be warped with an element of wishful thinking about one's ability to act. Survivor's guilt may lead to self-punishment, crippling depression, self-blame as well as the projection of blame and harmful feelings onto someone else. The guilt of survivors' show that the best qualities in humans - kindness, love, concern and care - can turn dark by psychological trauma. Jon Krakauer in "Into thin Air" with great writing skills walked backwards in the traces of our Everest experiences and created a scenario that was consistent with his judgment of what happened and who ought to have done what. In my view, Krakauer wrote a great dramatic account, constructing interpretations that work fabulously for storytelling. Attempting to objectively depict what really took place for all present on Everest and why, is not realistically possible, because we were spread out on the mountain and had very little, if anything to do with each other for the extended period of our respective expeditions. Pretending to have it all figured out and subjectively interpreting sequential happenings is just not possible and reading about who did what, when, is truly intriguing, but might not be conducive with real events.

"Everything is so tainted by the bad shit that happened," Krakauer says.
"There's no getting around it, my success is tied up with the fate of others."

The response to our incomplete enactment can be perpetual self condemnation. Self-condemnation related to that we failed to act, leading to a permanent, traumatized "self" that is still to some degree frozen in a state of perceived helplessness. Guilt presupposes the presence of choice and the power to exercise it. Survivor guilt may sometimes be an unconscious attempt to counteract or undo the helplessness we experience in too taxing situations. The idea that one somehow could have prevented what happened may be more desirable than the frightening notion that our trials were completely random and senseless.

In the aftermath of Everest, several participants on our expedition express a profound need to hear from fellow mountaineers, who had also survived the storm, what transpired where they were. A few had been unconscious or semi unconscious and we were all trying to piece together the puzzle of who had been where, with whom, when and what had happened to those who were not in our proximity. On the first day, back at base camp, we sat down together and started opening up, re-counting individual perspectives from the summit attempt. Relating self-experienced fragments of the bid for the summit and what each one of us lived through during the storm. Fragments, as objective as realistically possible, no interpretations, blame, speculations, just sharing what we individually carried with us down from the mountain. Day two, I noticed that some in our group were already altering what they had shared the day previously. Thus it continued. Over the years, I have followed individual perspectives change. Often times it seemed and seems as if the single person tells a story that is conducive with the picture we humans want of our conduct and ourselves. Sometimes it's innocent and does no harm. Other times it is a direct construct painting a heroic act, where there was none and thereby diminishing reality as well as the person who rightly deserved the honor. We who were high on Everest in 1996 all experienced shortcomings due to lack of oxygen and exhaustion up high. What we write whether the reality we choose to construct through our books, interviews and films, are close to reality or as far from what happened as proper fiction, it is there in print forever. It becomes part of Everest history. As time passes, what we write stands out as the truth, even though we are all biased and self-serving. The truth is what actually transpired, not what any one makes of our fates, to serve their own purposes. Altering factual reality through our subjective recollections as well as projections is a normal human well-researched process and happens for all of us continuously. The human psyche is designed to protect us from becoming flooded by traumatic circumstances and therefore alters whatever is needed, for us not to go under due to psychic strain. For some who were on Everest the reality-descripting, probably makes it possible to deal with the facts and traumas. Guilt can occur not only in relation to what we ought or ought not to do, but in relation to our views about what we ought to be. What is possible under normal conditions, however, is often not possible under traumatizing circumstances. Therefore, assessing responsibility based on normal conditions for what happened during the traumatic events may result in faulty assessments. Psychological projections by which humans defend themselves against unpleasant impulses by denying their existence in themselves, while attributing them to others, tends to come to the fore in normal people at times of crisis. Projection is a defense mechanism that involves taking our own unacceptable or admirable character traits or feelings and ascribing them to someone other than ourselves. Projection works by allowing the expression of the desire or impulse, but in a way that the ego cannot recognize. Through this psychological defense mechanism, anxiety is reduced to a level we can cope with.

May 10 1996 lives on and on in a myriad of contexts, presenting a sounding board for several walks of life. My perspectives and analysis might differ from some of what was reported and written about Everest, particularly the importance of specific actions or lack thereof. What is the truth about all the individual destinies involved in what transpired up high? It depends on whom you ask. We all have our own agenda. No one can claim, without arrogance to present the full insightful picture. Some of the truths will never be told, as quite a few of the major characters that continue to live in the eyes of the public are dead. What happened to them and truly why? We can only subjectively guess and speculate. Anatoli is dead. Scott is long gone. So is Lopsang Sherpa. Rob Hall, Doug Scott, Andy Harris. Certain knowledge perished with them. But I find it disturbing, if and when, we who still exposes our version of Everest distort facts to an extent where it is directly harmful or untruthful. And to what end? What exactly happened on Mount Everest in 1996 during our climb will never be completely clear. The factual truths are gone for good. I warn people who contact me for advice and guidance on how to climb Everest. Do you have children? If they have, I bluntly tell them that I do not want to have anything more to do with them. I find it fundamentally irresponsible to undertake high-risk adventures when you have children.

Next, if not, I stress that they must gain enough experience to be able to save themselves no matter what the promise and lure of advertising, commercial expedition enterprises promote. I will never coach anyone to become ready for climbing Everest. I know you risk dying. So go for it, but I will have nothing to do with it. Neither will I guide another mountain as I have done after Everest. I just do not want to have the responsibility for less experienced people's lives in an environment, where they involuntarily place their trust in me. Learning from experience, studying what transpired when I were on Everest, combined with the myriads of expeditions, consisting of more or less experienced climbers, individuals driven by a similar quest that drove me to the summit in 1996, confronts us all with brutal facts. Very few individuals are capable of helping suffering mountaineers above 8,000 meters. Virtually no one thinks about the other climber above or below. Everyone has to get down, on their own or truly be prepared to be left alone, abandoned to die.

Most alpinists are too ambitious or obsessed to abstain from going up, instead of assisting ill-fated climbers if possible. Just think about the IMAX expedition, having lost several of their good friends few days earlier, literally stepping almost across their dead associates and colleagues in pursuit of shooting a sadly flat romanticized gender biased film. What does that tell you about the virtues of high altitude mountaineering? Friendships, bonding for life or I am myself nearest. With the rising number of people wanting to climb Everest, the cynicism and human indifference seems to spread. Is the mountaineering community at large becoming more indifferent to our fellow beings on Everest? Was decency ever a component for ambitious summit seekers? What repeatedly puzzles me, when being engulfed by the emotional undercurrent from Everest, is why Anatoli seems to have been singled out to be the ONE, the only one that ought to have acted superhuman, where other guides, clients and expedition leaders are not scrutinized? What is it about Anatoli that allows some people to disregard their own all to average conduct on Everest, not doing anything at all but saving themselves, to point their beamer at Anatoli and develop special standards of correct conduct that entirely seem to apply to this strong Russian mountaineer? Is it envy? Is it guilt? Survivor's guilt? When a risky adventure transmutes into tragedy, severe traumatic reactions caused by multiple losses can occur. In addition to deaths, parts of one's own nature, self-confidence and expectations might be altered or lost. Consequently we might project our own disgraceful self-assertion unto someone outside ourselves to be able to cope with the guilt that is a common response following loss and traumatic experiences with significant victimization.

    I do not advocate that Anatoli could not have contributed to a different outcome, had he been with us who ended up in the huddle. Neal dragged Yasuku Namba down the fixed ropes until he realized it was not me in the red down suit. I never even contemplated to attempt moving her physically, but tried verbally to encourage her to follow Klev and me down the fixed ropes, Yasuku got up, but was so slow; we did not dare to wait. Then Neal came and tried to drag her for a short distance, also having to let go, to preserve himself and our group coherence. Even so, Klev and Neal tried to drag Yasuku back with us, in our attempt to locate Camp 4 in the gale-force whiteout but both had to let go and leave her, to die. Would Anatoli have made a difference? Would we have found Camp 4 immediately if he had been with us? Depends... I guess. How affected was Anatoli by altitude and fatigue? Being the most capable mountaineer on the mountain does not make your into an infallible God. So maybe Anatoli could have escorted Yasuku down and we could have found Camp 4 and not have to remain in the ferocious storm. Just maybe Beck Weathers would have been less affected by frostbite and maybe Yasuku could have survived. I assume this could have been best scenario outcome.

    Would Anatoli have focused on Rob Hall's expedition members instead of us? Would he have been less incapacitated than everyone else on the entire mountain? I know from firsthand experience that Anatoli was the sole human being capable and willing to venture out into the storm and save three people, who might otherwise have died or suffered severe injuries as reality transpired and not in hindsight speculative "What if" scenario.

Did anybody but Anatoli make a difference in the outcome at 8,000 meters on May 10 late at night 1996? No! Not a single person as much as contributed in the act of melting snow for those who suffered. Nobody except Anatoli did anything but survive himself or herself. So harsh are the conditions at 8,000 meters. Nobody did anything. Not because they might not have wanted to. Most were completely exhausted and could not do anything but to try to remain alive, preserving their own lives.

Was it wrong of Anatoli to be the first one down? If you have not been to Everest and experienced "Business as usual", and therefore still expect a guide to be the strong, wise person who escorts you safely up and down and make sure that no harm comes to you, then naturally Anatoli made a huge mistake by being the first one off the summit. However, if you harbor the belief that someone like Anatoli is there to save you and do for you, what you are not competent enough to do under your own steam, you might be signing your own death warrant. All lies in the eyes of the beholder.

Anatoli acted as the highly experienced mountaineer he was. And he too suffered the effects of altitude. You cannot safely be on Everest and eliminate risk, no matter who is in front and who is not. Your best odds of surviving are placing trust in your own capacities, because you have accumulated experience to back that trust.

Rob Hall climbed with his clients, presenting a clear example of security seeking and controlled hand-holding by remaining close to the weakest client. On the surface for some, a much wanted guidance. Rob and Dough both reached the summit, Dough apparently heavily influenced by Rob Hall's desire for him to summit. Compelled by unknown reasons, Rob was never able to leave Dough Hansen behind close to the top, when Dough succumbed due to complete exhaustion. Rob postponed for too long, his feet freezing into solid ice, causing immobility. He triggered a lot of trouble for the clients on his team by not defusing the trust they bestowed him. He unwisely ordered Beck Weathers to wait for him to come down from the summit and escort him down to Camp 4.

It is outright stupid, imprudent and fatal to tell anyone to sit still in the mountains and for Beck to have adhered to such a devastating order was deadly. Even the most novice hiker, skier or mountaineer are acquainted with the survival rule, "never sit still in the mountains", such an order coming from a very experienced leader that ought to have known better contradicts all wishful placing too much confidence in leaders, on Everest and possibly anywhere. For Beck to comply to that was senseless and a proof of either lack of experience, inability to assume responsibility or the effects we all suffer under, lack of sufficient oxygen to be even as trustworthy as we might be at sea level.

Rob climbed in proximity of most members of the New Zealand team, but four died anyway, including Rob himself.

Whenever I take people into wilderness, I allocate an experienced person in the front and another competent co-guide at the rear-the sweeper switching places every other day. On summit night, Scott took the role of the sweeper with Anatoli leading in front. Leaving around midnight on the verge of May 10, Scott was at the back, probably because he was tired, needed Anatoli to fix ropes and expected to be slower than Anatoli. During our summit climb, Scott fell so far behind, that nobody joined or saw him until we passed him on our way down from the summit, except Lopsang, who waited for him on the actual summit. None on our team expected Scott to do anything in relation to our summit bid, so he was not missed. Neal was among some of us on the route from Camp 4 to the summit. Neither Rob nor Scott contributed to the safety of the expedition members I was in proximity of. Rob actively did the exact contrary and increased the risk by asking Beck to sit still, remain where he was and wait for Rob's return, as he coached an already exhausted client upwards. It proved fatal to Rob himself as well as Dough Hansen, when Rob somehow and for whatever reasons decided and managed to mobilize Dough Hansen to continue towards the summit in spite of Doug's initial decision to turn around, apparently himself realizing his drained and exhausted ailment, so straightforwardly observed by me, while waiting for Rob and Dough to scale the Yellow Band. Rob Hall was a true liability as a leader for those individuals who did not assume responsibility for their own safety. So how does reality comply with the wants and needs for expedition leaders to be guides, that warrants safety for the less experienced? If we simply attribute the tragedy on Everest to the inadequate capabilities of a few mountaineers, then we have missed an opportunity to identify broader lessons from our fates.

Scott never helped or guided anyone on summit day. Nor was he close enough to offer advice or actively influence anyone to do something injudicious. Nor did we expect him to or depend upon him to be where we were. Lopsang Sherpa almost exasperated himself, willing to escort Scott down the mountain, but during the night had to vacate Scott, not to die from trying like Rob might have done. One dead is better than two.

Lopsang saved himself and climbed down to beg for help from others to climb back up to carry Scott down. All wasted efforts, as no one came to assistance. Due to human frailty and limitations, Scott lost his life, alone. Apart from Lopsang, no guide, experienced climber or client did anything that was conducive to saving Scott's life. Moreover, he was not able to save himself. For Lopsang to make the decisions to leave Scott behind, to die, as it turns out so as not to collapse himself, must have been devastating, yet necessary. A decision anyone on Everest must be able to make and live with or die from not being able to carry through, when things goes less desirable than wanted and envisioned. Whoever summits Everest and survives will have to live with the amassed consequences. It might save lives if alpinists stop to ignore the conventional wisdom of fixing an ultimate turnaround time. A clear deadline advocating that you should turn back, if you cannot reach the summit by no later than one o'clock in the afternoon. I advocate strict adherence to a conservative turnaround time. Openly discussing how crucial it might become to get your butt off Everest before darkness sets in, would help protect against the tendency to continue climbing because of our substantial prior commitment of willpower, money, years of training and the dreams of what might follow standing on top of the world. Turning around at a specific time, no matter how close you might be to the summit, is something you can control yourself: an action that will add to your chances of surviving.

All Everest climbers using the southern route have to pass a group of five bodies, amongst them Scott Fischer. A memorial cairn for Scott can be found at the top of a hill called Dugla Pass, near the village of Dugla, on the trail to Everest base camp. A similar memorial plague is placed on route to the summit of Kilimanjaro. The mountain Scott and Wesley Krause explored back in their youth. I cried, allowing myself to acknowledge my grief, when I led people up Wesley and Scott's route back in 1997 and 1998. I was guiding Kilimanjaro, actually being responsible for less experienced people's dream of standing on the highest point on the African continent. Turning a few around due to altitude sickness and experiencing local porters become snow blind, due to lack of sufficient equipment and protection, lead me to a fundamental conclusion,

"I will never guide mountains again. I will never risk experiencing, someone not sufficiently capable of taking the full responsibility for themselves in a wilderness environment - becoming injured or die - when I am the leader." Consequently, I stopped guiding.

As of 2017, Scott's body remains on Mount Everest. Scott's family still hopes to arrange for the retrieval and proper disposal of his remains. In 1997 Anatoli ventured on his next expedition to Everest: this time as the leader, guiding an Indonesian National Team. He found Yasuku Namba's body on April 28, 1997. Anatoli constructed a cairn around her, to protect her from scavenging fellow climbers and a few days later apologized to her widower for failing to save Yasuku Namba's life.

33

"There are many questions, but I cannot answer because I am not a businessman, I am a climber"
Anatoli Boukreev

- The fulfillment of one vision is a new beginning.
- Decide what you want to do in your next life chapter.
- Generate a new vision.
- Set new goals, adapt, develop strategies and take action.
- Take action-inspire change through Human Innovation.

I dread that most of us affected by climbing Everest in 1996, have been altered some way or the other. Traumatized and never to recover to innocence as before Everest. "It is as if we never came down from the mountain." David Breashears exclaimed while filming and interviewing me in Boston a while back, for his Everest movie. We, who carve out our voice to let our version of what happened on Everest come into life, inevitably take a point of view in deciding what to convey, which version of the complex reality we promote and what sources we quote and how and in which context we utilize the puzzle pieces in our construction of the reality we want to convey. While the tragedies of 1996 were distinctive, they were certainly not unusual.

Climbers die on Everest every year, but the 1996 tragedy, offered satellite phones, internet access to devastating events on-line and a cast of grand characters that intrigued arm chair climbers and the common man. Our expedition's fate was practically a readymade news event. The Everest IMAX film from 1998 has reached theatres around the world and has given a simplistic view of the mountain and a chance for viewers to catch a glimpse into the incredible beauty that seduces us. Yet it is also biased and the IMAX team decided to climb only a few days after several of their longtime friends died on their route. The film Everest 2015, adds to the countless stories based on what transpired in the spring of 1996. Most of the people taking an interest in Mount Everest will never experience, the 40 below cold, the 100 mile per hour winds, the excruciating pain of moving your body up 3,000 feet in a day and trying to breathe, much less eat, sleep and drink at the 29,000ft mark. As the West decides who are the Everest heroes and desperadoes, the Sherpa of Nepal go about their business of climbing Everest in un-celebrated glory.

1996 was also the first season where guided expeditions began to outnumber ordinary expeditions. The guiding concept brought a lot of turbulence into the mountaineering scene and far beyond. In the aftermath debates exploded. Questions were raised about the responsibility of the guides and what expectations the client harbors, conscious or unconscious that the guide is omnipotent. "No guide can guarantee safety at extreme altitude: I offer my experience for hire. I will advise a group of people on how to reach the summit and I will help them, but I cannot be responsible for their safety. They understand that." Anatoli stated before guiding Everest in 1997. People without high altitude experience or climbing insight might think guiding Everest can be conducted in the same way you would guide a safari. You buy your progress through a guide because you do not want to invest the time or are not fully experienced to take the complete responsibility for all complexities and planning connected with climbing high. In reality, most people who want to pay huge sums for a guide are probably not fully capable of conducting everything that's needed to be established and carry through a successful voyage. So climbing on a guided expedition implies a certain negligence of the fact that at altitude nobody can truly help you when things go wrong. Guide or not, you should be able to carry through on your own no matter what. However, modern humans are in a hurry. We do not want to or lack the knowledge of how long it truly takes to master the skills of survival. Many want to "Bag the big E" as just another holiday adventure and therefore we look for someone presumably better and more competent than ourselves, so we can entrust our lives in their hands and succeed faster than we could have, if we had been left to our own hard gained experiences. Hiring a guide for a risky adventure in any environment has one main characteristic in for conducting a safe ascent and offer timely assistance when necessary? Including turning people around when they show signs of not being able to deal with the conditions for whatever reason. Aid on higher peaks than 8,000 meters cannot be compared with the type of help a guide can present in the Alps. Here you can have assistance available from professional rescuers and special rescue services that are equipped and prepared to arrive quickly with helicopters. People still die in the Alps though. Risks are always present in the mountains and at high altitude; the risks are incomparably greater and excessively complex.

Climbing as a guide is probably at least ten times more difficult and dangerous than climbing alone. Whether through a guide service or other type of apprenticeship, we most often learn to climb from others, some who for a while are more experienced and better at the task than we are. 1996 turned climbers into guides and we climbers who were not guides became clients. Above 8,000 meters, a guide can only count on her or his own strength and experience to help you avoid irreversible mistakes. What about the clients if the guide fails? Scott and Rob died and we were without them on our descent. Everyone who summits Everest must be able to move one foot in front of the other under his or her own steam and failure to you might die. No doubt there will always be differences as to what level teams are technically suited for the challenge. From the onset, there has been a huge variation in the actual experience level of those who are drawn to Everest. The concept of guiding has now long been a part of Everest. Bearing the development of the Everest climbing industry in mind, guiding has become the common way of attempting to summit Everest today. Dwindling the massive controversy stirred by the commercial expeditions in 1996.

Our expedition on Mount Everest probably became a turning point in Anatoli's ability for self-sustainability. Some fine inner perimeter appeared transgressed by the world in the aftermath of Everest. Maybe a confrontation with the lack of fundamental insight and brutal honesty by perceived fellow climbers of what it truly takes to be a mountaineer and survive, ate away some of him. Anatoli unfortunately did not live long enough to truly recover from "Everest". How he conducted himself on

Annapurna, I am certain is a consequence of the process following Everest, where Anatoli was thrust into a negative spotlight of criticism, speculation and inquisitive attention generated by Jon Krakauer's personal interpretation of what transpired on Mount Everest in the storm of 1996. Outdoor magazine rushed to publish an article that held Anatoli accountable for having done what he did and did not do in the storm and complex web of ambitions that was beyond his control.

A global controversy threatened to eclipse Anatoli's brilliance and unquestionable bravery and extraordinary strength and capacity at high altitude. I hope to reveal some of the uniqueness and incorruptibility of Anatoli and his extent as a human being. All western climbers I have meet have given up some of their integrity to make money and pursue public limelight to satisfy the trends of our time and the sponsors craving for product placement. Anatoli was not like them. I have heard admiring comments from people all over the world, where fellow human beings seem to recognize Anatoli's ethic, through books written of and about him. Anatoli's mentality and discipline made him stand apart from his contemporaries. He was better than most of us.

Question remaining, did pure envy from more average westerners play a part in the aftermaths of Everest? Anatoli was one of the most experienced, strongest, wisest and profoundly disciplined mountaineers on the mountain, qualities worth respecting in themselves, but Anatoli was admirable on more profound levels due to his unsoiled love and understanding for the high altitude. Petty intrigues were beyond Anatoli's ideology; his zest for climbing was above slander and character slaying. He loved the Himalayas. Their unsoiled pristineness, for him was life itself. It is possible to achieve what Anatoli did, if you know what you want and work as hard and determined as he truly did. He is a grand example of human capability and also when it comes to living moral authentic ethical standards. Anatoli was a genius in the mountains and a wise philosophical human being. He was decent. He lives on as an inspiration in me.

When a human being has been stretched to the extent of Everest and the rewarding influence of being capable on summiting and surviving intertwined with the traumatizing impacts of so many dying, our brains are wired differently for the future. In the first year following my summiting and survival on Everest, I was disproportionately overemotional, grief and exhaustion made me excessively vulnerable, exposing my rawness in tears flooding relentlessly to the few I let in behind my successful façade. I turned myself into a workaholic - opportunistically utilizing the unique openings the global craze - following our expedition kindled worldwide. I had planned to immigrate to the US, entering into partnership with Scott, positioning myself for a guiding position in Mountain Madness. Making the transition from Denmark to the US smoother and more financially sound, following the successful summiting of Everest as a member of Scott's Mountain Madness adventure. Instead, at this juncture I was left with an emptied vision, the glory of the future we dreamt up distorted by the sobering reality of the irreversible death.

Instead of moving the card boxes in my flat into a new life on the other side of the Atlantic, I decided to utilize the global branding and unique opportunities being the first Nordic Woman on Everest actually boosted. I focused intently on work, working, lecturing, writing the first ever Everest account about

May 1996, participating passionately in the book launch process in Denmark in the fall 1996, then Germany, Holland, Italy, France etc. followed by a too packed three months US promotional road trip in 2,000. A successful global branding strategy set in motion, pursuing the intention Scott and I had co-created - airborne - due to the massive attention, only catastrophe seems to mobilize. A conscious coping strategy that left me completely flattened and with no room for either washing my hair or even peeing. At least I was carving out a niche for myself, celebrating the actual success I had accomplished, in exchange for the shared adventure focused future on the American Continent, which had been a considerable chunk of the motivation propelling me up Everest. I was pushing myself, saying yes to all offers in my "five Minutes of Fame window" of opportunities, burning out slowly but surely. I didn't realize how utterly outright exhausted I worked myself into being, before I had to be flown back to Denmark from a Trekking Documentary Film shoot in the Austrian Alps, no longer able to suppress the signs of physical degrading with painkillers.

I had accomplished much of what I dreamt could happen if I summited Everest and survived to tell the tale. But even fame and success come with a price tag. Being strong and trusting my physique to bear whatever I exposed myself to, I ended up feeling nothing, emotionally numb and blissfully freed from all vicissitudes. I exist with the imprint that it takes extraordinary sensory triggering before I can feel anything, but resigned distance, continuously seeking equilibrium and inner peace.

On Everest I experienced human nature when pushed beyond its uttermost limit. My interpretations of interacting unconsciously make me distrust or not respect human beings, until they have proven as worthy as Anatoli. Why invest tons of loyalty and love in someone or several, only to discover their self-servingness if things get tough? Formed by the facts in my life that the ones I cherish the highest perish, I observe that I have removed myself from city living, withdrawn in to nature, keeping a distance to civilization and enjoying the sounds of the wind, birds twitter, attracting mates during the lush spring months. Freed and puzzled by a feeling of not needing to accomplish any more great deeds. A modus of existence that is new to me: an untouched novel alleyway to be reconnoitered.

Who are to be the judges of who are really qualified to make an attempt of summiting the highest mountain in the world? What if we leave the verdict to Everest itself? We could conclude that those who come down alive, were qualified as well as lucky no matter what they have on their climbing c.v. Those who do not survive were not qualified at this specific point in time, under whatever uncontrollable circumstances they perished. But is this accurate? Who are to judge? Those who climb themselves or onlookers attempting to understand the earnesty, brutality, heroism and the lack thereof that is a part of belonging to the group of people with a psychological profile that make us willing to confront the risks of climbing high. The majority of humankind would never choose to attempt this endeavor.

34

"She is free in her wildness; she is a wanderess, a drop of free water. She knows nothing of borders and cares nothing for rules or customs. 'Time' for her isn't something to fight against. Her life flows clean, with passion, like fresh water."

Roman Payne

Everest is a long time ago but I believe all that occurred is still influencing me on profound levels today. Those of us who have summited the mountain seem unable to forget it, as if the experiences seeped into our genetic fiber. Actually the newest cutting-edge research seems to prove that profound impacts as well as traumas, actually alters our genetic dispositions. I breathe in a crisp day in the fall, as I receive an e-mail from a woman I do not know, Charlotte Bøving, an Icelandic actress it turns out, is playing "me" in the 2015 Everest Film. Thus, learning that Hollywood has invested 65 Million USD in yet another version of our destinies on Everest May 1996, provokes long buried and hidden emotions connected with Everest and the loss of Scott, Anatoli and Lopsang. They all died in the Himalayas within a year.

Having learned to live without their lively impact in and on my life, I again have to come to terms with the fact that others will choose their version of our reality, without consulting us, who are portrayed on the big screen and alive to tell our own tales. I know it is professionally wise to write another book in the wake of the Everest Film hype.

Nevertheless, I have been procrastinating and dawdling, for good and sound reasons. Not wanting to dedicate time backwards, prioritizing the past instead of living those same hours in the present. Everest, and me summiting, and surviving Everest in truly adverse conditions have revealed that my urge to break barriers stems from resources causing me to pursue unconventional life quests. I truly have what it takes to dream and pursue my vision until it comes true, in spite of extraordinary taxing challenges and setbacks. However, I still intensely want Scott and Anatoli to be alive, granting me the opportunity of sharing yet another adventure with my audacious, life zest inspiring companions.

Not wanting to turn time back, I have been postponing working on this book because I assume I will be re-confronted with my longing, loss and being stuck in impossible idealization of the deceased. I do not want to risk becoming engulfed in the sentiments intertwined with not having Scott and Anatoli in my life any more. I have been feeling slightly depressed lately, trying to escape the numbness of low energy and lack of lust for life: my three kids mirroring my inside grayness through our conflicts and lack of joyfulness.

The Everest Film might have poked a hole into protective layers, shielding me from the experiences and losses in my past. Triggering unwelcome intense response to my old traumas; causing me to experience sudden panic, irritability, anger, grief and vague "sinking" feelings that sometimes seem to come "out of the blue." Such reminders of our buried pasts can be obvious or they can be so subtle that you may not easily recognize them as connected with the ordeal. You may find that, quite unpredictably, you dissolve under ordinary stress that you would usually take in stride. You might find that music is intolerable, that your children's behavior or noise is hard to take, or that you can't watch television.

    The emotional overload from the past traumas inflicts on my here and now. Although my sentiments can be very intense at times, at other times they may be so much the opposite that I feel dull, empty, numb or completely shut down and depleted of all energy. Year after year, I have felt emotionally extinct, like a humanoid without feelings. I feel detached and estranged from others. You may feel that you can't even generate feelings of love in your most treasured relationships. You may lose interest or feelings of enjoyment for your favorite pastimes, eating or sex. Even though others may think you are doing well, it may alarm you to feel so benumbed and lacking in feeling. Again, this is a part of the normal response to trauma. My system mobilizes to protect me from being overwhelmed after trauma by numbing my feelings. For months, I have preferred to avoid negative emotions and to delay the stressful task of opening up the past through writing this new book. My procrastination has resulted in stress, anxiety, a sense of guilt, crisis and severe loss of personal productivity. On the other hand, my procrastination has been useful in identifying what is important to me, my kids and horses, as it is rare to postpone, when we truly value the undertaking at hand. It is perfectly normal to procrastinate to some degree. Putting off an undertaking is not procrastination, if there are rational reasons for doing so. I can easily invent plenty: I have published several books since I first published "Climbing High - Everest - Vejen til toppen" in Denmark back in 1996, making me the first of numerous to publish my account about what transpired on Everest. Being a small country with a minor language, it took years for my book to hit the global market even though it was a best seller in Denmark for a long period. I do believe it was healthy for my emotive survival, that I was not dragged into the global mud throwing that took place in the immediate aftermath of Everest 1996. I assume I have endured healthier psychologically, because I was withdrawn from the worst biased exclamations.

Looking at pictures of Anatoli after Everest, he appears burnt out and inertly deflated. Not having had enough time to regroup himself and restore a new way of being him, before he died. I blame Jon Krakauer and the media for contributing to Anatoli's disgrace as an ethical human and purist mountaineer. I am convinced that the aftermath of Everest where Anatoli became singled out, inflicted upon the way he climbed on Annapurna. As I meet his Italian friend, who witnessed the avalanche that caused Anatoli's death, I discerned the style in which he climbed was rather unlike Anatoli's former prudence, for whatever reasons.

The 2015 Everest Film was a constant undercurrent in my life since I was made aware of its production through Charlotte Bøving. 1996 is truly numerous years ago, lot of lived life and altering experiences. Nevertheless, the truth probably is, 1996 still shapes my present. I assume I might be more resigned than others might at my age, due to having lived an ultimate vision, fulfilled a monstrous dream and survived to live on without the mobilizing force of striving towards an almost unfathomable goal. Even though the latest Everest movie handed me a re-branding opportunity "Out of the blue", I buried the bidding to dive into 1996 all winter. Susceptible to the practice of deferment, daily carrying out less urgent tasks in preference to more urgent steps towards materializing my strategy for approaching the global market, preoccupying my mind with more pleasurable here and now oriented investments, in place of the anticipation of a less pleasurable writing process and thus putting off the impending tasks of finishing this book.

Having shaped a lifestyle, offering serenity and nature, I dillydally, not wanting to wake my companions from their icy dwellings, distancing myself from contemporaneous lifetime with my kids by going down memory lane and feel the thrill and love, I have not been able to replace since my inspiratory and adventuresome companions perished. Believe me, I have tried to the point of resignation. I have forced myself to grow accustomed to existing without my unconscious urge to adventure, in search of the replacement of Scott and Anatoli in chance encounters, scavenging for men out of the ordinary. I have lived long and experienced the full impact of their passing to be forced to accept that life was a grander place when Scott and Anatoli were alive. Eventually, lack of energy and increasing foul moods drove me to initiate the writing process.

Now - 20 years after Everest - I have one more time confronted myself with profound loss: Scott's death on our expedition May 10 1996, followed by Anatoli being swept of Annapurna by an avalanche, Christmas day 1997. The true extent of those fatalities, has become severely evident over time as I unwillingly acknowledge still missing both of them for their individual values and assets, over and over again. Dream-feeders for humankind and me are irreplaceable. I am marked by fate, my life taking paths it might not have, had I not encountered and been bidden to share life with these two grand personalities.

"I just saw the Everest film" Wesley Krause wrote to me. "Pretty disappointing. Of course their main goal is selling tickets and it is Hollywood but they could have tried harder. The Scott portrayal is pretty grim. First of all - why did they have a skinny dark haired guy with a full brown beard play Scott? I can deal with the "Oh wow man - we're all out here having fun no need to get up tight about the plan" part, but having a Scott character not be energized about life and inspirational with that infectious let's go energy he had, was a downer. Awesome if you can write something that sheds light on the other side of the story."

Wes and Scott had been friends since they were kids.

"Of course I still miss the guy. We grew up together adventuring around the world. We were in a number of ugly, tight spots at deaths doorstep and we would always say to each other. "What, are we going to do Homestead here?" as a way of mustering what we needed to keep on. I would have never thought Scott would give up and sit down. He was obviously in a tired, weakened state. Of course, he should have had faith in his leadership team and even bragged about the fact that he could stay behind as the "wiser old guy" and call the shots from below. But he wasn't that mature in life yet and had to stroke the ego still. We've all been there, but luckily for our kids, not when the stakes were quite so high. Scott was in Tanzania in March and really talked about making '96 his last Everest climb, I guess he succeeded and went on to say he was coming back to TZ with his kids. He at least had change in his heart: sad."

Wesley Krause and Scott Fischer

Immersing myself in the hundreds of photo's I have from our journeys yet again makes me gratefully realize how fortunate I am to have shared life with extraordinary personalities like Scott and Anatoli and how changed I have become from not being able to replace Scott and Anatoli with significantly enough other people: except my three kids. Hard as I have fought for my life to develop differently, replicating what I would have pursued had Scott still been alive, I have had to admit, that without Anatoli and Scott, I am not what I could have been. My time with adventure is something I speak of in past tense. Until this hour, I have not been able to fix a deadline to work towards accomplishing this book project. Just a few minutes ago I realized, this book, my hymn in veneration for the impact on who and what I am today, adding a few more human details to the portraits of two extraordinary humans, will be ready for the Global Market on May 10th 2016, 20 years after Everest 1996. Some personalities are unique, genuinely authentic enough to truly be inspiration for generations. Some people are irreplaceable, because we, who might not have the equivalent driving force, can create revolutions with the inspiration of these extraordinary human beings. When they perish, the world does close in upon itself. I am grateful to have shared some of life's wonders with Anatoli Boukreev and Scott Fischer. Two extraordinary people, whom I have as yet not been able to replace with living specimens of equal caliber and believe me, I have tried. Two men with whom I cynically measure any man who tries to venture into my life: a sadly impossible task, as time tends to bury the less than optimal character traits of those we loved. This keeps me aloof and withdrawn from emotional entanglements: a coping strategy that keeps me out of harm's way emotionally but has a definite isolating effect. What makes a person worthy of veneration? What does it take to feel deep respect for the dignity, wisdom, dedication and talent of one individual? A human icon is an individual, who retains original purity, stays uncorrupted and unsullied. One who becomes an enduring symbol for others to be inspired by and is therefore considered great: the so-called larger than life personalities.

What are the characteristics of these driven and globally respected iconic humble human beings? How can we - you and I - pursue decency in spite mass materialism and the global trends of focusing on material values before we focus on human values? How can we - you and I - develop character traits to inspire and contribute, to make the world a better place?

Lene Gammelgaard NeuroLeadership Business Talk

Due to my experiences from my Everest process and my passionate fascination for the potential for innovation in people, I have established myself as Global Motivational Speaker and Business Innovator utilizing the unique Branding Everest 1996 implies. I founded my company Human Innovation and I am now widely acknowledged as a specialized human innovation-activating lecturer. Mobilizing visionary quanta jump development processes in people, initiating innovation in individuals, in organizations around the globe. Life can and should be an adventure; after all we only live once. Our lives should be utilized from beginning to end.

And we can consciously program our brain to mobilize us in the desired directions. "The Everest Way".

Human Innovation through self-programming of our brains.
NeuroLeadership

In my lectures, Keynotes and books I share my experience-based strategies of how we can program our brain to support us to achieve what we dream about. I am genuinely motivated to discover and share the most effective strategies to make the most of our lives, because I passionately believe all human beings have untapped potential and a quest for seeking meaning from existence - to become fulfilled.

I wholeheartedly commit myself to continue to reach out to as many people as possible in the humble hope that those who are seeking more from life might find inspiration and ongoing fighting spirit through my life philosophies.

Numerous people I have encountered on the subject of Everest have certain concepts of what an expedition is like, what such a venture must be, the camaraderie, the leadership, the responsibilities, strategies, decision making and the teamwork. The friendships the outsider romanticizes will arise between mountaineers that have suffered through what we survived. Sometimes people become puzzled, almost offended, if the hands-on experiences I share do not correspond with their imaginings. The guiding concept for example raises awareness. Guides on Everest expeditions are not rescue services that pick up weaker individuals along the way towards the summit. Those on the mountain, who might have extra resources must be selective as to whom they try to help and who not, in order to preserve their own lives in the process. Experience levels vary, but we definitely all have to be prepared to take responsibility for making some decisions along the route - to assist fellow mountaineers or not - in the course of our pursuit for the summit or ultimate survival.

Most alpinists do not help others, while pursuing the summit or seeking personal safety during descend. Only the rare individual is ready and capable of assisting other mountaineers during a catastrophic scenario. Dozens of journalists, authorities and old-school mountaineers deprecate the commercialization of Everest; others ask why relatively unskilled climbers are allowed to be on the mountain at all. Everest is a realm where attempts to summit, is a commercialized big business; no longer a matter of one or two climbers with their Sherpas' heroically alone in the majestic landscape.

Since 1996 there is virtual traffic jams of well-off middle-aged guys from all over the world being conducted up to the summit by professional guides: individuals old enough to have amassed the money to pay the fee of $65,000, but also old enough to not be at the summit or peak of physical fitness. As an armchair interpreter, one must bear in mind that those who choose to attempt Everest do so on our own volition. Most fatalities are caused by avalanches, injury from falling, ice collapse and exposure or health problems related to the extreme conditions on the mountain. Numerous bodies remain on the Everest massif. Due to the difficulties and dangers in bringing corpses down, those who perish on the massif remain where they drop; some are moved by blustery weather and ice shifting over time.

In 1996, unprecedented 17 expeditions - we were hundreds of climbers - attempted to scale the highest Himalayan peak. The innovation of commercial expeditions expanding the number of client climbers assembled on the slopes. Back then in the aftermath of May 10 we became witnesses to intensive criticism of the Nepalese system, allowing too many, unskilled individuals unto Everest. Today's mass climbing tourism to Everest and the sheer number of permits issued makes 1996 look like the purist old times. In recent seasons, up to 2000 individuals assembled at

Base Camp, contradicting "speed equalizes safety up high". Bottlenecks are documented on photo's that scares the living daylight out of me. Nature's forces continue to claim lives in spite of a significant development in the available technical equipment that can now predict weather systems etc. On April 18, 2014, sixteen Sherpas' were killed in an avalanche that struck Base Camp. In addition, a number of climbers were caught in the avalanche; some were recovered but others remain unaccounted for. On April 25, 2015, at least 19 people, in a preliminary count, were confirmed dead in the avalanche hitting Base Camp following a powerful 7.8 earthquake, which killed at least 6,000 people in Nepal and injured more than 8,000. It is the worst single-day death toll ever in the history of Mount Everest. I did not consider the risk of earthquake when I was on Everest in 1996. None of us even remotely considered that particular added risk. I since expanded my knowledge about Katmandu being a known epicenter, when I lived there 14 months fighting for the rights to bring my adopted child home. Therefore, for those who aim at summiting Everest from now and onwards, it is crucial to add the calculated risk of falling victim to the new hazard of the mountain: earthquake.

Wannabe Everest climbers ought to be aware what actual risks dealing with the highest mountain on earth involve. Why not learn from Everest history what to expect from a guided expedition and what not. First and foremost, I at all times stress that you must have enough experience and endurance to save yourself no matter what transpires. Be certain that you can get yourself out of whatever situation - life and death - you might face. Never trust anyone with your life. Placing trust in a leader or guide, no matter what they promise and you wish for, might plain and simple, be the root to disaster and failure to accord an outsize mountain the immense respect it deserves.

Awaking Anatoli and Scott from the dead - through the process of writing this book, which I have procrastinated not to face the memories of what happened on Everest and the profound loss and loving, melancholic longing for the adventures we shared. Once again facing the depressing fact that I am not able to replicate the fun inflicted bold lifestyles, we pooled entangled with an amplified sense of connectedness to those with whom I experienced Everest. Procrastinating for long and now not wanting the writing and shifting through my photos process to end - because I then again have to live in the world - my world - without Scott and Anatoli. I sit back and smile, remembering, allowing myself to enjoy the voyage back in time to when we had fun. Mount Everest taught me invaluable lessons. I summited Mount Everest on May 10, 1996. I got lost and I could not find Camp 4 at 8000 meters. I was in the eye of the storm. I was in the huddle where we fought to remain conscious and keep others alive. I survived and am still alive today. Several of my adventuresome companions did not survive to turn 40. No more choices, no more bills, no more fun, no more life. I am convinced death is the end of all and everything. When you are dead, you do not have to bother anymore. Consequently, no matter what obstacles you might face in life, as long as we are alive we at least have the option to do something about it.

As long as there is breath in me, that long I will persist. I will force myself to create a new beginning. Everest taught me one of the greatest principles of success; if I persist long enough I will succeed. I will continuously choose to live my life with perseverance, enduring when it gets tough and uncomfortable, so that I can achieve some of the fulfillment that I dream about, in areas I have not yet succeeded to create the optimum that might be nice. I choose to continue to finish what I initiate, regardless of the obstacles that stand in my way. Trying to muster renewed fighting spirit when life's petty chores drain my lust and focus on momentum. Steady persistence in spite of difficulties, obstacles and discouragement will get me somewhere. I will never again expose myself to the amount of objective risk, which is inherent in the process of wanting to climb to the highest pinnacle on this globe. Never! And I will consciously set myself free from the last 20 years of existing in the shadow of Everest. I attempt to liberate myself from the past as possible ones I have this book off my agenda. Surviving Everest May 10, 1996 propelled life opportunities. I got lucky and rode the wave of success for a decade, breathing a sigh of relief when I gradually dwindled back to being incognito. Helping the process of just becoming me, whoever I am now, enjoying the freedom by withdrawing into living with nature as my only neighbor. Inwardly I still evaluate life and everyone in it according to my Everest standards. Grand for project fulfillment, but over time it does have an isolating effect on my social life. Therefore, I will invest focused effort into leaving Scott and Anatoli in their icy dwellings and discover what life has to offer, if I allow others not to have to live up to their standard. It is hard to beat the person who never gives up. A winner is just a loser who tried one more time. I will give myself fresh chances in life, leaving Everest for good. Change perspectives and modus operandi. I will dream new dreams. Not as big as Everest. Plan and take action to transform my aspirations into reality. I will learn new stuff. Life goes on, and change is inevitable. It has to be done and it might be fun!

Being alive is precious.

Life is so short.

Use it!

About the author
www.lenegammelgaard.com

Lene Gammelgaard was born in Denmark, a small Scandinavian country with 5 million inhabitants and where the highest point is 171 m (561 feet.). Lene Gammelgaard became globally famous when she summited and survived climbing Mount Everest in the spring of 1996. She survived the storm that killed many of her contemporary climbing friends. Pursuing her inner visions Lene is living proof that the most extraordinary is possible, no matter where you come from. Lene has been fighting for women's equal rights since her youth and summited Everest to prove what women are capable of when culture ceases to oppress their potential. She is therefore devoted to Innovating humans through Human Innovation in this period of intense transformation. Focusing on the demands from the future - we need to change now! In the high-velocity economy, where faster is the new fast, it's your ability to adapt, change and evolve, that will define your potential for successful survival in a more and more competitive globalized world. She dares to articulate how success can be difficult to obtain. You have to be stubborn and willing to conquer any obstacle you may encounter. She represent a new generation of female pattern breaking intellectuals, with a strong emphasis on action! Her unique processes contribute to install renewed fighting spirit and the will to want more in individuals as well as organizations. Lene Gammelgaard can motivate you to another level. She does not sugarcoat anything. For more than 20 years she has focused solely on helping people and organizations reshape their vision of what's possible. Her talks leave a lasting impact. Apply her strategies and your life will change. Her powerful messages of opportunity, self responsibility and action create startling and powerful change in organizations and individuals worldwide. She is best described as an understanding, compelling, empowering and compassionate tutor who has inspired thousands of people to go for their dreams. Her extensive knowledge is shared through her books and seminars worldwide. She is a global speaker, bestselling author, single-mother by choice and became the 35th woman and 1st Scandinavian female to summit Everest in May 1996.

For more than a decade, Lene Gammelgaard has worked in 15 countries with management and leaders to develop their potential. She has lectured for more than 600.000 people and her client list includes some of the world's top companies. CEO's invite her back to share her latest insights and boost their efforts to successfully prepare for launching groundbreaking projects. Lene knows adversity and strives to study the latest research mapping the human brain to constantly adapt her work with leaders and organizations to stimulate maximum capabilities in any given situation. Lene has hands-on experience with vision creation, succeeding as a woman in male dominated environments and circumventing hardships and tragic setbacks. Her first encounter with the possibilities of the humongous powers driving a person from within transpired when she with 18, finished college and decided to leave for the Caribbean, sailing, working as a deckhand and chose to risk what she had initially set out to do: crossing the Atlantic. This ocean crossing quest changed her life possibilities.

Fundamentally, she discovered that it was possible to transform aspirations, dreams and visions into reality. When she was 22 years old, she lost one of her brothers in a tragic accident, which propelled her into a rough confrontation with some of the unpredictability and unfairness of existence: formulating the quest; Get busy living or get busy dying. If you were to die in 24 hours, are you then living life the way you find meaningful? If not what are you willing to do to change it? Your life is not going to improve until you change your way of thinking and acting. Lene has a law degree, is a journalist as well as a trained psychotherapist. She is the founder of Human Innovation and continues to fight for equality for all. She as the first Everest survivor published Climbing High, published by Harper Collins, available in 13 languages. Climbing High became a global breakthrough. Lene has since published three books combined with 20 years of successful inspiration and mobilization of others.

In 2017 Lene started collaborating with one of the leading fertility clinics in the world – as Mental Endurance Specialist.

Printed in Poland
by Amazon Fulfillment
Poland Sp. z o.o., Wrocław